AUGUST 19

AUGUST 1914

England in Peace and War

Mark Rowe

Mhow

November 2013

CHAPLIN BOOKS
www.chaplinbooks.co.uk

Copyright © Mark Rowe
First published in 2013 by Chaplin Books

ISBN 978-1909183-34-6

A CIP catalogue record for this book is available from The British Library

Design by Michael Walsh at The Better Book Company

Printed by Imprint Digital

Chaplin Books
1 Eliza Place
Gosport PO12 4UN
Tel: 023 9252 9020

www.chaplinbooks.co.uk

In memory of my mother's father
John Nunn 1894–1973
who did not want to go to war, but had to

And his brothers
Joseph Nunn 1895–1916
and Harry Nunn 1897–1918
each buried near Albert, France
who did not want to die in war, but had to

CONTENTS

PART THREE: WAR ABROAD

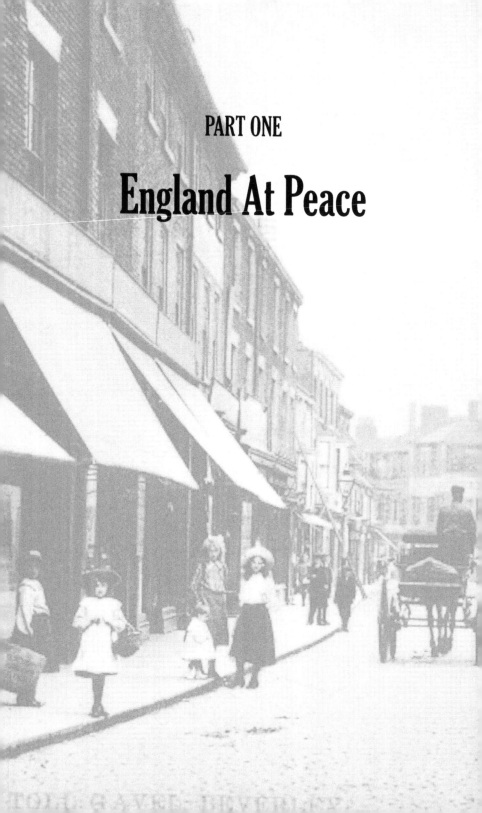

PART ONE

England At Peace

1

First Shots

The works of man's hands are his embodied thought, they endure after his bodily framework has passed into decay and thus throw a welcome light on the earliest stages of his unwritten history.

Ancient Hunters and their Modern Representatives,
by Prof W J Sollas (second edition, 1915)

I

The Honourable Gerald Legge began 1914, the last full year of his life, in Sudan of all places. Other upper-class young men left midwinter England for Switzerland, the south of France, or Egypt, with friends and family. Legge passed through the Suez Canal at Christmas, on 'a nice empty ship', landed at Port Sudan, and took the train to the capital Khartoum. He went further, where few travellers have ever been, into waterless Kordofan, so waterless that he had to send camels 30 miles to wells: "They leave here one morning and get back two days later," he told his father in a letter in March. You suspect from his letters that only in the harsh but simple wilderness did he feel truly himself.

He had wintered far from England before. Born in 1882, the second son of the sixth earl of Dartmouth, he had served in the Army from 1900 to 1905, and had since gone shooting as far as Newfoundland and Java. The Kordofan country was very like the Kalahari, he told his father, 'but the climate even better'. "Our hunting is usually done on camels as it is too hot to walk very far in the day time when we have to be chary with water. As soon as we strike fresh spoor we leave with camels and then go on foot and if we kill anything the camel has to carry it. I like these camels, they are wonderfully patient beasts and very forgiving; if only they didn't stink and groan so much I would like them. I took a toss off one, one day; I was in a hurry to get off and shoot a guinea fowl and somehow managed to get off quicker than I expected but luckily I fell on my head, so wasn't hurt," he joked, "but missed the guinea fowl."

Legge was disappointed not to see oryx, but shot gazelle. The game was very wild and wanted good stalking, 'and I am just as fit as blazes', he wrote. On January 31 he arrived at El Obeid, the main place in that region, about 400 miles from Khartoum, paid off boys and camels, and went by train to Kosti on the Nile to find a boat. The country had hold of him already. He wrote of the 'knowledge that you are bang away from every white man; the Nile will be all ginger beer bottles and orange peels, nearly as bad as East Africa I expect'.

He wrote again in February 'on a man of war on the Nile', which had been waiting at Kosti. The inspector there had been at Eton with Legge. "It is the most luxurious form of travelling possible, bathroom, deckchairs, etc etc … I am not much impressed with the bird life on this river after hearing so many wonderful accounts of it. It isn't a patch on Ngamiland [in the Kalahari Desert] for that but maybe it will improve as we go south." He noted storks, herons and cranes: "We have shot a good many duck mostly our own northern species." Legge had skinned the ducks, 'and a bad job it is as they are all so fat and greasy that each skin takes a very long time to clean'.

The hunters shot anything, but the bigger and the faster the animal, the better. The day before he wrote, a fellow hunter, named only as Jack, had shot a water buck and a white-eared kob. While Legge was stalking through some very high and thick grass, he nearly trod on a lion. "He jumped up grunting and growling within four yards of me but of course I could see nothing except the grass shaking as he bolted. I ran like mad after him in hopes of seeing him cross an open space somewhere but never got a glimpse." Legge shot what he was stalking and left some of the meat there in the hope that the lion would find it. Legge and his companion went after the lion early the next morning. A native shouted 'Asser! Asser!', meaning lion. Legge recalled: "I saw a great brute prowling around still a long way off and tried to get nearer but it was very flat and open and he saw me and slunk off. We ran after him and he started lolloping away so I had a long shot and got him plumb in that portion of his body least immediately fatal as he was going dead away but the bullet raked forward and he was dead in five yards. As soon as I fired Jack said he was a hyena and he was right! A great big devil too. So I had all the fun of shooting a lion without getting him."

The game was much tamer than Kordofan. The men set off in the dark at 4am to hunt buffalo, to get away from the river. Legge shot wide, and back at the river-boat, found that Jack had shot two bulls. "It was hard not to appear jealous," he admitted. Another day, Legge shot a bull from 20 yards away. He wrote how he went for 'the thin part of his neck just behind the head where his spine, windpipe and big blood vessels are close together':

At the shot he just rolled over without a kick but another bull I hadn't seen jumped up and started looking about. I didn't want to shoot another and expected him to clear off but no! he would wait for his pal and he just stood looking from me to his pal and back again. So I yelled and screamed at him and so did the man with me but he wouldn't move. I liked him for that! He wouldn't leave his pal. Then I fired in the air over his head and all the notice he took was to walk towards me looking very truculent. We still shouted at him and I was determined not to shoot at him but he

*just came on so I shinned up a tree with my rifle and cursed
every hair on his enormous body. He came to within 40
yards and then turned and walked back to the dead one and
stood there on guard. It was now just about dark so I came
down off my perch and left him master of the situation and
made a detour and came home. I have a greater respect for
a buffalo now than before even. What a splendid beast to
bluff me out like that. I am glad I didn't shoot him. So this
morning I went back at dawn. In hopes of finding a lion
at the dead bull but nothing was there. But my friend of
last night had been butting the corpse really hard to make
him get up I suppose … now I can take it easy as I have
got what I came for.*

According to its postmarks, the letter, addressed to his
mother the Countess of Dartmouth, left Khartoum on
February 18 and reached the family estate at Patshull outside
Wolverhampton by March 1. She was not there, so the letter
followed her to the family's London residence in Berkeley
Square. On March 10 Legge was writing again before he
returned to Khartoum. He was not sorry he was finishing his
hunt on the Nile, calling it 'altogether too tame and touristy'
and grumbling: '… the whole trip is a hold-up from beginning
to end and this Sudan steamers department are robbers of the
worst kind'. He returned to his costs at the end of the letter:
"I hear rubber is up but have seen no paper. I hope it is true
as I am spending money like water here." Legge had been
working on a rubber plantation in Java in November 1907,
when his sister Dorothy married Francis Meynell. ('How are
you? Married, settled down and lived happily ever after! Good
for you,' Legge wrote to her then, sounding like a man who was
not for settling.) Usually, he kept his letters to his shooting: 'the
rest of my news will keep till I get home,' he wrote on April 11,
from Port Sudan Hotel. A boat was sailing on April 14, and he
expected to arrive home on April 26, in time as it happened for

his 32nd birthday. "Dear Mother, Just back from the hills as hard as nails and so fit!" he wrote. "Real hard work down there, with here and there a bit of climbing that nearly frightened me to death. Jack got what is nearly a record ibex, a real fizzer. I got two, one small, the other only moderate, but quite nice heads. But I am rather proud as I found them, stalked them and shot them with no-one to help at all and was previously told they could not be stalked!' Legge hoped to go into the hills again in 1915. "This country has fairly got hold of me," he had told his father in January. "I love it and the people. The Arab is the greatest gentleman I ever met; I wish some of the things that think they are gentlemen at home could live out here for a bit and pick up some wrinkles from the Arab."

II

The brothers Clifford and Sydney Gothard, too, began 1914 with a bang. January 1 in their native Burton upon Trent, the Staffordshire brewery town, was fine all day, frosty then thawing, 'slightly misty and dull in afternoon'. So Clifford wrote in his new Boot's Scribbling Diary. In the morning he and Syd cycled uphill to Brizlincote, looking over the Trent valley, where his Uncle George Startin farmed. "Had a short chat with the two Miss James, uncle and auntie and went out shooting with Jack. Shot a cat which was ailing of some disease and killed a few small birds. Had lunch and then went out shooting again. Killed a few sparrows for the ferrets and enough blackbirds etc for a pie for them. Had tea, cleaned guns etc and played bridge. Syd and I v Uncle George and Miss James for three rubbers and then Jack took Miss James' place for four more. Miss Nancy James and Aunty Louie went out to tea and only turned up again just as we started to have supper. Cycled home, roads very slippy and went to bed." Next morning a thaw set in; Clifford went into town and bought the diary. He cycled to Bretby, and 'shot two or three birds for the ferrets'.

The shooting by the young Gothards – and many other farmers and their friends – had its uses. Besides ridding farmland of wild animals that might eat seed or grass, Gothard fed his ferrets. In a memoir in old age he explained further: "… the rabbits brought in were cleaned, hung in a game larder to cool and taken out the next morning in the milk float to the milk customers with whom the rabbits found ready purchasers. This brought a little income for the farm which far more than paid for the cartridges and had the advantage of keeping rabbits down to reasonable numbers."

III

In India, British Army officers shot for pleasure, and kept the dead skins as souvenirs; and, they could claim, saved Indians from dangerous animals. One Royal Horse Artillery officer, Alan Brooke, wrote to his mother how in February 1914 he and a friend and fellow officer Ronald Adam shot duck and snipe. They found a tank snake, 'a real big fellow, about eight feet long and about as thick as my wrist', which they did not want to shoot for fear of disturbing ducks. "So I first chased him with a stone, but he defeated me by getting into his hole. However I caught him by the tail as he was going down and pulled him out, then I swung him by his tail while Adam tried to drop a rock on to his head. At last I put my foot on his neck and we finished him off. They are not poisonous but have got a very nasty row of teeth with which they could give one a nasty bite. I skinned him on the spot and have sent his skin off to be cured. It ought to make a very nice belt and perhaps a card case also." One morning, news came of a panther in a cave. "So I went out in the afternoon. When I got there she had come out of her cave and was sitting out on rocks. I had a herd of goats moved about at the bottom of her hill to try and divert her attention while I climbed the hill and tried to stalk her." But the panther had gone back to her cave. Brooke waited until dark when he heard the panther kill a goat. He switched on a lamp:

> *The panther was sitting like a great cat looking at the dead goat. It was not a very easy shot as I could not see my sights well and I let fly. There was a roar and I saw a streak of yellow and spots come straight at the lamp which was at my feet. In my excitement I took my finger off the switch and the light went out. The panther dashed past within a yard of me making the most unholy row. I heard her making a noise for some time then when everything was quiet I followed her up with the electric lamp and I am glad to say I found her stone dead about 150 yards away. It was only a dead rush that she made at the lamp but rather unpleasant for all that. She turned out to be quite a fair female six foot six long. While I was skinning her I found two large bullets in her neck with the wound quite healed over which accounted for her being such a cunning old brute and for her temper not being of the best.*

As Brooke's story suggested, the hunter did not always win, and he gave the story of a subaltern named Shaw, who shot a panther which had killed tame animals nearby. "It charged him, pulled him off the rug which he was sitting on by his leg and they had a rough and tumble together till the shitari came up and hit the panther over the head with the second rifle and drove it off. They got Shaw in by the next train and pushed him straight off to the hospital where he is now." Despite having a hand amputated, Shaw died of blood poisoning.

IV

Here, then, is a reason why most of Europe went to war within a few days in 1914. Just as men thought nothing of killing other creatures with a gun, so nations sent their young men with guns to settle an argument with a neighbour, or to conquer some other continent. Which alliance your country was one of, how democratic you were, made little difference. Men – and women – from Europe turned to violence, if it suited them, or merely to pass the time. Eva Tibbitts gave the evocatively big address of 631 105th Street, Edmonton, in an undated letter from Canada to her mother in Gloucester. The only clue to the date was that she was 'sorry the war broke out when it did as I had just worked up a connection in the colony'. She furnished studios for a living, and was living in a house with 'artists and professionals'. Her 'man', Billie Stredmond, had taught her how to shoot, "and we make up a party amongst the boys and girls here nearly every week and go duck pheasant partridge and prairie chicken shooting. We have a motor car and drive on a bit and shoot and drive on again and shoot till we get 50 miles out. Last week we had a bag of 60 birds and 20 rabbits." Her free days sounded as rich and, at root, empty as the rest of her life.

War, like shooting, made a change from the boring working week; or from routine, if you were too rich to have to work. War was like the jar of mustard or the bottle of beer in your pantry. You might not even like mustard or beer, or only seldom had a taste for it, or only kept it to satisfy some visitor. Yet the chance was always there that you might bring them out one meal-time, and pour the bottle, or spoon some mustard on your plate. Even if you wished you hadn't, you could not very well put the mustard back in the jar, or unpour the beer. That was how the brewers and the makers of mustard made their money.

2

Ways to Die

And now the time has come when we must part, and go our respective ways – I to die, you to live; and which of us has the happier fortune in store for him is known to none, except to God.

Socrates; from *Marginal Notes* by Lord Macaulay, arranged by Sir George Otto Trevelyan (1907)

I

Clifford Gothard had his life ahead of him in 1914. On June 9, he was 21; on Friday June 12, he took the last exam of his last-but-one year at Birmingham University, where he was taking mechanical engineering. He began another carefree summer: shooting hares as they fled the wheat-fields at harvest; planting strawberries in the garden; playing tennis at the family home in Winshill on the outskirts of Burton; some light study. He had some growing-up to do, however, in the early hours of Thursday July 9:

At about 2.15am mother came and called us. 'Do get up, dad is so ill.' And I hastened to his bedroom and found him lying on his back and breathing heavily. His face being a trifle bluey. I raised him slightly and felt his pulse. It got very weak and so I wanted to give him some brandy but was afraid to pour it into his mouth as it may choke him. I dipped my finger in the brandy and then moistened his lips and mouth with it. It failed to revive him. I put a hot water bottle to his head with Syd's assistance. He breathed less and less heavily and finally breathing ceased just before the doctor arrived here. He said death had taken place two or three minutes before he arrived. (He was not above ten minutes in coming from the time we telephoned to him.)

As the eldest son, Clifford took charge. He drove with Dr Holford the three miles to his mother's unmarried brother and sister at Home Farm, Bretby – where James Startin farmed, and Sarah kept house. Clifford knocked at the door and summoned his uncle: "I told him. Auntie guessed when she knew that it was me." That day Clifford Gothard began settling his father's affairs, taking letters to friends and relatives – 'nearly 50 in all' – telephoning others, having an interview with a reporter from the *Burton Gazette*, one of the town's two daily papers, and before lunch going with 'Auntie Sallie' (Sarah Startin) into town 'to see bank manager where I opened an account'. Suddenly he had to become a man. They buried Frederic Gothard on the Saturday afternoon, July 11. Clifford, and Syd, worked for the rest of the month on their father's papers. When on the Wednesday, July 15 – according to his diary his first break from the accounting – Clifford took his father's guns, 'to kill a rabbit or two at Bretby', you feel the son was turning to a favourite pastime for comfort, and symbolically taking his father's place.

Clifford had much to live up to, for Frederic Gothard had risen in the world. The son of a tailor on the high street, Frederic had studied chemistry and became the head of the brewing and malting departments at Worthington's brewery – the man to make sure the beer was right, thanks to Burton's underground water – and a company director. He was 57. As the local newspapers remarked, Mr Gothard had not given any sign of illness. Whether he had worked too early in the morning on the private bowls green opposite his home was the most the papers could speculate. If Frederic Gothard had felt unwell in front of his family, Clifford wrote nothing of it in his diary. No matter how high your place in a town, death could strike you any night.

II

Death found the Gothard family; William Thomas Pickbourne sought it. Not that he wished it on his wife and four sons, or anyone. He did go to his brother-in-law's funeral in 1912 – in Winshill, as it happens. He and his own could hope for long and healthy lives: his father turned 90 in April 1914. The old man still enjoyed his food when he stayed with the Pickbournes in Northampton for a couple of months in the summer of 1911, though he was growing ever more deaf. Pickbourne took him one Saturday on the train to the Crystal Palace in London, 'though it nearly knocked him up', as Pickbourne put it in his diary. Pickbourne had a busy but comfortable life; once a commercial traveller, then a colliery agent, and for decades a part-time Methodist preacher. Whether in his own, Regent Square, chapel in the village of Upton, or around the district, or sometimes on invitation much further afield, he took services every Sunday. He never wrote in his diary about his job; only chapel. In March 1914 he told of a Sunday at Brixworth, the other side of Northampton:

> *Mrs Allcock, whom I visited for many years passed away about a fortnight ago in great peace … she has been bedridden for years and was a great sufferer but oh so happy, so peaceful and so thoroughly <u>ready</u>. After tea I visited her relatives and three or four other families between tea and Service as I generally do and at night we had a very fair congregation turned out. Brixworth people however do not hurt themselves by too many services on Sunday. <u>Once</u> generally suits them. Some of our officials even stay at home and sleep in the afternoons! Rather cool I think. I verily believe nothing short of an earthquake would startle some of our so called Methodists into earnestness. They do want waking up!*

Pickbourne was hardly the only, or the last, man to grumble in his diary about people's shortcomings that he could not say to their faces. Pickbourne had a point; he was going to some trouble for these people. On the morning of July 12, 1914, he cycled over six miles to Moulton, the other side of Northampton – a fair task for a man who turned 54 the next month. He found a congregation of nine: "... not a very inspiring number but nevertheless they were there and wanted all the help they could get and I must say they <u>did</u> get help. On my own way home got caught in a shower and got wet through, had to change my clothes." As so often, he took a young men's class in the afternoon, and was 'at his own place' in the evening.

Methodism bonded these men and women, even unto death. In July Pickbourne recorded the death of a fellow preacher, John Perkins: "A week ago he fell in his bedroom and seemed to quite collapse." Dead also was a Sunday school teacher 'and a very earnest worker', a young woman, Miss Burnett: "She was only ill two or three days." And as for an old man that Pickbourne visited, Mr Rushton: "He too is fast reaching his end, gets weaker every week and he too will soon be joining the majority in the upper country."

Just as Pickbourne tried with his preaching to help his listeners, to make sense of their world and to prepare for the next world they believed in, so he, too, was helped. Christianity, when it all came together, felt real to the believers. When in 1912 he went to the Methodists' conference in Liverpool, 'from the very beginning we were conscious of the presence and power of God', he wrote. In February 1914 he felt 'the master's presence', and after one Sunday's nearly full chapel 'a very gracious influence rested on us all especially at night and I am certain a good spirit was doing His office on many present'. That grace – as wonderfully and tantalisingly available to the common people of Northamptonshire as it was to the apostles – had to be something powerful, to take Pickbourne and his congregations (even the small ones) from one Sunday to the next.

III

Anyone could take time off work for their own funeral; that was about as far as the rights of workers went. Robert Blakeby, who lived in a room at 25 Great Portland Street in central London, received a letter on Wednesday May 12, 1914 from his brother Harry, 'to say that Dad died suddenly last night'. Blakeby, then 29, worked in the advertising department of Peter Robinson's, a draper's on Oxford and Regent Streets. On the Saturday, he bought a black suit for 22 shillings, a pair of braces for a shilling, and a pair of trousers for seven shillings and sixpence – the last sum the same as his rent each week. On the Wednesday, May 19, he got up at his usual 6.40am, and walked into work as usual before 7am. He left work at 1.10pm, walked to his mother's home near Edgware Road, 'changed my clothes and had a wash and shave, then to dad's funeral (at Finchley) with mother, Aunt Ellen, Minnie (my sister), Bill and Harry (my brothers) and back to mother's to tea. Changed my clothes then back to work at 25 to 7pm. Left work at eight min to 9pm. Walked home to mother's and had supper there.' That was a long day; not much longer than his usual working days. Blakeby took meal breaks, 'breakfast, dinner and tea', and otherwise worked regularly from 7am until 7.30pm. He might leave work at 8.15pm, have supper at his mother's, and return to do 'LU duty', or locking up. His employer allowed him not quite five-and-a half hours off work to bury his father.

IV

These deaths may have been distressing to watch, drawn-out and agonising to go through; at least they were all *natural*

13

deaths. Death could come to you before your time, where you worked, on the roads, even at home. Harold Fencott was playing with other four-year-olds under railway arches at Bushbury near Wolverhampton in July 1914; he slipped into the canal going after a frog and drowned. Anything hot, heavy or high could kill you. A man could fall from a cart at hay-making time and break his neck; a boy given a ride on the cart could fall under the wheels and die; horses frightened by a passing motor car could throw the carter to the ground. Wagons crushed shunters; cranes knocked apprentices off girders. If anything could go wrong, it did. As the local Church Lads Brigade marched through the town of Beverley in August 1913, a dum-dum bullet in a firearm, thought to be harmless, went off, hit the road, and then a watching boy. He recovered. In May 1914 grease caught fire on the apron of Edward Fletcher, 52, a stoker who had worked for Walsall Glue Company for 34 years, and burned him to death.

Mines were even worse: gas underground could explode or poison you, roofs could fall on you. For every accident that an inquest coroner and jury heard about, and that made the newspaper, many more near-misses and injuries left people bed-ridden or degraded, unfit for their old work. Some workplaces looked after their injured; if a railway shunter lost an arm or a leg, he could work as a signalman, or a night-watchman. Most cases never made the news, or never went beyond the nearest workmates or family. They had to accept the hardship, because they could no more expect anyone else to help them than they could help others. They had to shrug – unless the pain did not even allow that.

'My dear nephew,' wrote Sarah Pick to William Thomas Swift, on Monday July 20, 1914. Swift, a retired and widowed schoolmaster in the village of Churchdown between Gloucester and Cheltenham, read the letter the next day. She thanked him for a letter of his, then told him:

You will be sorry to know that I have had the misfortune to put my shoulder out. It happened up in my room, I hitched my foot in the carpet where it was unsewn, I fell and struck my shoulder against the doorpost. The pain was almost unendurable until Dr Phelps and his partner came and put it back in again. The pain is still very bad now I have no use at all in my arm yet. But I suppose it will come back.

A relative was staying until she felt better, she added: "He cannot bend his leg and is still on the club but he does all he can and Mrs Mower bandages my arm and dresses and undresses me." 'On the club', so obvious to Pick and Swift that she did not need to spell it out to him, must have been a friendly society or some such savings club, that paid out at such times. Swift must have answered her at once because on the Friday he had a postcard reply: "I am a little better. My arm pains me a good deal and it has made me feel very poorly in myself. I shall follow your advice to be as cheerful as I can and not worry. Hilda, Sybil and John are coming on Monday for a fortnight."

What could cheer Sarah Pick? She could tell herself, though she had no way of knowing, that others were worse off than her. At least she had not tripped on stairs, which could kill; as inquests heard elsewhere. Miner's wife Polly Henworth, living in what the coroner described as a 'miserable hovel' at Bloxwich in Staffordshire, went downstairs one night in March 1914 to fetch the iron plate from the oven, to warm the bed for her ill, visiting, sister. She must have tripped on stairs – called by the coroner 'the most awkward he had ever seen' – while carrying a lamp holding about a quart of oil. Frank Henworth awoke to his wife's screams and found her, in her nightdress on the kitchen floor, in flames from head to foot. She died 13 days later. Even such a sad story did show how families looked after their own. Also sleeping in the Henworths' one bedroom – divided by a partition – was the dead woman's mother. You could shudder at such overcrowding; or understand the sharing. Here, then, in the accidents that made life like a guerrilla war, may have been one reason for such public interest in the loss of the Titanic, in 1912. The passengers on that boat, kept apart by the class of their ticket yet with one fate, were a metaphor for Britain. Rich people, who could imagine themselves on such a ship, could see that an accident could catch even them. For the poor, who could only dream of travel, the Titanic's story spoke of the harsh choices in their own lives. Thanks to the failings of others, beyond the power of the passengers to remedy or even ask about, there were not enough lifeboats, actual or metaphorical, for everyone.

V

Though Lord Charles Beresford was a bigoted hypocrite, at least as a hypocrite he could take something as embarrassing as the Titanic and not only put the best face on it, but make it sound glorious. He was just the man for the unveiling of the statue to the captain of the Titanic, Commander Edward John Smith, at Lichfield on Wednesday July 29, 1914. Beresford, a Conservative MP, wearing Royal Navy uniform, had made several voyages with Smith. According to Beresford, Smith was 'an example of the very best type of British seaman, and of British gentlemen'. Hear, hear, the crowd said; the listeners wanted to hear something good. Beresford and other speakers that day described Smith as brave, gallant, and heroic (and, none of them added, dead). They left out the ignored warnings about the icebergs, the missed distress signals, the false pride of the Belfast shipmakers that called the Titanic 'unsinkable', and the avoidable lack of lifeboats. Instead Beresford recalled Smith's last command, as the waters rose to the bridge of the Titanic: 'Be British!' (Had anyone really heard that?)

So much for the figure of the man now in Lichfield's park, because other places more to do with Captain Smith, such as his birthplace of Stoke-on-Trent, didn't want him. Beresford continued the metaphors, by praising the 'black squad', 'those who served below in the engine room and stoke hole, those often forgotten heroes because being out of sight they were out of mind. That so many people were saved was no doubt due to those who remained at their posts working the dynamos, keeping the lights going, although they knew for hours that the ship was doomed.' Here Beresford praised the world as the Tories saw it; men at the top and, literally, at the bottom, each did their duty at their posts despite certain death. Never mind that efficient seamen would not have had the accident in the first place; rather, Beresford claimed that the British way *worked*, avoided panic, and saved some of those on board.

Beresford ended in the present, by calling the Royal Navy and the Merchant Marine as 'brothers of the sea': "The Navy were the police of the sea, so that if unfortunately they were called upon to fight they could keep the Merchant Marine still plying between our shores and distant climes to provide them," the listeners, that is, "with raw material and food." He was hinting at the crisis on the Continent of the last few days; the day before, Austria-Hungary had begun war with Serbia.

3

What is an Englishman?

Still in thy right hand carry gentle peace
To silence envious tongues. Be just, and fear not.
Let all the ends thou aim'st at be thy country's,
Thy God's, and truth's.

Henry VIII by Shakespeare;
a quotation pasted into Arthur Ross' scrapbook of
Beverley Church Lads Brigade

I

Even as Beresford was giving words of comfort about his old ship-mate Commander Smith, though so one-sided as to be deceitful, the journalist Philip Gibbs was at work on an article, 'What I saw of the Servians', for that Saturday's edition of the weekly illustrated paper *The Graphic*. On his way to Bulgaria to report on the first Balkan war a couple of years before, the Serbs had arrested him for sketching reservists at Belgrade railway station. The Serb interrogator could speak only Serbian and it was so obvious that an Englishman would not be able to speak Serbian, that Gibbs left it unsaid in his article. Eventually someone came who could speak to Gibbs in German, and the Serbs told him that 'as I appeared unmistakably English I might depart in peace'. Yet much more intriguing than the point of the article – how warlike Serb men (and women) were and how they hated Austria – was the question of why the Serbs let him go. What about Gibbs – what possessions, clothes or manners – was so English that foreigners recognised it?

18

Not that men who had never been to England and spoke not a word of English had any more idea of an Englishman, than the English understood foreigners. A shorthand sufficed. The English were stolid, whether because of the diet, the weather, the give and take of parliamentary government, or the military habit of waiting for the enemy to come to you that worked so well at Agincourt, Waterloo and Omdurman (less well at Hastings and Isandhlwana). The French by contrast – to quote the editorial of the *Wolverhampton Express & Star* newspaper on July 29 – had a 'ferment of emotions' personally, and revolutions politically. The stock Irishman, in newspaper cartoons during the Irish Home Rule affair, was someone short and shabby, like a leprechaun. To say something was 'a bit Irish' was to call it disorderly, or stupid. This prejudice served – in England and other countries – to make you feel the best, or at least better than someone. No matter how daft, or dangerous, such caricatures did point to differences between countries.

And what was wrong with that? "My friends say I am full of prejudices. I am," Guy Paget wrote in a private memoir, *Stray Shots by a Guards Gunner*, after the war. "I love my school, Eton. I love Mother Lodge; the Scots Guards; and I love my country, England. There may be as good but I know damn well there are none better." Even such a short, and frank, burst of national pride showed contradictions. His surname suggested his ancestors took English land after the Norman Conquest. He owned land, and Sulby Hall, on the borders of Leicestershire and Northamptonshire. He recalled: "The murder of the Archduke Franz Ferdinand and the Archduchess in June 1914 found me with my wife at Aix les Bains. We were there for her health. She had a very bad breakdown due to overwork at politics in my old division of mid-Northants." Paget had stood there for the Conservatives at the last election in 1910. Like many of his kind, he took every chance to holiday abroad (to avoid common Englishmen?). Perhaps the best test of what it was to be an Englishman, or anyone, was what it made you do in extremes. Your sense of who you were would decide the tugs between competing loyalties, even if your choice, or denial of a choice, hurt you.

As the title of his memoir suggested, Paget had pride in being a Guards officer, one of the elite of the British Army. On about Wednesday August 6 – after a long story, as it was for all the English fleeing for the Continent on the outbreak of war – Paget sailed from Dieppe. Paget saw a 'boy', who was dirty, without a collar, with a three-day beard, and an unclean hanky around his neck; 'but still obviously a gentleman'. Paget asked him to have a drink. The boy replied that he would rather have a sandwich, as water was free. "He had travelled three days in a cattle truck from Switzerland, penniless. I discovered his name was Whitbread and he was in the Coldstreams. I cursed him for not calling on me for aid as he saw I had a Guards tie and said I hoped I did not look such a bounder as to be thought unentitled to it. He replied he was so dirty and for the honour of the Coldstreams would not like me to go to the club and say how he looked." That, Paget wrote, was an example of the Guards' discipline (that lasted through the war, he added carefully). Here was much of what made men tick – perhaps not all Englishmen, but *gentlemen*, the sort that could afford to go abroad, for months at a time.

Paget had tried to reach his wife at Aix with 200 gold sovereigns as spending money, only to give up at Paris, as France began war with Germany. Whitbread – such men as Paget spoke of their fellows by their surnames, formally – preferred to suffer silently, rather than admit he could not afford to keep the usual standards, even though it was not his fault that he could not shave. A tie (or a handshake for a freemason such as Paget) was an unspoken signal for strangers to recognise they had something in common. This required trust, because anyone could wear a particular tie and pretend to belong to something. Men like Paget gave those guilty of such a fraud the name of 'bounder'; that was not a crime in law, but against custom. How could Paget tell someone was 'obviously' a gentleman? That came with experience, from being in a country longer than a mere visitor or journalist. All the places you fitted in – the schools, churches and friends' homes you went to; all the things that you, and people like you, took in – the newspapers and books, the conversations, the accents, the clues from posture and gait, let alone the outward clothes and cleanliness – all equipped you to judge the man or woman you met. In no time, you could tell if the other person was like you, and welcome them or keep a distance accordingly. You were like a sensible man who did not go to extremes of trouble to check that a gold coin or (less often seen) five-pound note was fake; instead, you satisfied yourself with a sign that it was genuine. Sometimes, when the coin or banknote was strange, if you were not in your usual places and met someone new to you in the same boat as yourself – literally, in Paget's case – misunderstandings could arise.

You could not check a coin or banknote *that* carefully, nor did you want to, because most of your fellow countrymen would be as unknown – as incomprehensible, even – to you as any foreigner. Travel – by taking you out of your home, and your workplace if you had one – more often threw up encounters with people unlike yourself, even though people unlike you might not notice social differences, nor care (which was itself one difference between 'gentlemen' and other men). The weekly *Tamworth Herald* printed one example, signed only 'WM', about a train journey in July 1914 – maybe by one of the newspaper's reporters on a holiday to Scotland. He began on a London and North Western Railway (LNWR) Sunday midnight express north. In third class, he wrote, you could always expect to come across 'sons of the Empire on furlough or on their way to their outpost'. At Crewe, two seamen came into the carriage. One burly man dumped his box in the corridor, sat in a corner, 'and then genially pulled a large bottle of beer from an inner pocket and invited all present to have a drink from it'. WM did not say if he or anyone else in the compartment took a swig; he, and his readers, may have taken it for granted that it was bad manners to sip out of a bottle, let alone after a seaman had put his lips to it. "He afterwards placed the bottle under my seat and left it there untouched for over three hours while he retired to sleep. Happily the window remained open and we had fresh air." Again, WM implied, without having to spell it out to his readers, that the seaman might not have washed lately, and might smell, and the other passengers would be glad of fresher air. WM had chosen to buy the cheapest class of ticket, and so was in the company of the sorts of people who could not afford anything else. "The other seaman was inclined to take a nap on my shoulder," WM went on – readers with imagination would feel how unwelcome that invasion of privacy would be – "so I engaged him in conversation and found he was a stoker just arrived at Bristol from Buenos Ayres and on his way home to Glasgow to his wife and children. He considered the trip from England to Buenos Ayres the hardest a stoker could have. It means 40 days' continuous stoking ... the poor chap was worn and thin. He was travelling in his shabby go ashore clothes and had no bundle or money, not even a match for his pipe, but he had a Board of Trade certificate for his full pay and would draw the money at Glasgow." The midsummer dawn came in Cumberland, the train arrived at Carlisle at 4am, and WM had two-and-a-half hours before his next train. He watched the overnight work – hard, unsociable and out of sight, done by men like the stoker. Porters tumbled empty milk churns from handcarts and shivered the air under the glass roof of the station with thunderous noises. Post Office officials came out of the mail trains carrying coats and umbrellas. They lit their pipes and went home. Morning papers from Liverpool, Manchester, York and London littered the platform. Even on the historic edge of England – if you saw Scotland as a separate part of Britain; and Guy Paget, who loved England and the Scots Guards, did not – men spread the things that bound a country together as tightly as the string that bundled the mail and the provincial newspapers on their way to breakfast tables.

II

Eric Bennett, too, was on his way home from Buenos Aires in July 1914 – but on a different ship than that unnamed Scottish stoker's; Bennett's landed at Tilbury. In a memoir in old age he was mistaken when he suggested war was looming when he sailed. According to him, the German, French, Dutch and Danish passengers were 'hurrying men', and 'the one thing we were bursting for was news', on a ship carrying mainly refrigerated beef. Without wireless, the only messages came from passing ships by semaphore. His brother Harry met him at the docks and took him into London to their booked room at the Imperial Hotel in Russell Square. Harry had tickets for the big boxing match: between the Frenchman, Carpentier, and the American, Gunboat Smith. The fight, for the 'white heavyweight championship of the world', was on the Thursday night, July 16, at Olympia. Not one in a million in Europe, except perhaps the Austrian and German emperors and the men around them, was even thinking of a war within a fortnight.

Carpentier arrived in London a couple of days before Bennett, by boat to Folkestone, and train to Charing Cross station. What the newspapers called the 'French colony' in the city, and Londoners too, mobbed the boxer, his manager and sparring partners. The crowd unyoked the horses from his carriage and pulled it – flying a tricolour – to the Hotel Metropole, where Carpentier was to stay. On July 16 the *Sheffield Daily Telegraph*, for one, sniffed that such enthusiasm

– anyone close enough patted Carpentier or shook his hand – was 'not entirely admirable'. That said, as Carpentier had already knocked out two English boxers, this public tribute to a Frenchman was 'about as effective a token as could possibly be given of the reality of the entente cordiale'. Again, the writer had no way of knowing England and France would be in a war together within three weeks.

The newspapers, the commentators on fashions, did not know what to make of boxing, or to be exact what the *Sheffield Telegraph* termed the 'over-idolising of crack boxers in general' by 'sensation-seekers'. The Bennett brothers sounded as if they were seeking sensations; Eric and Harry met Alfred at Euston station, went sight-seeing and, Eric recalled 70 years later, 'had a marvellous meal of steak and chips at the Holborn Hotel'. At Olympia, in one of the contests before the main bout, as the boxers broke from the clinch, one knocked out the referee by mistake. "The main contest proved to be a bit of a farce," Bennett recalled, a common view at the time, "because in the fifth round Gunboat Smith caught Carpentier with a good punch felling him to his knees; whilst in this position Smith struck him again and was immediately disqualified." The brothers took the train to their hometown of Stoke-on-Trent the next morning; that afternoon Carpentier collected a cheque for £3000 from the offices of the *Sporting Life*, and Smith's manager Mr Buckley (the 'beaten' boxer not showing his face) picked up £2000. Carpentier left London – smartly dressed as ever, in suit and tie, carrying gloves and cane – on the Saturday morning train for Paris, having already promised a match against one of the Englishmen he had beaten before, Bombardier Wells.

What made the people paid to have an opinion on such things unsure about boxing? At least some of the watchers were rich enough, as the Bennetts' spending proved. The newspapers deplored the rougher sorts of men drawn to watch boxers, seeking the thrill of a knock-out blow. It reminded those who harked back to the Roman Empire of how the commoners of Rome enjoyed rather too much for comfort the gladiators' fights to the death. On the other hand, as the *Sheffield Telegraph* admitted, men in the sport of boxing were now of an 'improved type', making boxing a 'healthy and manly recreation among all classes'. Boxing taught you to take a knock, and give one back according to the rules – rules that everyone had to follow, even the failed challenger for the title of white heavyweight champion of the world. Boxing could channel the anger and sheer spare energy of young men, that otherwise might spill out into drunken, disobedient 'mafficking', named after the mischief that used the patriotic celebrations for the relief of Mafeking, in 1900 during the Boer War, as an excuse. It was no accident that the Army taught boxing, nor that the Church of England was behind something as military-sounding as the Church Lads Brigade. The Army and the Church were not looking to put out the violent fires in young men, but to discipline them. Likewise countries did not necessarily keep armies to start a war, but to punch back if someone picked a fight; or at least to stay on their feet long enough until someone stood by them. For a war between nations, even ones as civilised as France and Britain, might not carry on, or even start, according to any rules.

III

As Captain Neville Hobson, the captain of the Beverley company of the Church Lads Brigade, said at the opening of the east Yorkshire market town's new drill hall, in May 1913, drill and discipline were 'a means but not an end'. It cannot have felt like that for at least some of the 'lads' aged 14 and over, judging by the journal of one of the sergeants. The 18-year-old Arthur Ellerker Ross plainly cared about the Brigade enough to keep a handwritten diary of it, and in July 1914 to become joint secretary of the new Old Comrades Association – new, because the first Lads like him were becoming old enough to have to leave. Even so, Ross tells a truer story of the Brigade than the forever favourable newspaper reports he pasted onto the pages – some articles surely written by his father Harry Ellerker Ross, a reporter for the weekly *Beverley Guardian*. The same things that attracted lads to the Brigade – the smart uniforms, the comradeship – they rebelled against, when carried to extremes. At an evening inspection on Thursday January 29, 1914, for instance, Captain Hobson sent a lad, Walter Welburn, home 'to change his jacket, because it had some grease on'. Incidentally, to belong to such a group, with its white shirt, brown tie, puttees, haversack and boots, and the cost of keeping them clean, took some money. Capt Hobson left the parade, meaning that when the inspecting officer – from the East Yorkshire Cyclists Territorials – arrived, Arthur Ross had to take charge. Afterwards, Ross 'went to see Welburn and after persuasion he went down with me to say he was sorry to Capt Hobson. His parents did not like it and they sent in Walter and Tom's resignations'. Other times, lads tried to fool around or stir up trouble. A sergeant's lot was a weary one, of telling off one lad for 'slodging feet', and perhaps being told off himself for not being strict enough.

Why did anyone stick it? Not every lad did; several of the 55 or so in the Company were made to leave. They may have hung on, much like the adults in the Territorial Army, for the entertainments – the fund-raising social evenings, the sport, the exercise, the parades around the town, and the camp every August. For instance on the Whit Monday holiday in 1914, the lads took the train to nearby Cherry Burton and marched to Dalton Park for manoeuvres. Then they took on Dalton villagers at cricket. Dalton were all out for 55, only for the lads to lose five wickets for nine runs; then Tom Welburn, presumably one of the brothers who resigned over a greasy jacket in January, made 28 not out and Beverley won. 'Tea was provided at the village inn,' Ross added, 'after which a short display of drill was given on the cricket ground.' After a church service, they marched back to Cherry Burton and caught the 9.13pm to Beverley. It might not sound much of a day, except that in 1914 it offered more than anything a lad could hope to do by himself. Like-minded lads made friends. The Brigade – and similar groups such as the Boy Scouts – appealed to young men, and their parents, because they saw it as another way to rise in the world. Arthur Ross worked for John Bickersteth, the clerk to the East Riding County Council in the town. Ross pasted uplifting quotes from Shakespeare in his journal, and lived in a terrace of villas next to a house called, to this day, 'Enterprise Cottage'. Far from everyone wanted to, or could afford to, submit to uniformed groups; Ross tallied 157 Lads, Boys Brigade and Boy Scouts on a parade in May 1914, out of a Beverley population of 13,600.

Often, however, those on parade were the ones in any town with something about them, such as Arthur Allinson. One Saturday in July 1914 he was walking to the cricket ground, when he saw a runaway horse, yoked to a cab: '... dropping his cricket boots he ran to the horse's head, seized the reins, and brought the animal to a standstill after running with it for about 100 yards,' the *Beverley Guardian* reported. Allinson may have learned the skill from his father, Beverley's police inspector – police textbooks taught that exact method of halting a runaway, quite a common hazard. Allinson may have known horses, in an era when Beverley and most small towns were physically and culturally not far from fields. Or the lad – who worked in a railway drawing office at York and came home at weekends, and who held a silver bugle as best bugler at Church Lads Brigade regional camp – may have had the very thing that all the uniformed groups were trying to drill into boys: in a word, 'pluck'.

Pluck, another word for courage, tellingly, is a word long gone out of fashion. Was it something any man, or any organisation, could drill into a boy? To have pluck, like Arthur Allinson, you not only had to *do* the right thing, and not leave it to someone else; you had to *know* right from wrong. By having to set up groups such as the Church Lads Brigade, were you in fact admitting that modern life no longer gave someone pluck? What was stopping young people doing plucky things, such as risking their necks for the good of others? Was it the machines taking over ever more of life, the easy-come pleasures of the 'picture houses', spectator sports and the seaside? The worship of money, and the advertising everywhere? If men of pluck won Britain the Empire, and if it would take pluck to protect it against envious rivals – not only Germany, but Russia, and maybe France; Japan, even – did Britain have enough lads of the right sort, the men of the future?

4

The Quid Pro Quo

A compromise .... is not always the negation of two opposite policies and the adoption of a middle course between them.
Twenty-Five Years: 1892-1916, volume one, by Viscount Grey of Fallodon (1925)

I

England could not agree on anything – even whether all the disagreements were healthy or not. Conservatives, also calling themselves Unionists, believed in the old and trusted authorities: the army, the monarchy, the aristocracy and the church. Liberals had their own beliefs: in liberty, in a life without the nearest priest or lord telling them what to do. Liberals could claim they had won centuries-old battles. They had their freedom to think, to worship God the way they wanted (or not at all, even), and to make money (and spend it) without the state taxing much of it. In 1914 the Liberals had been in power eight years and had won the last three elections. They knew that they had work to do still, and said so, partly as a tactic to keep their side keen, partly because it was true, and they had to explain their shortcomings away.

Rather than go through the politics from 1906, as done and spoken about by the main and best-known politicians – Herbert Asquith, prime minister since 1908; David Lloyd George, chancellor of the exchequer; and Winston Churchill, First Lord of the Admiralty, to name three – it's of more use to follow the lower-rank politicians. Ministers had to compromise to get anything agreed, and had to mind what they said in public, in case the other side used their words against them. The lower ranks could speak their minds, whether they were men who used to be of top rank, such as the former Unionist chancellor of the exchequer Michael Hicks-Beach, made Lord St Aldwyn; or the Liverpool Liberal MP Richard Holt, starting in parliament after working in the family shipping firm. (Were they freer to speak because they were not in office; or because fewer people were listening?)

Lord St Aldwyn toasted the health of the heir of Lord Harrowby, Viscount Sandon, at his coming of age celebrations, on Thursday July 23, 1914. The estate tenants and workers at Sandon, north of Stafford, ate lunch in a marquee. St Aldwyn admitted that they did not always hear good of the aristocracy. "But were there not black sheep in every class?" he asked, as a local newspaper reported later. "There were commercial men who were not always absolutely honest and there were even labouring men who sometimes scamped at their work. To pick out particular incidents of black sheep and apply them to a whole class was an unfair and a wicked thing to do." The diners clapped; as their present and future masters were paying for their meal, and watching, they could hardly do otherwise. Even at such an event, where everyone knew their place – or did not have a place at all, as the garden party and a ball later were for grander guests than the common people – the lords had to admit things were not going their way. "They lived in a democratic age," St Aldwyn went on, "but he was not sure that democracy was not tending towards bureaucracy. For the present, the power was with the democracy."

St Aldwyn made a shrewd point. Meanwhile, Richard Holt, so he wrote in his journal in July 1914, was "active with business men and some survivors of the Cobden-Bright school of thought against the ill-considered and socialistic tendencies of the Government finance ... we have certainly travelled a long way from the old Liberal principle of 'retrenchment' and

I deeply regret it. The more I see of socialistic developments the less I like them – the stronger I feel in favour of leaving individuals the maximum of personal freedom including the right to make a thorough mess of their own affairs." This was Liberal philosophy as argued generations back by John Stuart Mill. Lloyd George, making old-age pensions and national insurance, talked of fighting poverty. Liberty, to the reformers, looked like an excuse to leave people in ignorance, in dirty houses, downtrodden by all; as bad as anything by the Unionists. St Aldwyn may have spoken about democracy with a sneer that the reporter could not or dared not carry into print. St Aldwyn however foresaw that 'socialism', whatever that meant, might turn the poor – the drunks and the workshy and the decent sort alike – into new serfs, or the mob of ancient Rome, living forever off the state.

Not that politicians or anyone ever had such a debate. They seldom met under the same roof, apart from parliament. The goodwill – and the means of holding such a debate, until the radio – were lacking. Liberal and Unionist politicians, and newspapers, spoke to their own. A speaker would show how bad the other party was, by jumping on a rival's reported remark; or would simply misquote. The speaker and his side had the right ideas for the country and worked in a statesmanlike way, the other side made plots. A cleverer Unionist speaker would claim that the other side used to have leaders of principle – men now safely dead, such as Gladstone, and Bright – but not any more. In truth a politician the same as any man had to smile, shake hands and do deals with men he might not like, to get through the day. If the party-political speeches were worth listening to, it was because each side said things that the other side did not want to admit even to itself.

Unionists mocked the Liberals for taking no interest in Home Rule for Ireland, until after 1910, when the Liberals needed the 'Irish Party' of Irish Nationalists to give them enough numbers in parliament. The Liberals accused the Conservatives of hypocrisy. Unionists warned of civil war in Ireland, spreading to England, if the Protestants of Ulster could not stay in the Union. Did Conservatives *want* Ireland to look bad, to make the Liberals look weak? Would some Tories only be truly satisfied if Ireland did fall into civil war? Both sides felt strongly that they were in the right. After a speech in his Walsall constituency in April, someone in the audience asked the Unionist MP Sir Richard Cooper which he hated more, the Home Rule Bill or the Parliament Act (a Liberal law to reduce the power of the mainly Conservative House of Lords). Sir Richard replied: "Let me be quite frank" – always a sign of a politician steeling himself to say something unusually revealing – "we hate them both, and there is an end of it." Such hatred in politics – the sense that one side was unlike the other – ran deeper than over Ireland or any single issue. Richard Holt and his wife decided to move into Holt's old family home in Liverpool, after his father died there in 1908, "a home too big for our requirements but from its excellence and size nearly unsaleable – and I should hate to part with the house my father built and loved – perhaps to a Tory". Hence neither side liked a politician who left one party for the other, such as Churchill (and his changing back again after the war would not help).

II

... I think that most strikes are due to a longing for a break from the deadly monotony of a repetitive job.
The Lonely Sea and The Sky by Sir Francis Chichester

The lack of trust between Liberals and Unionists over Ireland – 'the great burning question of the day' as the Unionist MP Sir Richard Cooper put it in a possibly unfortunate phrase – made what the two main parties agreed on, all the more significant.

Usually the agreement was of a taken-for-granted kind: the monarchy, for example. When people did come into contact with royalty, they might not be impressed, or at least they said they weren't. In May 1914 Charles Wright wrote from Oxford to his sister Dorothy about a tennis match:

> *After tea I had another single with a Trinity man and the Prince of Wales was playing on the next court. He is pretty bad!! His balls with E on and ours with TC on (Trin Coll) kept getting mixed up. He has a beastly squeaky little voice.*

Few, however, came so close to royalty to form a human opinion. At most they would see the king at a distance on a short formal visit to their city, or in a passing horse-drawn coach or motor-car. Few people genuinely queried the monarchy, whether because the king was popular or because all authority stemmed from the crown. While Richard Holt grumbled in June 1911 that royalty was "a horrible nuisance on its ceremonial side tho' probably the best institution for this country", he was happy to attend the coronation of King George V that month in Westminster Abbey. Similarly, Liberals and Unionists alike would beware of any groups that did not answer to them, such as trade unions and the Labour Party; and the suffragettes, the campaigners for the vote for women.

Trade unions and socialists talked well. Ben Tillett, the dockers' union leader, told an open air meeting in Walsall in June 1914: "They were taught that the king was really the king and their children were taught to sing God save the King [here the audience laughed, according to the local newspaper report] but in any real sense there was neither control nor real power in either the cabinet or parliament. The real power belonged to those who owned the land, the wealth of the country, and the machinery of production." Tillett then predicted (wisely) that even a Labour cabinet, under the present system, "would be as supine, as stupid, as was the present government". Tillett was hinting at revolution as the only answer. Until then, socialists

– who wanted political change – were not working for *quite* the same things as trade unionists, who sought better pay and hours for the men in their union. Seldom did anyone ask whether the workers not in a union, and even the workers who were, might well be happy with the way the country was run, and merely wanted a better deal in it. Tillett hit home when he told working men that everything – schools, the national anthem – was for a reason, to make them, and the generations to come, know their place. Even if Tillett's audience laughed in agreement, what were they going to do about it? As Tillett foresaw, striking for a penny more, or for an hour less, or voting Labour, would not change who was truly in power. Was Tillett good, however, for anything besides talk?

Apart from the socialists, as sure, as faithful, as talkative and as few as the Christian apostles, most people wanted, or at least said they wanted, fairness and things done 'sportingly'. This did not mean that men wanted to carry the sports they played into the rest of their lives; many using the name of sport may have been too old to play sport any more, or never did play. Football was a battle without weapons that left you hurt and dirty. Instead, people were appealing to what people thought sport stood for; they were trying to make a political demand sound more reasonable by sounding less political.

In sport as in politics between Liberal and Unionist, one side faced another. Each side felt it ought to win; but had to tussle, and abide by the result. To be 'sporting' was to play within the rules and to either accept defeat or not crow too much in victory. You could tell winners and losers in politics or business, by who made a profit and who won an election. Beyond the obvious numbers, you had to contend with morals, the law, and groups with their own followers and interests. A Unionist parliamentary candidate, Philip Ashworth, made no sense when he said in Stafford in April that the Home Rule Bill was 'framed on un-English, unfair and unsportsmanlike lines'. If Home Rule was, as he was suggesting, like a match between two sides in some sport, surely the stronger side in the end would win, and the other lose? What he might have been trying to defend was a principle, that people should be allowed to keep what they had – whether a geographical region like Ulster, the ownership of things such as property, the respect due to a name or title, or the going rate for a job. To sum up, if unionists in Ireland gave something (loyalty to the United Kingdom), they wanted something in return (their own way over Irish Home Rule, and no parliament in Dublin where they would always be out-voted).

This sense of wanting a fair deal – a quid pro quo – ran deep, though was seldom aired. An anonymous watcher of cricket, signing himself 'Quid Pro Quo', put it as well as anyone, in the *Walsall Observer* of July 25. He complained: "When I go to a county cricket match I get a good, sound comfortable seat commanding a good view of the game, for sixpence. At Gorway [Walsall cricket club's ground], for a Saturday afternoon league match, I am charged ninepence, and can take my choice of a front seat on a ricketty old bench which is likely to let me down if I attempt to lean back, or a back seat on an uncomfortable plank with a backing of pailings, the whitewash of which adheres with sorry results to the attire of those who are misguided enough to rest their backs upon them. This, surely, is not fair value for ninepence." He closed by wondering what the three-penny seats were like; next time, he would try them; 'they cannot be much worse'.

Here, then, was a metaphor for England that men from one political extreme to the other – Lord St Aldwyn to Ben Tillett – could recognise; though they would argue over what (if anything) to do about it. All classes paid to enter; the more you could afford, the more comfort you could expect. If you did not care for the deal, you could try elsewhere. You could emigrate as Eva Tibbitts did, or go on holiday to miss the winter, as the very richest such as Gerald Legge did. What if, like Mr Quid Pro Quo, you wanted to stay where you were, because for all its faults you liked it? St Aldwyn believed, against the democratic tide of the time, that labourers, shopkeepers and landowners ought all to accept their place. Quid Pro Quo felt differently: paying a few coins gave him the right to say how a cricket club (or a parish, or country?) ran its business.

This wish for a fair deal was widespread – wider than any political party, let alone a movement such as socialism. It made England sound like the supposedly more equal and progressive Australia. It suggested some national unity. As St Aldwyn hinted, all classes had duties as well as rewards. Shops and factories could sell at a profit, but had to be fair to staff and customers. Lords had more wealth than labourers, and more responsibilities, as charitable leaders of their district, especially in hard times. Men could disagree over what was fair and what was 'taking a liberty', but agreed those were the terms of the argument. As in a good marriage, if you took, you had to give. What indeed about women in all this?

III

History has been kind to all three of the main protest movements around 1914: few would now deny women the vote, or workers the right to combine in trade unions; and if Nationalists and Unionists are each unhappy still with what they have in Ireland, at least they can be happy that the other side is unhappy. Of the three, the suffragettes have the best reputation, whether because half of Britain can always identify with them, or because of the shortcomings of later trade unionists, Nationalists and Unionists. Odd, then, that in 1914 the suffragettes should have been so despised. They had failed, and gone to extremes, itself a sign that their campaign was not working.

To take two of many court cases: on Wednesday morning, July 15, Mr McKinnon Wood, secretary of state for Scotland, was on the doorstep of his Portland Place home, speaking to his butler, Walter Hanscomb, when Janette Wallace and Bertha Watson rushed up. The butler seized Wallace while Wood warded off Watson with an umbrella. A nearby policeman claimed to hear Wallace say: 'You Scotch pig, if you don't stop forcibly feeding we shall smash you up and you can't say you haven't had a thrashing from a woman.' Watson meanwhile told the Liberal minister: 'You are a dog and a lot of hounds and stop forcibly feeding.' When searched, she was carrying an egg with the words written 'refreshing fruit'. When fined £1 each – or two weeks in prison – they screamed and had to be carried out of court. A few weeks earlier, Watson and another woman, who would not give her name, tried to chain themselves to railings in Downing Street. Fining each £2, a Bow Street magistrate told them: 'There was a time no doubt when you had a case which might have been worth fighting for, but you must recognise now that it has been killed by you and your friends long ago.'

Where to start with such sorry – and unladylike – behaviour? The suffragettes had, on purpose or by mistake, allowed their grievances to get in the way of their goal. Hence Watson's call to the minister to stop forcibly feeding the suffragettes starving themselves in protest in prison. How did the suffragettes expect to be taken seriously, as seriously as men, if they acted childishly in court? How would they ever have the ear of politicians, if they were hitting them about the head with riding whips? As for public goodwill, the suffragettes – again, whether deliberately or stupidly – only hurt or offended men and women, every time they interrupted a church service, set fire to places, poured some sort of tar in postboxes, or broke windows. By going to extremes, the suffragettes were not campaigning harder; they were showing their contempt for everyone but themselves. Suffragettes by 1914 had turned from calling for the vote to fighting against every institution. They were the first modern campaigners. They were not proposing something but flailing *against* something; things which later would be as varied as the United States in Vietnam, South African apartheid, airports, power stations, and the testing of animals in laboratories.

All such protesters believe in how important their cause (and they) are; historians generally agree. That women did get the vote after the1914-18 might give the impression that the suffragettes succeeded. Only the fact that the suffragettes stopped their campaign in August 1914 – when even they understood that Britain had no time for them any more – made success possible. Even before Continental war, the public had lost patience with suffragettes. On July 23 – the third day that King George hosted the Nationalist and Unionist leaders, Mr Asquith and others at Buckingham Palace, to seek some agreement on 'Home Rule' – a woman tried in vain to enter the palace forecourt. When she shouted something about the king receiving rebels, but not women, the crowd gave such answers as 'duck her in the fountain', 'what about your husband's dinner', and 'you ought to be ashamed of yourself'.

That suffragette did have a point; why one rule for Irish men, because they were threatening bloodshed, and another for women? While we have no way of knowing who in the crowd made those taunts, or even whose side the crowd was on, presumably the crowd was fairly representative of the country: the curious and well off, of any political side, who could spare the time to gawp outside the place of most political drama in London that day. Some, evidently, believed a woman's place was in the home. Someone, at least, felt the suffragette should feel shame, or even felt shame for her; because what the protesting woman shouted cut both ways. Trade unionists and the Irish, Nationalists or Unionists were not – yet – burning buildings and breaking things, or people; only suffragettes were. An interesting speculation is what would have become of trade unionism or Irish nationalism, without war in 1914, if a few extremists in each movement had, like the suffragettes, decided on violence. Irish Nationalists did take up arms, in Easter 1916, and after 1918; and won independence. Trade unionists stayed peaceful, because they and their members were working men, bettering their pay and hours to feed their families, not to become revolutionaries.

The few aggressive suffragettes had almost become outlaws, sheltered and paid for by outer rings of sympathisers and donors. Suffragette leaders such as Mrs Pankhurst were physically ringed by bodyguards, carrying 'Indian clubs', as a confidential memo from New Scotland Yard's criminal investigation department told police forces in the regions in July 1914. The Metropolitan Police sent the memo – with photographs and pen-pictures of 80 of the most militant suffragettes – because, in another tactic which was to be taken up by twenty-first century protesters, the suffragettes were shifting to less relevant, but easier, targets; away from London, where the police knew them too well, to the provinces.

The suffragette movement, by 1914, did not add up, partly because it had rival leaders and was no more united than the trade unions or Irish nationalism. Partly, and again like later protest movements, some suffragettes at least had given up trying to convince others – or had never felt like it in the first place. They had become anarchic, like the woman in the Met memo pictured with her tongue sticking out. (The apologetic police explained that the woman had not co-operated in having her picture taken.) But for the war, these few fanatical suffragettes could only have become yet more extreme, becoming what we would call terrorists.

IV

A sign of how the suffragettes bewildered the Liberal Government, and the country, was the lack of punishment for their crimes – which sooner or later, by their use of explosives for example, would kill people, if only themselves. Suffragettes boasted of how they went to jail and came out again to do the same again. This was not because of weak magistrates or judges: courts readily jailed trade unionists for assaulting strike-breakers, for example, on dubious evidence. Nor was it that the courts – all run by men – shied away from punishing women, for soliciting for example. No: then as now, the British courts had no answer to people who did not want to reform their ways; whether burglars with no other work skills, or fanatics for an idea. The country could tolerate those staunch law-breakers, because they were not making too much trouble, and because making allowances made England what it was; not Prussia or Spain.

England was what it was; neither divided happily by class as St Aldwyn wished; nor split in two between sensible Liberals and wrong Unionists (or the other way round). Some, like a boxer, or the faithful of a political party, would always see themselves in the mirror of their rival: Liberals and Unionists, Christian and godless, town and country, suffragette or socialist and the uninterested rest. England was like a kaleidoscope, with changing patterns at every turn. You had those who worked with their hands, and those that did not; the rough and the drunken, and the respectable and sober; the educated and articulate, and the ignorant and silent; those who sought change for the better, and those who feared change for the worse. And whether in a family, a workplace, a sports team, or the filthiest 'court' of houses backing onto one yard with one water pump and toilet for dozens to share, there were those that did the work, and those that let them.

5

On the Brink

What is war? I believe that half the people that talk about war have not the slightest idea of what it is.
John Bright speech of October 1853, from
Selected English Speeches from Burke to Gladstone
(World's Classics, 1913)

I

Robin Page Arnot in spring 1914 went from Glasgow to London, 'like so many writer Scots before me'. He went halfway back in the second half of July, as far as Barrow House, on the shores of Derwentwater in the Lake District, for a Fabian Society conference. While seeking a start on a newspaper in Fleet Street, he had become secretary of the Fabian research department. "Instead, like so many people of my age and indeed of almost any age, of having to work at something not of my choice," he typed in a memoir 60 years later, "I was doing the thing I most wanted to do in all the world." That was: working for socialist revolution. He and his new friends wanted to end capitalism, and what they called superstitions (such as Christmas, and birthdays); and to reform dress, language, ranks, and titles, even 'mister'. This summer fortnight in the country was their chance each year to live as they wanted, earnestly and simply. In the morning they heard reports; in the afternoon they went bathing, rowing and climbing; and later, more speeches. "When the din of discussion had died away each evening I could hear before I slept the tinkling sound of the Lodore Falls within the grounds of Barrow House," Arnot recalled.

The Fabians made camp in tents beside the lake, or stayed in hotels. Early one morning Arnot went to the jetty, testing the water with his toes. Swimming between the islands of Derwentwater was 'a bearded, good-looking lean figure of a man': George Bernard Shaw. Meeting for the first time, the playwright said to Arnot: "The temperature is very even." Arnot, and others, duly went in. Such was Fabianism; you left the world (and your clothes) behind, and chose a new element, so cold that only the most determined would go through with it. Once you became used to it – the talk of guild socialism, collectivism, provision for maternity, and the like – you could tell yourself you were enjoying it, and look down on everyone else as too stupid to follow. Except, if socialist reforms were so good for you, why weren't more people there? As Arnot admitted, he saw Americans, Indians, Scots and continental Europeans at the conference, and fairly few English.

Everyone was looking forward to the arrival of the French socialist leader, Jaures. As the fortnight ended, on August 1, Arnot wrote: "I saw the face of Beatrice Webb turn white as she learned by the morning papers of the assassination in Paris by a warmonger of her old friend Jean Jaures. It was this more than any flood of frequently contradictory telegrams in the daily papers which made us all realise that war was very near indeed; that it would be hard to prevent it; and that the first blood sacrifice had been made ..."

The Fabians left the Lakes by train at Keswick, for London. "We were leaving a world of keen and animated Socialist discussion and planning of how to end Capitalism, of what was to take the place of it, and of how to provide the means to build up a new society. But this which had seemed so near, so actual, so full of *zeitgeist* was already far in the past." So Arnot claimed. Whenever the train stopped, they bought newspapers, and their gloom lifted. "On the facts as known to us there seemed no likelihood of Britain going to war. It was fantastic, utterly needless and groundless. Apart from the overwhelming repugnance of the mass of the people to war (not to mention the reiterated pacific intentions of our Government) there was no reason for it."

II

"The first sign of war that we heard of was on the wedding day," Alan Brooke wrote on board ship in mid-August. He had sailed to England from India in June, in a full four-berth cabin 'no larger than a dog kennel'. In the mornings he studied German and an 'excellent new book on tactics'. His main homework was to marry, in Ireland, Jane Mary Richardson. His bride, like him, was a child of County Fermanagh. "Day all went off splendidly," Brooke wrote on Wednesday July 29, the day after the wedding. They drove to St Michael's Church, Trory, by brougham (a closed carriage drawn by a single horse) and left by hired car. Just as the couple's change of transport showed a world on the brink between real horse-power and machines, so the weather was a sign of a hopeful future. The sky cleared, Brooke wrote, 'and the sun was shining brightly on us when we came out of the church'. The guests, who had decorated the car with slippers, pelted the Brookes with rice. "It was a great relief to get off, away from the crowd and to find just the two of us breezing through space. It was quite one of the happiest moments of my life," Brooke wrote.

Army officers had to make the most of all-too-brief months at home – the Brookes had been planning to marry for six years – compared with years in India. After a reception at his wife's family home at Rossfad, they took the train to Gweedore

Hotel, in neighbouring County Donegal. They honeymooned quietly. On the evening of August 1 they went out to fish the river running past their hotel, 'and I caught a few small trout, but nothing worth keeping,' Brooke wrote. They planned to stay a week, return to Rossfad, and pack their presents, and Brooke would sail back to Bombay on August 11. A hint of war was on their wedding day, when a guest from the Royal Navy had to leave after the ceremony, 'but of course that was more or less of a precautionary measure'.

III

If Ireland was near to civil war – so near, said Lord Harrowby to Unionists in Stafford in April, that they might hear any day of a massacre of Ulstermen – how did a Ulster couple manage to marry, in Ulster, without any mention of it? If anywhere in Ireland would see conflict, it would be Fermanagh: then, as now, it was one of the most mixed counties of Protestant and Catholics. So was Ireland on the brink, but Alan Brooke kept quiet about it in letters, so as not to worry his mother in France? Or were the only ones talking of war the English, who had nothing better to do than poke their nose into other people's business; and a few Irish politicians, such as the Ulster Unionist Sir Edward Carson, who were boosting their careers? Guy Paget admitted after the war: "I was on the fringe of the gun running with Carson and the Ulstermen. How near we were to civil war during those months will never really be known. The powder was ready and lots of people were striking matches all over the place." At the time, some feared that war, or the danger of it, in Ireland might tempt unnamed foreign powers to attack England. When continent-wide war came, some claimed that Germany took advantage of England giving all its attention to Ireland. This was crediting Germany with more cunning than it had, and assumed, wrongly, that foreigners worried about

England before they made their moves. Certainly neither the Unionist nor Home Rule sides in Ireland held back in case of what foreigners might do. As Paget admitted, men like himself made civil war more likely by sending weapons to Ireland; and not all for the Unionist side.

On Sunday July 26, a 29-year-old Army officer, Gordon Shephard, on leave from his regiment, took the tram from Dublin to the fishing port of Howth. There he directed the landing of guns by boat for the Nationalist Volunteers. He wrote in a letter soon after that "the whole was carried out in a most orderly manner though there was some scrimmaging at the start. The Volunteers marched off when all was over." Private armies were against the law, and had been since the Wars of the Roses, for good reasons. The Nationalists knew they were doing wrong: a 'Cycle Corps' of their men watched for the police. Yet the day could not have been that secret, because newspapers ran photographs of the cyclists; and of Volunteers in their Sunday best suits, marching with rifles over their shoulders.

Shephard had an impeccable background. Named after the imperial hero Gordon of Khartoum, he combined his love of sailing with some amateur spying on German harbours. He may have aided the Irish Nationalists because he had become a Roman Catholic; yet the reason he offered in a letter was one more, daft and irresponsible, example of an Englishman's wish for life to be like sport. He reckoned that because the Unionists had guns, it was 'fair play for nationalists to have a counter-consignment of weapons'.

Now that both sides had the means to fight, men who denied civil war could happen were as dangerous as the likes of Lord Harrowby, who merely made themselves look silly by exaggerating the risk. In Ireland in July 1914, the same as before or after, it made no difference to most people where they were ruled from. They wanted a quiet life; they no more thought of spoiling the Brookes' honeymoon than the newly-weds thought of it being spoiled. It would only take a few hot-heads, drunk from the feel of a rifle in their hand, or plain drunk, to upset the other side, and the other side hitting back, harder, and it would be like a schoolyard or a pub fight – no-one asked for it, or remembered how it started, but once a punch stung you, you would not be satisfied until you had unstung yourself by hurting someone else. That was how wars began. In what looked to some like the last effort for peace, King George V hosted talks with English and Irish politicians at Buckingham Palace between July 21 and 25. Even this offended some Liberals, as the King appeared to lack confidence in his Government. In any case, the conference came to nothing; the elite of politics and London in general had their summer holidays to head for, starting with the race meeting at Goodwood. Paget was right not to know where interfering with Ireland would end.

IV

William Swift, the retired Gloucestershire village schoolmaster with the injured aunt, rose a little earlier than usual, before 6am, on Monday July 20, the day that Sarah Pick wrote, no doubt painfully, her letter to him. He was 'busy at housework most of the morning' and had jobs to do for St Andrew's, his parish church, drawing out cheques for coal and 'vino sacre', and for Walter Organ, the village's young coal haulier. Swift sent cheques to a local solicitor and parishioner, John Henry Jones, to sign. In his diary Swift wrote: "He goes to Ireland probably next Friday or Saturday; he told me this yesterday," presumably at church. "He thought the Irish might very fairly be trusted with Home Rule. 'Look at Canada with several parliaments, and why not Ireland?'" So Swift quoted Jones as saying. "Germany got on very well in the matter of religious fairness and why not Ireland? &c."

Swift's daughter-in-law Annie came in the afternoon for a couple of hours, to pass on gossip. "She said it was reported that Uncle William had applied for relief to the Guardians so as to make his son 'brass up'." This offers an interesting insight into family thinking; that old uncle asked for state help, not so much because he was poor, but so as to shame his son into looking after him better.

Swift, who turned 73 in 1914, was slowing. In the last two years he had had 'faints' and 'swoons'; 'housemaid's knee' from kneeling; and lumbago. In February, when he asked Boots in Gloucester for something for his rheumatic pains, the chemist had told him about new tablets: Aspirin. In May, he had to stop when walking because of a tight chest. It is given to no man to know the hour of his death, and Swift was not to know that he, like Gerald Legge, was in the last full year of his life.

He kept his routine. He rose around 6am, cleaned and swept – women's work, but his wife Rosena had died in 1907. On Saturday July 18, he picked the last of the broad beans for Sunday meals and dug some of his potatoes. He had to ask a neighbour, Mrs Gilkes, to get some earth out of his left eye: "She then sat for half an hour." Emily Gilkes, the wife of Daniel the village railway stationmaster, gave Swift some gossip too, about the renovation of her house: "Then of scandalous behaviour of our young neighbour. CP aged 14 and three lads at the school. L upon hearing of CP received the complaint with great apathy and indifference. Lastly that the children at the school did not learn their tables. And Dorothy Locke had just lost L chance of good employment in consequence of this and bad spelling; this is a blot on our school." Wisely – though Mrs Gilkes was moaning about the school Swift had run for three decades – Swift did not, at least not in his diary, become angry about something that was no longer his affair. Who 'L' was, is a mystery, but 'CP' was probably Cyril Phelps, the eldest son of another neighbour, Hubert Phelps the baker and his wife Priscilla.

Like the householders around him, Swift had a physically demanding life, helping and helped by neighbours and family. Dorothy Hill, the young niece of Mr and Mrs Gilkes, picked the last of the raspberries and currants. Though busy, Swift had time to read good books: the Bible, Boswell's *Life of Johnson*, Shakespeare, and the French fairy stories the *Contes de Fées*, which on July 22 he finished for the 45th time, as dated by him on the cover. As a man of habit, thanks to such attention to detail, he had kept a diary for more than 50 years; a Pepysian feat, one of the great unappreciated recordings of English life. If he had great emotions, he seldom gave way to them in writing. What he had to say was the unexciting stuff of a village; of attending near-deserted church services (on that July 22, he and Mr Phelps were the only ones in church that morning, apart from the vicar); and of occasional train journeys into Gloucester to buy the few things the village could not provide. Swift and the people around him had no quarrel with Ireland, or Germany, or anywhere.

V

The Army officer Donald Weir was scratching around for news all July for his weekly letter from India to his mother at home. He had little to do except run the regimental rugby team in the afternoons, and go through the usual rounds of dinners and golf. He was playing a long game; when the colonel asked if he wanted to go 'to the depot', in England, he said he was not keen: "For one reason only," he admitted to his mother, "that I hope to be in for a year's leave next February or March though I have little hope of getting more than nine months, whereas if I went to the depot I might get three months at Christmas and that is all."

On Wednesday July 29 he wrote a few lines before lunch, "as I will be playing in a football match this afternoon and after that I have got fids of work to do so much so that I am going to make a night of it, not dine in mess but have cocoa and biscuits in my quarters and work up to one or two o'clock if needs be. Anyway I have to get answers written to a number of Mil History papers and hand them in on Saturday so there is little time to spare." Beyond that, he knew his next few months: rugby tournaments in Lucknow and Calcutta, then to Delhi, then manoeuvres. As for the news from home, he called it 'pretty bad':

> what with the trouble in Dublin and the possibility of a general conflagration among the different European powers. I am afraid our King cannot feel very happy at the way matters are going alone just now. The remarks about the King in the Radical press after the conference at Buckingham Palace are disgraceful. Of course we only get just the general outlines of events in the daily telegrams; so much goes on at home which we do not hear about until a fortnight later. We have been having incessant rain for days past now but it makes the air so cool and though rather depressing I like it.

Weir still had home leave on his mind. "All said and done I have only had eight months leave in six and a half years out here so feel entitled to a winter at home especially as I get that bally hay-fever in the summer."

VI

Frank Balfour had a routine as much as William Swift; plans for a holiday as much as Donald Weir; an Eton education like his near-contemporary Gerald Legge; and marriage on his mind as much as Alan Brooke, though more in hope. Otherwise his life had little in common with any of them. On his hunting expedition early in 1914, Legge may have passed Balfour, who worked as the inspector of Berber district in Sudan, beside the Nile north of Khartoum. Having returned to Sudan in

December 1913 after leave in England, Balfour wrote that he was 'up to the neck' with:

taxes, trade, prices of grain and animals, cattle-plague, sanitation (if any), schools, crime, markets, the state of the river, date trees, police, and all the thousand and one things one has to deal with here. One falls straight into it at once – even my dog greeted me as if I'd been away four days, not four months, and barring the big difference of having run up against you, I feel as if I'd never been away at all.

The 'you' was 'my dear Irene', the Honourable Irene Lawley, an aristocratic beauty he had evidently fallen for the previous autumn. For the next months, and indeed years, he had just about enough maturity, and good humour, to express in letters how he felt about being thousands of miles from her, and the rest of civilisation; without going too far by becoming too self-pitying or menacing. At times it was a close call; he admitted he tore up some of his replies, and on June 2 was reduced to 'collecting all the back Tatlers in the club, and going into the deserted Billiards Room', to search for her picture, 'for a clue as to your whereabouts'. On June 23, he received a 12-day-old letter from her, "as I sit sweating under the office punkah [swinging fan], and I can't do any work till I've answered it. I salve my conscience by using the cheaper brand of Government paper." He had plotted to 'lure' her to the Austrian Tyrol. Instead, she was planning to travel to America. He hoped to meet someone called 'Baffy' early in August, probably at Salzburg, "and drift home. I want to see Munich among other places. I was choked off it last year by home-sickness and a Wagner festival." The dream of meeting her again plainly kept him going, though he managed to keep his tone playful: "I hate the idea of having to wait till September to see you, and I'm not sure I shan't pursue you to America … I only ask you for a chance – I'm not in a hurry and I won't hurry you or pester you with what the Victorians called 'attentions'!"

In fairness, it sounded as if he was indeed pestering her with (already a quaint term) 'attentions'. Why did she put up with it? She may have liked him. They did have friends in common; on July 26 he reported that 'Baffy tells me that you are going to have an operation to your nose which horrifies me'. It must have crossed Balfour's mind that he was probably not the only smitten young man writing to her; nor was he. As the sort of rich young lady who had nothing better to do than be seen in places where *Tatler* magazine might photograph her, she might have enjoyed reading and answering letters of the sort that ended "I am, if possible, rather more 'yours' than usual, Frank." His letters, besides, told of a genuinely out-of-the-ordinary life, an odd mix of the exotic and the leisurely European – he had ponies to ride, 'and very good tennis every afternoon' he reported on July 3; again using works notepaper, this time from the Governor's Office. A week later he described enduring two hours of the 'haboob':

First a little bright yellow cloud on the horizon across the desert to the east – in ten minutes it covers all the sky in that direction ... – in the interval you stow away everything that could possibly break loose, double mooring ropes and drive in the pegs. Then it falls on you in a hill of wind and sand against which you shut doors and windows in vain – there is nothing to be done but sweat in misery till it's over, and then go and wash the mud out of your eyes and ears.

He knew by then that he would be on leave from July 26, and in the Tyrol 'in little over a week'; only his holiday seemed cursed. His relief at the governor's office missed a train, and his relief at Berber came down with diphtheria at home. On July 26 he wrote to her that he had been 'buried under papers and people' at Berber. He made a rare comment on current affairs:

The Buckingham Palace show seems to have ended in smoke – and it almost looks as if we might only be saved from civil war by an European one – anyway I don't believe Asquith and Co will dare force it to a fight in Ulster – I don't see why the King shouldn't make them dissolve.

Frank Balfour – a nephew of the former Unionist prime minister Arthur Balfour – had political work of his own, before he could begin his leave. He had to go 150 miles down the river, pick up camels, and trek back, on the way meeting the local sheikhs and kings. In a letter dated July 28 he told of a perilous and primitive crossing of the Nile. A native, Osman, whose father the British had shot for shooting a colonel in 1885, 'and the local charon' – meaning a ferryman, Balfour showing off his classical Greek – paddled with two sticks, 'to the end of which were bound bits of old sugar boxes'. Balfour, in the bows of the boat, having taken his shoes off in case he had to swim, 'bailed for dear life'.

Back on land, a sandstorm blew. Balfour ate what dinner he could in under a blanket hung on the side of a native bedstead; he tied his head in a towel,

> *and pretended to go to sleep – after about an hour of that when I was on the verge of being buried alive, Osman came and said there was a house near by – they dug me out and we staggered to it. At least ten men left it as I arrived and they had a fire in the middle of the room for cooking. Further description of the atmosphere is unnecessary – it was better than the sand though, and I slept the sleep of the just till dawn.*

August came as Balfour rode on camels back to Berber. Despite the 'desperate' summer heat of midday, when men had to halt, recent rain meant mud even in sandy country, 'and a camel in mud is the most despicable of God's creatures', Balfour reported.

VII

The collapse of that Buckingham Palace conference left 'the country and the Empire with the greatest danger they have known in the history of living man', the *Times* wrote rather dramatically on Saturday July 25. Only then did the newspaper turn from Ireland to what it called 'Europe and the crisis'. In the last 36 hours, it said, 'a grave crisis' had arisen, between Austria-Hungary, and Servia, which the *Times* summed up, as only it could, as 'a small and excitable Balkan kingdom'. It seemed to the *Times* even more of a crisis than the ones of 1908-9 (when Austria took over Bosnia, which neighbouring Servia resented) and 1912-13 (when much of the Balkans went to war with Turkey, or each other). The 'conflagration', as the *Times* delicately put it, might catch all the 'Great Powers'. Most likely to start a war this time was Austria-Hungary, which seemed set on breaking Servia, before Servia broke it. Given this sniff of a war, some reporters would do anything to follow the story – because they had to if they wanted to stay in the job, and because they wanted to.

The war correspondent E Ashmead Bartlett, for instance, left London on the Sunday, July 26, under orders to cover the Austrian Army. He took the train, running as normal, down the Rhineland to Frankfurt. Germans he spoke to laughed at the idea of European war. Inside Austria, however, he found the railways disorganised. At Vienna he found he would be at least five days behind the armies, and the authorities would not give a time for warcos to leave. Bartlett decided on Monday to try to join the Servian army, at Nish, 'where I knew I would be welcome, having made the campaign against Bulgaria with the Servians in the previous year'. The Austrians, obviously, would not let him pass into Servia. He would have to take the long way round, first on the 4.50pm to Budapest, crowded with 'Roumanians, Servians, Bulgarians, Russians, and a conglomeration of Levantines, all seeking to regain their own homes before communication entirely broke down'. If it ever struck Bartlett there was no point heading for a battlefield, if he had no way to tell anyone his news, it did not stop him. The urge of the true reporter, as ever, was to *witness* – such as Austrian officers leaving for their regiments at the front, and the ladies of Vienna weeping for their husbands. What the newspapers did with his writing, or whether his despatches even reached home, he would worry about later.

Troop trains blocked the line. The travellers reached Budapest at 10pm. A train was leaving almost at once for Brasso, then on the frontier of 'Roumania', now Brasov in the middle of that country. Bartlett, and his baggage, made it – but only as far as a corridor. He had not seen a train so packed since 'the flight of the entire population of Thrace after the rout of Lule Burgas', he reminisced. 'The guard blew his whistle, and we moved slowly out whilst a despairing scream arose from hundreds left behind.' Bartlett was taking himself hundreds of miles out of his way into one of the most backward parts of Europe. After a sleepless night the train crossed Hungary, stopping at every station, on the Wednesday, July 29. Men had to set off for their regiment as they had been dressed when given the slip of paper of mobilisation: peasants in their smocks, small farmers in riding breeches and bowler hat; clerks with pens behind their ears. All 'to fight for a cause which not one in ten understood and in which not one in a hundred was really interested ...' Bartlett raged. "They had ceased to be human beings in the eyes of the Government; they were now so many living creatures capable of bearing arms, mere numbers to be counted and killed like sheep, so that Austrian statesmen could boast that their country could put 1,600,000 men in the field." Most of the called-up men looked surprised, not anguished, Bartlett reported. "Such is human nature – nothing appeals to the mass of mankind so much as excitement and a change."

Did Bartlett have enough self-consciousness to think that applied to him, too?

Bartlett changed at Brasso and arrived at Bucharest at midnight. In the Roumanian capital on the Thursday he bought kit – he had left London without any – and asked around. The government was neutral, its army wanted war with Austria. The people, as the ones who would not have to do any fighting, showed how they felt: "Whenever soldiers marched through the streets they were received with tremendous enthusiasm. At night time in the cafés the officers, who always wear full uniform, stuck large bouquets in their buttonholes, and sang patriotic songs." At 7pm on the Friday, July 31, Bartlett took the train to Sofia. Bulgarians seemed peaceful, Bartlett noted, though (or because?) their small country of a few million had lost the colossal number of 140,000 men in two wars the previous year. At midnight, after well over 1200 miles and five days of more or less non-stop travel, Bartlett pulled into Sofia. "There was no news of any sort."

VIII

At least Bartlett was looking for news. For every other English man and woman on the Continent – whether there for work, or through marriage; usually for pleasure – a time would come when even the blindest noticed that everyone else was changing. It depended on country, as each – first Austria-Hungary and Servia, then Russia, Germany and France – began mobilising. Few ever holidayed in the Servian capital Belgrade, near to the border with Austria, and shelled on July 28. Few English people went further east than the Tyrol, for the reason raised by Ashmead Bartlett's thousand-mile journey. If you had only one or two weeks away, you could only take the train as far as, say, Switzerland, Marseilles, Dresden or Vienna, or else you would spend half your holiday *en route*.

With so much to see and so little time, the Continental holiday did attract the sort of man who would exert himself half to death, take a month to recover, and for the next ten months look forward to the next holiday: men such as A T Daniel, headmaster of Uttoxeter Grammar School in the Staffordshire market town. As soon as school finished for the summer he went cycling in France, leaving his wife behind. On July 31 he wrote to her – clearly having heard that war was looming across the Continent – that war meant at most a heavier income tax and a fall on the stock exchange; a 'Mafeking night' (when, naturally, England won) and a few exciting pictures in the illustrated papers; something distant and theatrical. "Here, with the merest threat, the poor folk see their crops trampled down, thousands of soldiers passing and a bereavement in every family ..."

'Here' was the far east of France, only 30 miles from the border with Germany, since France had lost Alsace and Lorraine to Germany after the war of 1870. Ever since, France had wanted to fight Germany again, if only someone else would join their side. Late on August 1, in the dark, Daniel reached Verdun:

> ... and I had some difficulty in passing groups of horses that were being brought in by soldiers. The entrance to the town is through many forts and to be quite sure of my way I asked a soldier if that was the proper entrance to Verdun. He rather gruffly told me it was but seemed suspicious. After some trouble I found this hotel and went to bed but did not get five minutes' sleep. The mobilisation had at last begun and all night long groups of reservists came marching up the stony street singing the Marseillaise with stirring fervour.

Daniel doubted if anyone slept in Verdun that night, because 'nearly every ten minutes heavy motor trolleys of ammunition and other warlike gear came rumbling past over the uneven pavement'.

6

The Island Club

For some time before the war broke out a belief had been gradually extending and strengthening that modern warfare of any magnitude between the Great Powers was now impossible, in view of economic interdependence among the nations.

The History of the Great European War: Its Causes and Effects, by W Stanley Macbean Knight (September 1914)

I

You could soon see why, within a week, most of the countries on the Continent went to war with each other. Russia was sticking up for Servia, and above all for itself, looking for land from the faltering Turkish Empire. Germany felt it had to stand by its ally, Austria-Hungary. As it had invaded so many neighbours lately and taken land off them, Germany could easily feel ringed by enemies.

England was an island; which was not the same as saying England had nothing in common with the Continent. Northern France looked much like southern England; the Low Countries, much like the flat eastern counties of England. England had traded with neighbours, and neighbours of neighbours, since before recorded history. Nineteen-fourteen marked 200 years since the first English king of the house of Hanover, the German-speaking George I. For the romantics who still wished for the House of Stuart, some newspapers noted that the rightful ruler was another German – Queen Marie Thérèse of Bohemia, married to Prince Ludwig of

Bavaria, who became king of Bavaria in November 1913, in place of the quaintly titled 'Mad Otto'. She, reportedly, did not wish to be Queen of England.

Royalty spread family webs across the continent. The German Kaiser Wilhelm II was a grandson of Queen Victoria, the same as the English King George V. The Austrian Franz Ferdinand and his wife had visited England in autumn 1913; they hosted the kaiser a month before their deaths. A German torpedo boat gave a tow as far as the north German island of Borkum to the kaiser's boat, Meteor; and to Captain Sycamore, a yachtsman from Brightlingsea, Essex, on his way from Denmark to Cowes for the annual 'week'. A telegram from Berlin on July 27 ordered the Meteor to Cowes, only for headwinds to keep it in port. "I did not believe the German emperor himself expected war with England," Sycamore told East Anglian newspapers. Even if the captain and the newspapers each puffed up the story, it showed at least the Europe-wide calendar that the cultured and rich lived by – boat-owners, music-lovers, businessmen.

The rulers of Europe could still clash, despite their shared interests, destinations and backgrounds, just as members of a family could. Yet it's striking how many middling people, not only the idle rich, had dealings with countries that turned out to be enemies or allies. While Fabians were bathing in the Lakes, Labour politicians were talking with Jaures and their continental equivalents at a conference in Brussels. Bishops were in conference at Constance. English football teams were on tour, and old players were coaching continental clubs. Bretons toured England as sellers of onions, Frenchmen worked in London as cooks, Germans around the country as waiters and pork butchers, Italians as ice-cream makers, Hungarians as violinists. Adventurous young people then, as now, used a musical or other paying talent to see the world; or they gave language lessons to the studious, such as Clifford Gothard. He went to Hamburg in 1911, to learn German, as the language of engineering. Germany even touched William Swift in the village of Churchdown. Cropping up in his diary in the summer of 1914 is a Mr Walker, whose daughter Florence Browne was in a lunatic asylum in Surrey and whose son-in-law had placed a 'little boy', presumably a grandson, in a 'creche infant asylum' in Munich. In mid-July Mr Walker was planning to take free passage to Hamburg with a 'sea captain of Mr W's acquaintance' and then take the train to Munich to carry off the boy. 'Seems an awkward business', Swift noted.

The English, then, showed themselves as keen as the French or Germans to use other countries – keener, maybe, to leave their weather behind. In March 1906 the shipping company owner Richard Holt and his wife stayed at a hotel in Taormina, in Sicily, which Holt described in his journal as 'not good and very German, but with the best views of Etna'. As that typically English remark about 'views' suggests, the English might travel far for the sake of foreign landscapes, but found the going harder with foreigners. That same month Holt stayed at the Amstel Hotel 'as usual' in Amsterdam: "The object of my visit was to try to come to terms with the German Australian Co [company] but their representative, Mr Harms, was impossible: ignorant and grasping."

Each side could not help being the sum of their past. Germans had sprawled for centuries from the Alps to the Baltic, and newly united were still finding their political weight. For centuries England had been without land on the Continent, and had made an empire on other continents out of weakness – never something an Englishman would admit, any more than anyone else. To reach England, or leave it, you had to cross the sea for some hours, days or weeks; maybe hazardous, even impossible, in a storm at any time of year. When Louis Bleriot made history by crossing the English Channel in his monoplane in 1909, England could no longer boast of 'complete isolation'. Maynard Willoughby Colchester-Wemyss made this point in his monthly letter to the King of Siam in June 1914. "The passage from one country by aeroplane to the other through the air is now a matter of daily occurrence, dirigible balloons can easily make the journey and he would be a rash man who would attempt to limit the possibilities that lie before those engaged in the conquest of the air during the next ten years." The conqueror of the air might be halfway to conquering England.

Colchester-Wemyss makes an interesting and unusual source. An informed enough man, he was chairman of Gloucestershire County Council, a magistrate, and lord of the manor of Westbury on Severn. By setting out one topic a month, for his Asian reader, he went into detail that news reports and diaries of the day took for granted. He picked up that parliament, and French and Belgian senators, were talking about a rail tunnel under the Channel. This forced the English to ask what they wanted to do with their neighbours, because whereas flying machines were at the mercy of the weather as much as ships, trains would not be. Colchester-Wemyss wrote: "Now of course very large steamers pass across several times in the day, some of them specially constructed to reduce to a minimum the miseries of sea sickness and moving so fast across the Channel that much time would not be gained over a train travelling through a tunnel under the sea." Even the supporters of a tunnel suggested a dip in it, so that it could be easily flooded; or exploded. You could argue, a tunnel could save England; if England lost control of the sea, and France stayed friendly, England could import the food she needed. "But could we assume France friendly always?" Colchester-Wemyss asked. "No, whatever the commercial advantages ... we must always remember that each generation is in turn trustee only of the heritage of England and has no right to take any steps which might deprive England of an incalculable advantage ...", namely the advantage of being an island, making it much harder for a neighbour to invade. In isolated safety, England could mind its own business or poke its nose into other people's.

II

Geography worked both ways. Being an island made it harder for Britain to fight anyone on land; as the Continental countries knew well. Britain made much of its navy, to hold its empire together and to defend the seas – its borders. Its volunteer armies policed the empire and were in any case a fraction of the conscript armies of France, Germany, Russia, even Austria-Hungary. If Britain had wanted a war with anyone on the Continent, it would have built a larger army; it would have joined in more often in more of Europe's nineteenth-century wars. Peace for itself and the rest of Europe suited Britain; but as one power after another mobilised for war, would anyone listen? 'Europe ablaze', said the *Lincolnshire Echo* on Monday July 27. "War is not yet declared and a faint hope still persists that it may be avoided ... bellicose enthusiasm prevails in Vienna, Berlin and Budapest ..."

The next day, the *Echo* said: "Nobody wants war which can only prove disastrous to all the nations of Europe but then wars are never precipitated, as far as civilised countries are concerned at any rate, through the sheer wanton lust for battle. More often than not they arise through comparatively trivial causes. It can only be hoped that statesmanship will be equal to averting a catastrophe unprecedented in the annals of history ..." The *Echo* was at best half right. Somebody, plainly, wanted war; Austria-Hungary started it. The *Echo* in fact managed as neatly as anyone at the time to sum up the chain: if Russia, 'as head of the Slav nations' took matters to extremes, Germany would 'enter the field' as Austria's ally. "And France will carry out her obligation by supporting Russia." Were the 'trivial causes' worth a 'catastrophe', as the *Echo* – accurately as it turned out – put it? Three of the four rulers of those countries lost the war: the German kaiser had to leave his country, the Austrian empire split into seven, the Russian Czar Nicholas II was murdered. So much for their statesmanship. Why would they not listen to Britain? Lloyd George in his war memoirs came down on the Foreign Secretary, Edward Grey (by then dead) for his impartial but 'weak and uncompelling appeals to the raging nations of Europe to keep the peace'. Even Lloyd George sounded as if he believed stronger British appeals would have been compelling. If the British were telling foreigners – from the Irish outward – what was best for the British was best for them, wouldn't foreigners merely resent it as British hypocrisy, even if the British had a point? In any case, surely the time to appeal for peace was before any 'raging'? Foreign emperors, the same as Britain's leaders, did not listen to many people in their own country, let alone anybody else's.

In a democracy, the reader of newspaper editorials (let alone the writers) can easily make the mistake of believing that the right to vote men into power every few years, and the freedom to say what you think, also means you can expect those in power to heed what you say. As if those in power, who have worked for years to get there, would ever share decisions – with the ignorant, the uninterested and undecided, and their rivals. Political leaders did not ask for their country's views by postcard in 1914 for the same reason they do not ask by electronic mail in this century. Even inside the Liberal Government and around it – the friendliest newspaper editors, the king and his courtiers, relatives, friends, officials – few people even got a word with Asquith and the ministers that mattered, let alone had an influence. Richard Holt, as an MP, had some claim to a voice about whether to go to war. Reporters of parliament named him as leader of the Liberal 'millionaires' in the Commons, suspicious of big-spending Lloyd George. In 1913 the then war minister Jack Seely had 'most confidentially' consulted him 'about the conveyance of the Army to Armageddon'. As his flippant phrasing suggested, Holt was 'much amused'. A typical Liberal, he was set against war. His journal entry for the week ending Sunday August 2, 1914, showed his strong views, and that he had absolutely no say in what his government was doing:

We are all in the midst of the most miserable alarm ... Even a week ago we thought not much of it ... What England will do seems uncertain though it is almost impossible to believe that a Liberal Government can be guilty of the crime of dragging us into this conflict in which we are in no way interested. The fear of war has produced a paralysis of business, the Bank rate being advanced from 3 to 4 per cent of Thursday to 8 per cent on Friday and 10 per cent on Saturday. The stock exchanges in London and all the big towns being closed and also many of the produce exchanges. Today an Echo [in Liverpool?] has been published (how these horrors benefit the press!) and we are told that Russia and Germany are actually at war.

Holt cursed even the *fear* of war – the uncertainty, besides the loss of markets and materials – as bad for business, yet was sharp enough to notice that some, such as newspapers, were as quick to profit. In fairness, in the few days of this crisis, a leader only had so many hours awake, only so many people he could take views from. An able leader stayed in power as long as Asquith did precisely because he understood his friends, and enemies, already. Any minister only had so many letters he could sign, only so many meetings he could attend in a day. Lloyd George had enough work keeping the banks in business, Churchill with the navy, Sir Edward Grey urging diplomats to keep what was left of the peace. What was the point in asking for opinions when the crisis changed from day to day, as ever more countries went nearer to war? While the question was always 'what is best for Britain?' it changed from 'how can Britain prevent war?' to the more realistic 'should Britain go to war, or not?'

At least the men at the very centre of power could confer easily. Their work, and lives, did not take them far, physically. Partly, the things they relied on to take in news and send out decisions – letters, telegrams, the telephone – tied them to one place. Partly, keeping to a small part of London kept the rest of the world out. For instance J A Spender, the editor of the *Westminster Gazette*, wrote in a memoir after the war that he had little time out of his office before war broke out. He had two short talks with Grey:

> *I saw him again late in the evening at his room at the Foreign Office on Monday, August 3 and it was to me that he used the words which he has repeated in his book; 'the lamps are going out all over Europe and we shall not see them lit again in our lifetime'. We were standing together at the window looking out into the sunset across St James' Park and the appearance of the first lights along the Mall suggested the thought.*

The 'lamps going out' is the most famous and powerful metaphor of August 1914; what is striking but seldom noted is that Grey – who was supposed to represent Britain to the part of the world not British – stuck himself in a small patch of central London. Downing Street for cabinet meetings was around the corner; parliament, a couple of streets away. Ambassadors called from their nearby embassies; they, and Grey, did not have far to go for pleasure, even, if they had the time. Regular morning riders in Hyde Park, for exercise, included King George and his daughter Princess Mary; many army officers based in London; and Churchill. Typically politicians lived near Westminster, whether they owned or rented for 'the season' of February to July. The Holts usually took a furnished house around Sloane Square. They could give and take invitations to dinners and parties, from a ball at Buckingham Palace downwards. On July 21, 1914 the Holts' time at 112 Eaton Square ran out and Richard Holt stayed at the Reform Club, for the first time ('very comfortable'). To reach your club, usually around Pall Mall, you could stroll across the park or take a cab for a shilling; all these were chances to have those more relaxed conversations with fellows, that somehow proved so much more important than formal meetings. You could eat, and gossip with like-minded men – army officers, Liberals, clergy, or Scots. A club was one more way to get on. Even the Communists had a club, in much less fashionable and cheaper Charlotte Street, off Tottenham Court Road, as visited by the socialist Robin Page Arnot. Members' clubs belonged to the well-off – a club's annual fee might be more than £100, and it might cost as much again to become a member.

That instinct to club together was sound, and widespread; even in August, the holiday month; even if it was a forced holiday, because schools and factories shut. Some liked to be alone, fishing on a river bank, but, the *Burton Daily Mail* claimed on August 1, 'the great majority of people really like to take their holiday when all holiday places are crowded, simply because they are crowded'. Even at the best of times, mankind had an urge to be 'in it', whether a family, an occupational group, or an artistic or sporting interest; or, when abroad, bunching in the same hotel, quarter of a town, or favourite destination (and maybe copying the native French, Swiss or German crowd). Even the single-minded warco Ashmead Bartlett, who left Sofia on Sunday August 2 at 7am, palled up with his own sort, "a German newspaper correspondent whom I had known in the Turkish war. We were the best of friends, sharing our frugal repast together, talking of the past, and of our plans for the future." Bartlett's last 100 miles through the hills into Servia took eight and a half hours; at Nish, he heard that Germany had declared war on Russia. When the English abroad in France, let alone Germany, had to face the coming of war, what Bartlett called the 'longing to reach one's native land' would become over-powering; and telling.

7

The Long Bank Holiday

Thank God the press keeps us all, even diplomacy itself, well informed if a nation is going to quarrel with us and threaten war. We have at least some time to make preparations ....

An 1869 paper to the Society of Arts, from *Fifty Years of Public Work of Sir Henry Cole* (1884)

I

When Ashmead Bartlett had left home, one week before, Servia seemed the most important story in Europe. By the time he arrived, it wasn't. He described Nish as a 'strange state of affairs'; a country town of 20,000, 'about the size of Evesham', only with squalid houses of straw and wood, swelled by another 30,000 – the upper classes, royal court and parliament, newly fled from Belgrade. The locals and émigrés alike paraded through the streets and beside the River Save, like 'Hampstead Heath on a bank holiday'. Bartlett as an Englishman and a likely ally was welcome. Even so, as a bright and ruthless newspaperman, he faced the facts. He felt 'tolerably sure' that Britain and France would fight Austria-Hungary and Germany; the war in Servia would become 'of mere local importance'; he had to leave at once for France. The only way – in case Italy sided with its allies Austria and Germany – was through the Mediterranean. It meant he had to make for the port of Salonica, in the opposite direction to home. At 1am on the Monday, August 3 he took the train to Uskub (today Skopje, the capital of Macedonia), the same journey he had made in 1913 to the Servian army headquarters for their war against Bulgaria. His train had to stop to let troop trains pass. Four people filled a hot compartment meant for three, 'the height of misery and discomfort', Bartlett moaned. The 140-mile journey took 13 hours. As soon as the reporter's troubles became his main story, he had missed the story.

II

The man paid to follow the news, thanks to his very doggedness, was the wrong side of Europe. Without meaning to, A T Daniel the cycling headmaster found himself in one of the best places in Europe to witness the marching of an army to war.

From Verdun, after a sleepless night thanks to mobilising troops, he had the choice of turning back, or – like a spy – carrying on along the scenic Meuse valley, parallel to the German frontier about 40 miles away. He carried on. He rode into the town of St Mihiel and ordered lunch at a hotel. Almost all the diners were officers, who stared at him, but Daniel was used to being stared at. He had a good meal, 'the last for several days', and paid. Outside, his back tyre was flat. At a repair shop, two gendarmes asked for his papers. He did not have a passport; they arrested him. Daniel managed to convince the magistrate he found himself in front of, Monsieur Roult, that he was who he said he was, a tourist. "I noticed that he laid great stress on the fact that my tickets were issued by Cook, a household word apparently in these remote towns." The two men became so friendly, they had a drink in a café. Daniel shook hands with nearly all the men in town not mobilised. They toasted his English *sang froid*, 'le flegme de la nation'. As Daniel admitted later, 'it was in fact his ignorance', not his phlegm, that took him to what would soon become the battlefield.

So near the frontier, Daniel saw the garrisons of Rheims and Orleans arrive: "... trains came in at intervals of about

15 minutes and in less than ten minutes the men had formed up and started on their march with a heavy and varied kit that a French infantryman carries; all fine men with springing step often singing the Marseillaise with a fierceness that gave it a new flavour to me." The cheerful, soon to die marchers were, as Daniel wrote, 'a sight never to be forgotten'.

III

The French were rushing to their borders for the same reason the Germans were; because the other side were. As France and Germany each planned one big battle, all hinged on taking as many of your soldiers as fast as you could – by train – to where you wanted to attack. As Daniel saw, the French were hoping to take Alsace and Lorraine back. The Germans were going to attack through Luxembourg and Belgium, making them like two dogs trying to bite the other's rump. Much has been made of how August 1914 was war by 'chain reaction', or 'railway timetable', inevitable once one country gave the order to mobilise. The Hull MP and Yorkshire battalion commander Sir Mark Sykes wrote, characteristically bluntly, in a letter of August 1:

> *I at last have five min: to spare – at least I have slept – well things look worse and worse – by last night's paper Germany seems to have taken the plunge – as far as I can see this at bottom is a Russian attack on Germany – whether warranted or no of course no one can tell. I do not see any way to peace unless Russia cease mobilising ...*

A third world war in the 1950s would have been equally by timetable, as sure as a game of snap; if the enemy played one card, you played the other. The planners of atomic war assumed, incidentally, that their war would last a few weeks, much as the leaders of August 1914 assumed. What saved the world from World War Three was the very speed and ease of nuclear warfare, that made it like a shoot-out in an American Wild West saloon. If you truly did not want to die, if you ever spilt a cowboy's drink by mistake, you made it your business to apologise fast and keep your hands off your holster. In August 1914, by comparison, once a couple of cowboys had fallen out at cards and pulled out their pistols, everyone else urgently – yet taking several days over it – did the equivalent of knocking their chairs over and pulling out their revolvers.

Then what? A timetable of mobilisation itself did not fight. As Sykes pointed out, the trouble was the *lack of a way back to peace*. Straight enemies – America and Russia over Berlin in 1961, and Cuba in 1962 – could agree to put away the guns. August 1914 had too many guns pointing too many ways.

IV

War began for the same reason as mobilisation; men could not see straight, whether through fear or lack of it. A Tamworth man, H C Mitchell, left London with a friend on Thursday July 30, ignoring the signs of trouble; the closed currency exchange offices at Charing Cross, all the passengers on the boat from Dover to Ostend being German. 'Full of faith in the power of the English sovereign', meaning the coin, Mitchell and friend planned ten days in Belgium and the Ardennes. They made it as far as Brussels, where shops and restaurants would not take English money, or Belgian paper money either. As a last resort, the pair went to the travel agent, 'the mighty Cook', only to find a crowd of stranded English and American tourists. The Thomas Cook office advised them to go to the national bank. There they found 'a surging mass of humanity, vainly struggling for gold', the only thing people trusted any more. Mitchell came by some coins.

Refugees poured into the city from the German frontier by the hundred, and 'grim looking Belgian soldiers were marching out by the thousand'. Their light guns were pulled by dogs, "thoroughly imbued with a sense of duty and most apparent enjoyment of their task. It is difficult to say which were the most keen, the men or the dogs." Mitchell told his story afterwards light-heartedly; he was on holiday after all. He did have a serious near-miss, before he returned to Dover on the Sunday evening, August 2. As in Paris, on Saturday nights it was the custom to sit outside restaurants over wine, and be social. As Mitchell's friend only spoke English, and Mitchell made a few notes, soldiers and civilians threatened them:

> One man accused me in German of belonging to the fatherland. I replied in German that I did not. Several officers then poured out the vials of their wrath in most voluble French; in vain I tried to stem the tide of their eloquence. A passer by brandishing a stick called us German spies. Then a gentleman who spoke broken English called out spies. I understood. Immediately handing him my notebook, my railway ticket and card, I raised my glass and called out 'Messieurs, je suis anglais. Vive la Belgique! A bas l'Allemagne, vive la France!'

The Belgians took their hats off and shouted 'bravo, vive l'Angleterre!'. It did not make sense that a spy would be so obvious; nor did a few words in the local language prove that Mitchell was not a spy. It only made sense because the angry and frightened Belgians wanted to let out their hatred of the likely German invader on someone.

Daniel meanwhile, minus bicycle, took an evening train to Chalons, then more trains the next day to Rheims and Amiens. He never saw anyone with, nor anyone asked for, a ticket. Occasional trains passed, full of civilians – Germans, according to Daniel's fellow travellers, 'received with grim silence'. As in England at its time of crisis in the summer of 1940, any

Frenchman would speak to another: navvy with businessman, private to officer. When a couple said that if and when England saw an advantage, then she would join, they apologised when Daniel, smilingly, said he was a native of 'perfide Albion'. He then found it wisest to tell any new companions that he was English. None of the French expected England to land an army on the Continent. At most, they hoped the English navy would guard northern France.

For the previous few years Britain had had an 'entente', an 'understanding', with France; except that, the Liberal Government insisted, it was free to choose what to do. That begged the question, why have an 'understanding' at all? Did the French and the British 'understand' the same things? As Daniel pointed out, if Germany had attacked Britain at sea, the French would certainly not have fought on land.

Belgium made the difference. On the Monday, August 3, the *Hull Daily News* asked: 'Why should England fight?' The old treaty of 1839 that agreed Belgium was neutral gave the *right* to fight, if someone invaded Belgium; Britain, or anyone else who cared, did not have to. Two days later, that same newspaper said Britain had 'got to see it through'; 'it' being the hours-old war with Germany, now blamed for trying 'to fill too large a place in the sun'.

By August 4 Germany had threatened, and had begun, to invade Belgium and Luxembourg. According to a treaty of 1867, Luxembourg – like Belgium – was neutral. Few people in Britain even noticed Luxembourg, because it did not matter to them; Belgium did. Britain was ready to go to war against Germany not because of anything Germany did, but in case of what it might do. If Germany captured the Belgian and northern French coast, it would become too strong a threat to Britain. Better to fight now, with France, than have to fight Germany alone after it beat France. Hence the British demand on August 4 – though days too late for it to make a difference –

that the Germans stay out of Belgium; and when the deadline passed that night, the declaration of war: by Britain, against Germany.

Colin, later Lord, Davidson, was a 21-year-old private secretary to 'Lulu' Haldane, the minister for the colonies. When the 11pm deadline passed Davidson left the Foreign Office with a clerk, a major as a bodyguard, and a sheaf of telegrams in code to send to Britain's colonies to tell them they were at war.

We went out into Downing Street which had been kept fairly free from the crowds as Whitehall was simply packed with a seething mass of people. We fought our way up Whitehall and unable to get through Trafalgar Square took a route through some side streets by way of the Strand. We got to the post office in the Strand which was still open and went in with the telegrams. We walked up to the counter and handed the telegrams over. The woman behind the counter did no more than just look at them. We didn't even get a receipt for them … we then started back to Downing Street to find thousands of people milling around shouting and singing and bursting with cheers. It was all very unpleasant. They did not know what they were in for and they had this awful war fever.

Here is another of the most-repeated stories (with photographs) of the outbreak of war; the cheering crowds in the capital cities; not only London, but Paris and Berlin. For some it's proof that publics welcomed war. To anyone with business to do, the crowds were in the way. Davidson went back to the Colonial Office and waited for replies; Fiji, where it was the next day, acknowledged first.

What, if anything, were the gawpers there for? Did they catch, as Davidson suggested, 'war fever'? The men in authority plainly disliked having so many common people around. Asquith for example in his memoirs found it 'curious' that going to and from Downing Street to parliament he was 'always escorted and surrounded by cheering crowds of loafers and holiday-makers'. This was a burdened man, to say the least, angered by the ignorant and idle in his way. Were those people unwelcome to him because they, even without realising it, were holding him accountable? Or were they not anticipating war, but merely there out of curiosity? Even more vaguely, did the on-lookers wish to be around the making of history, something seldom on offer to them? If so, they were hanging around (it cost nothing) in the right place: the centre of government; politics; and, in nearby Fleet Street, newspapers. Some may have joined the crowds in London merely for the same reason everyone sat on the same seaside beaches, at Blackpool, Scarborough, and Skegness, every August; if so many were doing it, something about it had to be right.

In her memoirs Emily MacManus, then sister-in-charge of a ward at Guy's Hospital, told of how she and other Guy's men and women on August 4 'made our way through the evening crowds of restless, anxious people, to the great space in front of Buckingham Palace. War! Yes, it had come ... I was exhilarated ...' After that 11pm deadline to Germany passed, King George, Queen Mary and Edward, Prince of Wales went onto the balcony, to cheers and the singing of God Save the King. Even after their majesties went in again, thousands stayed. This went on before and after the outbreak of war. One anonymous reporter described the crowd as 'Cockneys from the East End, sight-seers, fashionable ladies and top-hatted swells, all showing their love for the Old Country and its Sovereign', waiting to see their majesties, and cheering at the slightest new thing, such as a raised flag and the guards. The noisier sorts sang patriotic songs and parodies of Germany, 'probably made up on the spot'. These 'loafers', as Asquith spotted, were tourists wanting to see something, or Londoners with time on their hands. The centre of London has always been the place to go after work, if you do not have meals to cook or children to put to bed. After all, during a bank holiday, bank workers among others were on holiday, and in case of a panic run on the banks Lloyd George ordered an unheard-of extra three days of bank holidays, for the Tuesday to Thursday. On that Thursday evening, August 6, Robert Ramsey stood outside Buckingham Palace for the second time that week. As he lived in Ladbroke Square to the west and worked as a solicitor in the City, Buckingham Palace was on his way home. After work (and dinner) he found 'a large crowd assembled … which gradually increased until there must have been four or five thousand people':

> …. cheering from time to time and singing snatches of God Save the King and Rule Britannia. At last towards ten o'clock the blind was drawn up, the French window thrown open, and the Queen appeared in white standing between the King and the Prince of Wales and remained for some minutes. The crowd cheered frantically as one man, waved hats and flags and sang God Save the King. One man had two large flags, a tricolour and a Union Jack which he held high to catch the king's attention. This continued until the royal party withdrew, the king pausing for a moment or two at the closed window. Then the crowd woke up and started away down the Mall in perfect order and good humour.

Some argued afterwards that people headed for the palace seeking a consoling figure at a confusing time. Or it may have been that the people were not paying homage to the monarchy, but showing their power, of a sort; they coaxed the king and queen to appear. As Ramsey went to the theatre and concerts – judging by the programmes between the pages of his diary – he, and we, can see something theatrical in it all: the crowd making music (as if wooing the king outside?), and the royal family – once *they* had dined – acting their part. Once the royals had made their bows, their public went home satisfied. Something may have drawn people to the palace; or nothing.

As Ramsey suggested, nothing came of the evening; it was an entertaining break from daily reality, like a dream ('the crowd woke up') or an evening at the theatre (only free). What was political, let alone warlike, about it?

In a world before radio, where someone from Britain's government had to walk to a post office to tell its empire it was at war, we should not forget that some people made for where news would break first: central London. The weekly *Willesden Chronicle*, the Friday after the declaration of war, recalled that instead of the usual bank holiday Monday 'gaiety of crowds', anxious people were 'eagerly waiting for the various editions of the newspapers as they came to hand', sold on the streets by 'Fleet Street runners' shouting the headlines. As ever, not everyone felt the same. Robert Ramsey in his diary wrote of that week: "Nights are now made hideous by people calling 'newspapers'."

The craving for news can explain at least some in the crowds in any of the capitals going to war, even Wellington in New Zealand. The thousands gathered in the grounds of parliament, to hear the governor repeat the first message of the war from the king – on Wednesday afternoon, August 5, their time – is the most poignant of all the scenes of August 1914. What drew the listeners was more powerful even than war. Some New Zealanders, like Australians and Canadians, felt deep home-sickness for the country they had left behind, that they called the 'old', or, tellingly, the 'mother country'. The guilt they felt for leaving family behind felt even worse now their homeland was in danger. The colonies offered England help so quickly because they hoped it might give them a chance to visit (on the cheap).

V

True, some greeted the outbreak of war with cheers, not boos. Cheers for what, exactly? For whatever it was their leaders decided? For dead men across Europe, at a cost of (so the *Hull Daily News* speculated) £1,000,000,000, that would have to come from somewhere? "All wars are popular on the day of their declaration," wrote Lloyd George in his memoirs, with the wisdom of a man after the event. People, even the people who went on to die in the war, cheered because it was something exciting; something for a change; something that had not done anything bad to them yet.

Arthur Ross and the Church Lads Brigade lads from Beverley were, as locals, among the first of 1500 lads, from Carlisle and Alnwick to Sheffield, to pitch tents at Seamer, three-and-a-half miles south of Scarborough. They arrived at the village station at 10am on Wednesday July 29, asked the way, and marched into summer camp with their kitbags, singing On The Mississippi. The lads had so little to do for the first couple of days, they were allowed to enjoy Scarborough all afternoon; walking the pier, eating ices and chocolate, sending postcards. Stepping off the 10pm train at Seamer they walked to camp 'singing wild to mouth organs, 'Hello, hello, who's your lady friend", Ross wrote. Their pleasures were as simple as the food in camp – bread and butter, or jam, or brawn; pork pie, and coffee – and the drum-head service after tea on Sunday: "The Bishop of Hull delivered a fine address and spoke of one of Rudyard Kipling's yarns." As in the Territorials' summer camps around the coast, the lads did some drill, and had plenty of time to read and chat, because their officers no more wanted a hard time than anyone else. It all became serious on Monday August 3, as captured by Ross' clipped prose:

> *Reveille 5.30. No hot coffee. Adjutant's parade 630 (company drill). Tent inspection. Parade 10. The brigadier*

made us a fine speech. 'England is preparing for a great war,' he said. 'If anything happens to annoy you, take it like sportsmen.' God Save the King was sung and then three cheers given. Half an hour afterwards a telegram came for the Brigadier and he left camp. He had been called up.

Everyone was excited and talked of the possibility of war. A visitor's *Daily Mirror* was 'nearly torn to bits, so anxious were we to see news', Ross recalled. The Beverley lads were that evening's camp guard. As Ross posted the first sentries, an officer told him of orders to strike the camp that night. Likewise, around the country, Territorials were going home early, to be readier to mobilise if the order came. The guards opened the gate to the first lot of lads marching out, singing Rule Britannia 'good enough to wake the dead'. This change from normal – and the strength in anonymity in the dark felt by a thousand lads – prompted a carnival. Or as Ross put it, the camp 'went mad':

We could see the mess tent lighted up and you could have heard the row a mile off. The voices absolutely drowned the piano. The guard was rushed twice by parties of lads not leaving till after midnight who wanted to go into the town first for a spree. We held them back the second but not the first time. I had a flash lamp and as the various companies left camp I was able to pick out my friends and say goodbye.

By 2.30am, only the local Beverley 'fatigue boys' who would have to unpack the camp were left. Ross, doing his duty, walked round the sentries, and with his commander Captain Hobson: "We saw the Bishop coming back to Camp. Although an old man he had marched to the station and seen the lads off and then walked back." The Bishop of Hull, Francis Gurdon, was in fact in his late fifties, and presumably looked old to the teenage Ross. The lads ate breakfast on the grass outside the guard tent – 'eggs, coffee, bread, butter tea and cakes' – and Ross bought a newspaper from a visitor for the war news.

They slept, and after tea went into Scarborough for a shave and to visit the aquarium again. On the Wednesday, August 5, a captain read from the newspaper of the declaration of war on Germany. "Bishop of Hull made a speech to whole fatigue after breakfast and sung national anthem. Bishop leaves camp in midst of cheers." Whether because camp was cut short, or because he wanted to grab every chance of leisure, Ross did not go home at once; he got off the train at Filey for three hours, walked the cliffs, and with three lads had tea in a cafe for three shillings and elevenpence-ha'penny: "I kept odd half pence as a souvenir." His father, no doubt anxious, met Ross at Beverley railway station at 8pm. The lads marched to the town drill hall, "some of us keen on joining forces, told Captain Hobson. He asked us to wait." The next morning, when Ross went into town after breakfast and a shave, he found the 'town in an excited state'.

VI

A good tree cannot bring forth evil fruit, neither can a
corrupt tree bring forth good fruit.
Matthew 7:18

Ross, in camp, acted like half a soldier already. He, Arthur Allinson, and other Beverley Church Lads volunteered to their Captain Hobson to become Territorials. Civilians meanwhile had no experience of how, if at all, to react to a European war. William Swift, the retired Gloucestershire villager, on his shopping visits by train to nearby Gloucester, similarly found that the supposedly more worldly townspeople were losing their heads. On Tuesday August 4, he rose at 6.15am and caught the 10.17am from Churchdown, to bank the cash from the church collection, only to find the extra bank holiday. A shop 'obligingly gave me silver for my coppers'. He bought bacon and kidney at Pardoe's the butcher: "Mrs P not in the most amicable state of mind and a man told her she seemed to have the war fever."

Swift bought some extra strong peppermints he was fond of 'and took a slight refreshment' – he did not say what – 'near the Northgate railway bridge'. As he returned in the company of 'Canon and Mrs Bedwell', he cannot have been too refreshed. Only he and the vicar were at evensong at 8pm; evidently the crisis was not sending the people to church. Swift closed the day by reading St Matthew's gospel and Boswell's Tour to the Hebrides.

While his home, garden and village life went on, four of his old scholars, as Territorial soldiers, had left by train. "A young man (Mayo's) who brings us the par-oil [paraffin] says some of the people seemed demented in trying to obtain as much as they could get; one man who usually has two barrels actually ordered 12." Everywhere, shoppers were buying flour, 'and anything that would keep', such as Quaker oats, canned fruit and Golden Syrup, as the weekly *Harrow Observer* reported on the Friday. Did a housewife have to stock up on syrup?

Some newspapers, such as the *Uttoxeter Advertiser* in Staffordshire, admitted it was a week of panic, that would only cause the shortages that the panic-buyers were trying to beat, and encouraged shops to charge more. Flour became 'practically unobtainable', the *Advertiser* reported; the price of sugar more than doubled. Whose panic was making it dearer for everyone else? "Private motor cars went away laden from some shops on Tuesday morning," the *Advertiser* said – that is, as soon as doors opened after the bank holiday – "and prices commenced to rise a little later." A solicitor in Walsall, Lenton Lester, made it even plainer at a meeting of town traders who was guilty – 'the wealthy', the few people who could afford a car, the very ones who could, as Mr Lester said, afford a penny or two extra.

The panic-buyers, naturally, did not offer their names to the public, or even admit to themselves that *they* were panicking. They, like the Gothard family, were only looking after themselves, and – as good customers – traders wanted to look after them. Clifford Gothard wrote for Saturday August 1 that he went to bed 'after letting in a man with a lot of groceries from Oakden's': "Everyone is afraid of a rise in prices all around; there was a panic rush for groceries this morning. We managed to get ours all right. We cleared Wright's and Oakden's out of biscuits by buying a very few lbs." That was as much as anyone would admit, even in their diary.

Traders, too, made excuses. Retailers could blame wholesalers, who could blame shippers. Some perishables, in fairness, became short right away. If fishing fleets could not sail in case of enemy warships, or because the fishermen who were also naval reservists had joined the fleet, fish would be scarce and cost more. Other costs would rise with time; ships could sink and cost more to insure. The question then became: if Europe's markets drew on the world, and all Europe – all the world, perhaps – was at war, what would be the new cost of doing business? Some shopkeepers had the courage to limit customers' grocery orders, or the decency to limit their profits. Others wanted to use the crisis to bump up their profits as much as they could get away with. It was the commercial equivalent of the main powers of Europe mobilising armies; if anyone above you in the chain of selling raised prices but you did not, you would suffer; if anyone below in the chain raised prices but not you, you were a fool. Often the profiteering businessmen were the worst-run or the downright crooked in peacetime, such as the Rhodesia Trading Company in southern Africa. Its joint MD Arthur Suter wrote to England from the capital Salisbury in August 1914:

The chambers of commerce have taken up a very philanthropic attitude as to raising the price of actual foodstuffs on present stocks and in Bulawayo practically threatened to boycott any Trader who did so. This has somewhat upset my proposed general increase of about 15 per cent but there are a few good lines on which we have managed to secure a very considerably increased profit and we must bide our time for the remainder.

As with any panic buying, people did not suddenly eat more, or burn more paraffin. The extra fuss during the panic evened itself out with quiet afterwards. The Hull architect, cricket-watcher and diarist George Thorp went into his regular grocers, Brown Cox and Holmes, on Saturday August 8, 'to learn the why and the wherefore'. Why had the flour they delivered cost two shillings and sixpence a stone – as it turned out, more than double the price before, and after? Why did the tinned beef not come at all? "Found them in a state of collapse, had been working for 33 hours on end. On the previous Tuesday had called with the usual order and found no flour or bacon was to be had. On Wednesday and Thursday they were closed." Thorp and his grocer saw the panic was over: "I believe I was the second person in the shop that morning. Parted good friends." At least Thorp had a grocer to go to; Kress, his pork butcher, was among the Germans arrested.

PART TWO

England At War

8

The News

We and the French had to defend ourselves;
it is as simple as that.
Within the Fringe: An Autobiography, by Viscount Stuart
of Findhorn (1967)

The horror of joining in the silly fray was less than the
danger of dishonour of keeping out.
The Mist Procession: The Autobiography of Lord Vansittart
(1958)

I

B ritain going to war against Germany ranks as one of
the most memorable pieces of news of the century,
like the assassination of President Kennedy, and the
death of Diana, Princess of Wales; or indeed the ends of wars
in 1918 and 1945, or the start of war again in 1939. As with
any object, however, news needs speed – as well as mass – to
have force. People remembered the start of the second war by
the speech on the radio by Neville Chamberlain – or claimed
to, because some wrongly thought Churchill was the prime
minister they heard. Nineteen-fourteen had no such broadcast
to unite listeners in a common memory.

The navy and – above all – ships at sea, were the exceptions.
Civilians had all the time they wanted to let the news sink
in, or to ignore it; sailors had to do as they were told. They
assumed fleets would clash as soon as they found each other,

the same as the armies on land. If anything, sailors wished for that great battle, to get it over with. G C Harper, a cadet in Devonport who joined *HMS Endymion* on August 1, admitted to a 'temporary depressing feeling' on the evening of Monday August 3, 'that perhaps after all England would remain neutral'. His 'frightfully old', 20-year-old, cruiser put to sea at 10am on the Tuesday, weighed anchor at 5pm, 'and went off at 15 knots around Land's End and up the Irish Channel'. Harper was in charge of two of the ship's four searchlights. An officer told him that Britain was going to declare war on Germany at midnight.

> *So when the end of the watch came and eight bells struck I thought, at last we have begun war with Germany after all these years of talk; now we will see. There was a ripping kind of air of perfect calm and efficiency about it. We knew that the Navy had been preparing for a week and everyone was ready. I thought of all the novels and scare-mongering magazine articles which all without exception prophesied a surprise and a very bad one for us when this war came off. But it struck me it was more of a surprise for the Germans.*

Harper arrived at Scapa Flow, the navy's harbour in northern Scotland, on the Thursday afternoon, August 6. Also on its way to Scapa Flow was *HMS Marlborough*, whose wireless officer, James Somerville, heard earlier on the Tuesday that war would be declared. "Revolvers and ammunition were served out to the officers today; I think I shall wear mine after all because I am the only officer on the main deck and if things go badly at any time there may be a panic; not my own people, they are too intelligent, but among the hoi polloi such as stokers etc." As that line suggested, Somerville felt under strain already – 'I hardly dare sleep for fear of something going wrong with the WT [wireless transmission]', he admitted in his diary. He expected 'to be blown up at any moment' as the ship steamed towards Norway. At 11pm, Somerville received from the Admiralty the king's message telling of war. "Somehow it

seemed rather banal ..." he wrote, evidently by now too tired to feel much; he went to sleep at 1am and had to turn out again at 4am, 'dead to the world'.

Typically people learned of the war in their own time, by a routine act – by reading a newspaper; or, even less dramatically, by having the news read to them. Those on holiday might well not have heard the news until hours after everyone else, which would make the event feel even flatter.

William Pickbourne, the Northamptonshire preacher, felt the war as much as anyone; his son Frank, as a Territorial, was called up. Pickbourne and two of his other sons had travelled overnight, uncomfortably, from London Paddington to Ilfracombe, arriving on Saturday August 1. "With the war news about however we felt we had better be getting home," he wrote; yet the Pickbournes carried on their holiday, taking a coastal pleasure ship to Clovelly on the Wednesday, the first full day of war, and only left Devon on the Friday. By the Monday, August 10, he was telling his diary 'a horrible crisis has arisen', and how his son Frank, camping in a schoolyard in Northampton, was about to go to Derby for training. Plainly it took a few days for the war to sink into Pickbourne – or he had not liked to leave the boarding house he had already paid for.

Once you heard of the war, what were you supposed to do? If you had been in uniform, you might expect to join in. Frank Balfour, back in his office in Berber after his trek by camel, let out his disappointment in a letter to the society belle Irene Lawley:

> I got back here to read a week's old Reuter's and find all the world in a blaze. And tonight comes the news that we have gone to war – and here am I consigned to simply carry on in this cesspit without a chance of a show at all. All leave is stopped. The one thing I've prayed for was a chance of a little real soldiering, and I've got to miss it and merely do what I'm paid for.

On the Tuesday, Guy Paget in Paris gave up trying to reach his wife in Aix – 'the military had monopolised all the trains' – and decided to return to England to get a job. To smooth his way home, he had what he recalled was 'a very important looking passport covered all over with stamps of eagles and things from having had it in Russia'. As Paget had met 'a Gordon Highlander called Hamilton' with a wife, maid and dog, Hamilton 'indented' his wife and maid over to Paget, whose passport was 'made out for those commodities'. Paget's other weapon was upper-class cheek:

Together we approached the Gare du Nord and ignoring the sentry we progressed to the office of the chef de Gare and demanded an interview. My French is limited but emphatic. They said the chef was busy and saw no-one. I replied dites lui Monsieur Paget est ici … allez vite.' The clerk was impressed and alleyed all right. We followed on his heels into the office. Who the clerk said we were whom he had let break unannounced into the great man's presence I know not but should not be surprised if it were the Prince of Wales incog. Flourishing my passport as if they were an order from the President I bowed and explained that under the present difficulties I should not insist on a special train but if the chef would have a first class reserved for me on the next train it would just do, but only just … The bluff came off! At 2pm I found an armed soldier at each door of my carriage into which a bowing official in gold lace deposited me cum spurious wife and maid and what he supposed to be I think my ADC.

The train took them only as far as Rouen, where they had to change and go third class to Dieppe. Once at London Victoria on the Thursday, August 6, Paget drove straight to his old regiment, the Scots Guards, and to the adjutant Roger Tempest. "He greeted me with, 'Where on earth have you been? You are the only one we had not heard from,'" Paget recalled.

As a free man not on the reserve, Paget asked the Guards to have him back. Tempest, going by the deaths in Britain's last war, against the Boers, reckoned it would be 18 months to two years before Paget could reach a battalion, because they were already full. "I said that the war might be over in six months at the most, so might I look for a job ... Roger agreed." Paget soon had all the work he could take, and never did join the Guards again.

II

The Army officer Donald Weir, writing his weekly letter from India to his mother in England on August 4, was following the crisis, Reuter's telegram by telegram, and guessing that war would come by 'the next wire'. They had been arranging mobilisation for three days in case of any sudden order, and all leave was stopped: "But this has no meaning for us as we will not leave India," Weir predicted.

The Army at home must be overjoyed at the chance of going for the Kaiser's dirty Germans and to fight side by side with the French. It is most disheartening for us out here to think that we are so absolutely out of it out here and that the latest joined warts and squirrels at home will probably be experiencing their first taste of war. Every soldier longs to see some fighting and here is the chance of a lifetime to have a dig at the Germans whom we have so long despised. It is doing something for one's country and in the event of being killed which is by no means necessary one can not wish for a more glorious death. This war will probably be the last of any size for years to come at any rate during our lifetime as soldiers and yet we in India can take no part in it, as we are compelled to remain out here and look after these dirty

*lieing blacks whom we hate so much that one would revel
in shooting them down by the hundred daily.*

"Am just going to pop off to the telegram office,' Weir went
on brightly, "only 50 yards away to see if there are any more
wires. No more news," he continued after that pause. "It appears
the cable via Suez is the whole while taking government
messages so something serious must be taking place. The cable
via Germany, Russia and Teheran has been cut."

9

Spies

Spying is no more ignoble than shooting; the cause is the thing that counts.

Spy, by Bernard Newman (1935)

I

George Rose lived in a flat in north London, worked as a clerk in an office, and at weekends went to his family home at Chipping Ongar in Essex. He played the piano, and was learning to paint and sketch. By late July the sensitive young man was wondering, over a map of England, where to go on holiday: on a caravan tour; or to Maldon, by the Essex coast? He packed on Friday July 24, and painted in the fields around Ongar at the weekend. On the Monday he and his family took the train from London King's Cross to Friskney, in the Lincolnshire Fens, where his brother Ted was marrying a farmer's daughter and George Rose was best man.

Rose began sketching the farm soon after arriving, but soon met the bridesmaid, her mother and sisters. Alice, a 17-year-old 'with clean cut features and sweet grey eyes' he knew from a photograph in Ted's room, 'and I have always been charmed by it,' he wrote later in his diary. "Now I am not a whit disappointed by meeting her in the flesh (not much flesh either!)." He played tennis with her and other ladies, before the wedding, addressed cards after, and after tea 'made a bad drawing of her'. He wrote that he was sad to leave on the Wednesday: "I have received enough invitations to allow me no time for anything else for the rest of my life if I followed them to their logical conclusion. But I shall not for the inviters only expect me to commit matrimony."

What made this talented young man, who plainly found Alice as interesting as she found him, so *ungallant*? Insecurity did not explain it, though he was unsure of himself. He had an ambition that women would only get in the way of; he longed to be an artist. As he may have seen it, he had little enough time free from work, without having a woman too. As a sign of his priorities, in his diary for Tuesday August 4 – by now, holidaying at Maldon – he noted the war with Germany, then wrote all about his afternoon outing with his friend, Duncan, to Osea Island nearby. First they had 'a good tea in a village shop'; "also we found corn fields both reaped and growing. Best of all was a family of little sandpipers in a dyke which we watched but better even was the grey harmony of colour when the moon was behind the white sailed yacht which followed us home." On the edge of Essex, with Germany beyond the sea, visitors with eyes only for scenery stuck out. On the Thursday they painted Maldon church tower all morning:

and in the afternoon we walked to Heybridge Basin where we had tea at the Old Ship Inn and sat in the comfortable window all the evening whilst it rained and we sketched and listened to the long-shoreman talking about the War News. After supper at our own inn I still had enough energy to start a sketch by the church tower, Duncan with me. We were then inconvenienced and much annoyed by being locked in the churchyard and accused of being German spies and we had to give our identity to the police and show all our works at the Swan Hotel to them. After this performance we stood drinks to the officers and went to bed.

Couldn't anyone with suspicions have talked to the artists, and seen they were genuine and harmless? As the wrongly accused, should the artists, not the police, have been the ones offered a drink? The most obvious hurt Rose felt was on the Monday: "Back to office after a fortnight's leave," was all he put in his diary. Rose knew his ache for more freedom, dulled weekdays by the routine of work, too well to put it into words.

At least his accusers knew they were at war. William Page of Burton-on-Trent and two friends, visiting Grimsby docks on Bank Holiday Monday, on the last full day of peace, tried to take photographs of warships in the bay. Soldiers with fixed bayonets took them to the Customs offices, where the trio showed their excursion tickets. "They could not have been satisfied with what we had told them, for before long we found ourselves being followed by an officer with his hand on a revolver which was, no doubt, loaded," Page reported later. The officer told him to stop smoking his pipe; why, Page did not know: "... and it was only by taking refuge on an excursion steamer and disappearing down into the hold in double quick time that we eluded our pursuer." If the officer thought Page was a spy, why let him go? Why believe his story; couldn't a spy buy an excursion ticket the same as anyone else? The soldiers were doing their job of guarding; you suspect, besides, that they enjoyed the chance to bully civilians, if only to make a change from the boredom.

In Walsall Wood, they didn't chase Germans; they punched them. On Monday evening, August 10, an 18-year-old miner, Bert Faulkner, went to have a look at the 'German' in his street. The stranger asked Faulkner (with swear-words) what he was looking at; and had he lost his dinner? Faulkner may not have grasped that someone with such command of sarcasm in English, was hardly likely to be German; or, the insults may have provoked Faulkner to hit the stranger twice, hard enough to fall on a doorstep. The 'German' was Edward Evans, a labourer from Barrow in Furness, who told Walsall magistrates he had walked from West Hartlepool seeking work. As a magistrate told Faulkner: "Why don't you join Lord Kitchener's Army?"

II

Evans had, so the court heard, been the talk of the street as a strange-talking 'German'. If Faulkner felt so keen to take the fight to Germans, what stopped him joining the army? As an excuse of sorts, Faulkner had said that he had 'only had three days to pick up this week', meaning three days of work. Short-time working was common in coal mines and factories where demand for their goods changed with the seasons. The poverty, and the ignorance that made Faulkner and his likes take a northerner for a foreign enemy, meant that Faulkner would never feel strongly about the rights of Belgium, or anywhere.

Not that only common people mistook their countrymen for foreigners. A Mr Durose, an accountant from Nottingham, reported to his local police on August 6 that while at Woodhall Spa in Lincolnshire he found a German prince was staying at the Clay Hotel, 'who was constantly receiving and sending telegrams etc'. Nottingham police passed the tip on, and the local force evidently checked, because a Superintendent Corden reported back that the man was Prince Frederick Duleepsingh, of Blow Foston Hall, Thetford, Norfolk, 'who is an exile prince from India who has come to Woodhall Spa for the last eight years and he has offered his services to the War Department'.

For every hothead like Bert Faulkner and nosey-parker like Mr Durose, many more people minded their own business. What did Mr Durose think he was playing at? Did it not occur to him that the hotel staff would have noticed a suspicious guest? Could he not have asked around the hotel, or indeed politely made conversation with 'Prince Frederick', before going to the police (and why wait until he was home?). Mr Durose may have wanted badly to do some good, and did not know how to. Seeing hidden enemies cost nothing. Anyone in uniform, a soldier on guard or a police constable, would always take a sighting seriously. The only sure way they could then stay out of trouble was to act on a complaint, no matter how foolish. Newspapers gave the Mr Duroses of every town their excuse. Fears in print sold more papers, and newspapers knew they could never be proven wrong. A *Burton Daily Mail* editorial late in August, for example, urged readers to join the 'hunt for spies', claiming that 50,000 able-bodied Germans and Austrians were at large in Britain – 30,000 of them in London. Germany had bred, the *Burton Mail* reckoned,' the most astute and unscrupulous class of spy yet known to Europe'. What, then, of the real Germans and Austrians in Britain?

III

As early as August 1, the order went from Lincolnshire police chief constable Captain Cecil Mitchell-Innes, a former soldier, to have Anthony Strenge, a marine engineer of May Villa, Barton upon Humber, 'carefully watched during the present crisis' as he was suspected of being an 'evil-disposed person'. Even before the war, clearly the authorities had some suspects, whether agents gathering information or waiting for the outbreak of war to blow up things. At 10.10pm on the Wednesday, August 5, Mitchell-Innes sent a telegram went to all his police divisions to "keep special watch to prevent aliens travelling by night by motor car for purposes of committing outrages. Motor cars belonging to Germans may be seized ... warn Motor Garages not to hire out cars to aliens."

Any Germans in Lincolnshire, a county facing Germany, were a risk not only for the mischief they might do, but in case they guided invaders. The military sent Lincolnshire police two significantly related telegrams on the evening of Friday August 7. First, the army wanted notices along the county's 60 miles of coast, from Grimsby on the Humber to Sutton Bridge on The Wash, warning people not to go on beaches between sunset and sunrise, 'as they might be shot'. Why else would the army guard the coast – or say it was guarded –

unless it feared a German landing? Next, the army asked for the arrest of all Germans able to bear arms. Fears persisted in Lincolnshire, even as the Germans attacked in Belgium. On August 12, Lincoln police headquarters rang the police stations near the coast, at Spilsby, Alford and Louth. Police were shortly to tell the owners of horses and cattle to drive their animals behind the wolds – in other words, well inland – if, after a naval battle in the North Sea, enemy ships beached on the coast: "and of course the obvious thing to do would be for them to land and do useful work for their point of view". Here was one of two dilemmas for enemy-facing counties in two world wars: in an invasion, should you stay put, and risk enemy capture and having to do his bidding? Or should you flee (but where?), and risk getting in the way of the defenders, and being called a coward? In both world wars, as this first time, the authorities made some daft compromise. Farm animals would flee, but villagers were best to stay at home, and (the police added hopefully) 'should not get alarmed nor go rushing about'.

Here was the other, connected dilemma: whether the authorities should *warn* the locals beforehand, so they would know what best to do (at the risk of panic by the weak and stupid ruining it for everyone else); or should the authorities *say nothing* (at the risk of panic if the Germans did come). In another unrealistic compromise, police at headquarters told local stations to explain to locals what might happen, 'but it should be done quietly and without fuss, so as not to cause any excitement etc among the community'. Headquarters did not say *how* constables should explain the possible invasion without giving people 'excitement etc'. HQs never do. If German sailors had come ashore, after a battle, would they have felt like capturing anything, let alone cows and horses?

Regardless of reality, fear of invasion lingered. Meanwhile police acted on another, intriguing, worry. On August 10

Mitchell-Innes sent a memo about the possibility that "owing to the discharge of industrial employees on a large scale in the big towns, their districts in course of time may well be visited by casual labourers and others severely affected in fairly large numbers and who may be in serious want and therefore likely to be troublesome". The chief constable suggested that police on their beats approach "representative members of the community with a view to their forming a local organisation impressing other sound and reliable men in subordinate positions such as farm foremen, keepers, stewards, game keepers etc throughout their districts". In other words, while police were short of men, because reservists had joined the army or navy again, and police were guarding railway bridges in case of sabotage, citizens ought to do their bit to protect their property. Around the country respectable men, in numbers, volunteered as special constables; George Rose did in London, for example. In early September 110 men swore at Newark town hall to 'keep the peace' in case of an (unspecified) emergency.

In mainly rural Lincolnshire, Mitchell-Innes was not only thinking of resisting what he called 'destitute strangers and wanderers' by force. He suggested that 'the unfortunates' out of work and wandering the countryside should have 'temporary relief', such as 'scrap food, old boots, old clothing etc'. How real was this threat of unrest from the very poor tempted, or forced, to steal to survive? Mitchell-Innes' need to reassure lonely-feeling farmers may have mattered more than the threat. By defending themselves, the panicky property-owners may have felt less afraid of losing their possessions. Homeless but otherwise sturdy folk from the cities did not invade the countryside in August 1914, but they did come; for Britain always had men and women down on their luck and tramping, as vagabonds, or whatever you wanted to call them. They seldom left a trace. One time that a pair of wanderers did show in print, it proved how such aimless people had no grand thoughts of overturning society; and society was far too strong for them in any case.

On Thursday September 3, William Hall, a warehouseman, went to work at 6am at a flour mill outside Southwell in Nottinghamshire. Hall wrapped his brown leather shoes in paper, and put them on a sack of wheat. He meant to take them home, but forgot about them. When he looked on the Saturday morning, the shoes had gone.

William Sharman, the mill watchman, opened the warehouse door on the Friday evening to let the dust out – which was probably why Hall had a pair of work shoes and another pair. Under the flour bags, Sharman found a man and a woman. Sharman asked the pair to leave, then let them stay, whether out of softness or because the couple were too tough to shift – if they would leave things alone.

At 5.50am on the Saturday, a Southwell shopkeeper, Abraham Bee, was sweeping. A man showed him shoes and asked sixpence for them. Bee told the stranger that he did not know that he wanted shoes. 'Some old toff gave them to me,' the man said. Eventually – to get rid of him, perhaps – Bee gave the sixpence. Bee must have guessed something was wrong, and said so, because later that morning police constable Copeland was on the vagrants' trail. First he found the woman – Bridget Hughes, a widow – lying in a lane; then the man, Charles Mackenzie, a seaman thrown out of work at Hull by the outbreak of war. Drifting south, Mackenzie had reached Southwell from Lincoln on the Friday and met Hughes. You wonder what other petty crimes Mackenzie had done in the last few weeks, though as Southwell magistrates sent him to prison for two weeks – Hughes went for four – this was probably the first time Mackenzie was caught.

Here lay another reason why English holiday-makers on the Continent rushed to the Channel ports for home, despite the discomforts and loss of luggage – or rather, they left their bags to be sent on, so they hoped; in truth someone, probably

French, Swiss and German hotel and railway workers, pilfered it. Even if the holiday-makers were not running out of money – and many were – they were not only fleeing danger. They sought their place in society again; while abroad, they were little more than higher-class tramps. A T Daniel, for example, ran out of trains at Amiens and had to buy a second-hand bicycle. Armed with a piece of paper stamped by the British vice-consul – 'without this my journey would have been impossible'– Daniel made for Abbeville, stopped at every village every few miles by 'ignorant and indignant patriots'. This must have been while England hesitated about joining the war because, as Daniel admitted, to many Frenchmen England was 'a false friend and little better than a traitor'. Having cycled the 70 miles to Boulogne, that left the cheeks of his bottom 'two huge blisters', he and a 'rush of Britishers unused to police interference' made a farce of the official check on the gangway to the ship home. "It was quite enough to proclaim yourself a British subject in no matter what accent."

Landing at Dover at 2am, the hotels were full, and the ship's cabins were forbidden. A railwayman offered Daniel a place to lie down in the telegraph office, adding cheerily: "We put the aliens in there!" Daniel rested there, but could not sleep, 'because of the shunting and clicking of the telegraph'. By now, Britain must have declared war:

> Shortly after four o'clock I got up and saw a brilliant sunrise and had conversations with policemen and watchmen. They were good fellows and one could not help thinking good material but they were singularly inferior in intelligence and singularly ignorant of foreign politics of foreign countries and anything but the very outside of things military. To them this was a war between England and Germany. Little Belgium was plucky, this they conceded but wait till the British Army got there, they would make the Germans run! They seemed to take no account of the French Army whatever.

Daniel went into Dover at 5.30am and found a small coffee house, filled with workmen, 'mainly of a very submerged type'. They showed no interest in news of the war: "To them the war was mainly a question of the price of sugar and bacon." One man, Daniel added disapprovingly, used all the expletives he knew, "of course he didn't know many! To denounce the government. I could not exactly make out why." Daniel was still 200 miles from home, but had reclaimed his place back in society already, as he was able to look down on (and fail to appreciate) his countrymen. Life-changing events, a war in Europe, made no difference to the thankless lives of roaming, labouring men, surviving on hard or odd jobs, charity, the workhouse, or what they could pocket and get away with.

IV

But to be certain of a situation is not to be certain of a human being.

Maurice, by E M Forster

And for all the fears of agents, invaders, and wastrels, what did the threat to England come to? The London representative of the German makers of armaments, Krupp, sent a petition to Winston Churchill at the Admiralty on August 16, pleading to be allowed home to Germany. On August 5, when about to leave with his family in the German ambassador's train, he was arrested in his Putney house for espionage. The police search of his letters and belongings had not uncovered anything; newspapers however had called him a spy. Major Kell of the security service did not want to let him go, not because of anything he might have done, but because he might be useful as a hostage or as someone to trade for Englishmen held similarly in Germany: 'Herr von Bulow belongs to an influential family'.

While a memo for Churchill agreed that von Bulow was not caught with anything incriminating, 'the Krupp firm like other armament firms maintained a system of espionage', and von Bulow 'very possibly' was part of it, or at least knew about it. This case hinted that British companies did espionage, the same as anyone else. Firms did it to keep ahead, or at least so they did not fall behind rivals. It was business, not necessarily done for the sake of a war. In any case, whether you believed von Bulow when he wrote his conscience was 'absolutely clear', you suspect that von Bulow's worst crime was to make the British feel tricked. In June, von Bulow had accompanied the company's chief, Herr Krupp himself, on a tour of British armaments factories and shipyards, as arranged by the Admiralty.

Churchill's decision was characteristically brief. 'Hold him WSC 19-8,' he scribbled.

10

Serving Men

'Why did you do it?' I asked.
'This? Oh, well, I couldn't wait about for a commission, it
might have been weeks.'

An unnamed sculptor, a private in the XVth Hussars,
in *The Garden of Ignorance: The Experiences of a Woman in a*
Garden, by Mrs George Cran

I

Another letter in mid-month to Churchill came from
Francis Grenfell, with his cavalry unit at Tidworth. "I
am in command of a squadron and can hardly believe
my good fortune of being in the prime of life a soldier at this
time," wrote Grenfell, knowing that Churchill as a former troop
leader in the Lancers would understand. On Thursday August
13 Grenfell had been in London for three hours, but had to wait
at the dentist, and did not have time to see Churchill before he
caught his train back to Wiltshire. "Goodbye my dear Winston.
We must teach these foreigners again what a great nation we
are, what England means." It was one of those letters that left
much unsaid, because written in haste, and because Grenfell
did not have to tell Churchill what he already knew: that an
older brother of Grenfell, a Lancer, had died in a cavalry charge
with Churchill at the Battle of Omdurman in 1898; and that
the chances were that Churchill and Grenfell might – thanks
to a dentist – never see each other again.

Such happy and patriotic thoughts as Grenfell's, brushing aside the prospect of death, have been the stuff of August 1914, on all sides. Whereas Germany and France had millions of men ready-trained putting on uniform, Britain's new war minister, the Boer War commander Lord Kitchener, began by advertising for another 100,000 men. If the war on the Continent would be over in weeks, as many in England (but not Kitchener) thought, even those first recruits would not reach the front line before their months of training. As Britain had never seen so many men recruited at once, for anything, it would take a while to clothe and arm them, let alone make them soldiers. Exceptions were men who already knew how to do special jobs, such as riding motorcycles to carry despatches: such as the later spy Bernard Newman, and the St John's College, Cambridge man J K Stevens. They, like Grenfell, were bright young men, well-off enough to ride (a motorcycle, not a horse), and smart enough to know how to get a job – because, as so often, it was a case of who you knew, not what.

Clifford Gothard, who rarely included world news in his diary, began noting war as early as July 27. He did not put his feelings in writing, not even on the sudden death of his father – with one exception. Even on the Monday, August 3, for example, when he wrote 'everybody seems very excited about the war', or rather the prospect of Britain fighting in it, he did not say if he was excited. "General feeling seems to be, go to war and smash them," Gothard wrote, 'them' being the Germans. However, when the next morning (still before Britain declared war) a letter came asking Gothard if he would take a commission, if asked, he confided to his diary: "To please mother, entirely against my own inclination, I signed off as unsuitable. I think it is the greatest disappointment I have ever had, having to sign off like that." For the next few days, Gothard carried on his usual round of shooting rabbits, and finishing the arranging of his father's estate, though the war was going on around him, and was evidently on his mind. "All the trams passing out house to town have a lot of Territorials in them," he wrote on August 5.

Did Gothard feel the shame of any young man who could not measure himself against his fellows in battle? Was his shame not so much a feeling of cowardice, but that he would look like a mummy's boy? Mrs Gothard, we can imagine, did not want to see her son hurt; did she insist as well that no son of hers was wasting his education by going in the army? As so often, did the mother with more experience know better than the immature son?

Kitchener's appeal for 100,000 men aged between 19 and 35 filled the newspapers. Yet such large advertisements, half-page and whole-page, not only told readers this was important; like any jobs that make the newspapers, perhaps these were the vacancies that could not be filled easily? Some men did seek to join the army, so that they had a place in what the *Ashbourne Telegraph*, like many, called 'the greatest war in the world's history'. Yet the average young man in the Derbyshire market town of Ashbourne had not had the least wish to join the army before August 1914; the pay was poor, the discipline alien, the routine boring, and the years away from home intolerable; as the volunteers were about to find out. Even so early in the war, the *Ashbourne Telegraph* had to talk up the army, to overcome the centuries-old sense that a civilian only joined the army if he was starving, a fool, or fleeing the hangman: "No man is too good to serve his King and Country as a private soldier. JOIN AT ONCE." Those capital letters, the printed equivalent of shouting in your ear, were in truth like the ever-more strident tactics of suffragettes: a sign of a losing cause.

Soldiers, in these first few days of the war, had something going for them; and they made the most of it. They were *needed*. It meant, first, that Territorials could get away with mischief. Usually drink came into it. Christopher Hollis, a 12-year-old son of a clergyman, recalled in a memoir that on the Tuesday, August 4, "a drunk leaned out of a carriage window at Taunton" as his family were going on their holidays and bawled to Hollis' father to pray for him. "My father promised that he would." And Frederick Jewitt, a gas stoker from Gainsborough, arrived at Beverley drunk on a train on Wednesday night, August 5. Jewitt threw himself across the tracks in front of a train from Scarborough; Mr Franks, the assistant stationmaster, rolled him clear. As thanks for saving him, Jewitt threw Mr Franks – by now trying to help the suicidal man onto the platform – over his shoulder onto the rails. Mr Franks hurt his back and stayed off work. As the town's chief constable, John Moore, put it: "If he wants to commit suicide he had better put himself in front of the Germans." The court let off Jewitt; not because of the woes he claimed – his wife had left him, he had four children, he had been drinking all day – but because magistrates simply sent him to his regiment, after a few days on remand.

Another court case shows that the authorities did give soldiers some respect, now their country needed them to stay alive, at least until they reached the battlefield. Herbert Strutt, a Derbyshire magistrate and a deputy lord lieutenant, was driving from his home at Makeney north of Derby on Saturday August 15, to (ironically) a meeting in the county town in aid of the war. Halfway there, at Allestree Hill, Strutt overtook, at crawling pace, some marching men of the 4th Lincolnshires. Another car driven by a chauffeur, Arthur Smith, pipped its horn and came round a bend fast – at 20 to 23 miles an hour, so Strutt reckoned. Some of the soldiers had to jump out of the way and Strutt stopped his car in a hedge bottom. Before the war, the men on foot might have had to shrug off the near-miss. Someone in a car, or on a motorcycle, was all too willing to be the fastest thing on the road and expected everyone else to get out of their way. Being the richest, the motorist got away with it. But now, as magistrates told Smith, drivers had to be careful because so many troops were about. The court fined Smith £5 and banned him from driving for three months.

Another car story suggests that soldiers understood – and played on – their new, albeit unlikely to last, prestige. Clifford Gothard asked a local man, a Mr Cherry, " if I would be of any service and to try to get a job as transport driver for Arthur Wardle"; Gothard's friend. The next day, August 12, Mr Cherry rang Gothard, to suggest Wardle could indeed get a commission in motor transport. Gothard set off into Burton-on-Trent on his bicycle with the news; on the way, on the bridge over the River Trent, he met Arthur Wardle, and a man called Arthur Linsley, in Linsley's car. Linsley offered to push Gothard's cycle home, while the young men drove on. The drama, fit for a silent film, had only started:

> When Arthur and I had just passed the end of Wellington Street we were stopped and asked to give a lift to two Territorials, one of whom had sprained his ankle and whose mates had carried him two miles and were about 'done up'. We willingly consented and after putting rugs and macs for him to rest his leg on we drove him down to Allsopp's maltings and then we put him in one of the buildings. We were told it was the wrong one and so Arthur and I carried the chap into the proper building and I asked the officer if it would not be better for the men to have some bags to sit on, so some were brought. Arthur shaking hands with the man with the bad ankle and the officer commanding.

Finally, Gothard told his friend to apply for a commission at Lichfield nearby. Arthur Linsley had earlier given a lift to the town's police superintendent, a sergeant and a constable, 'to try and capture a spy' in the suburb of Stapenhill, 'so he had quite a lot of adventures in one morning'. While Gothard did not say any more about the poorly soldier and his mates, and may not even have noticed their cheekiness, we can speculate what they made of their lift. But for the war, would two well-off young men – officer material – like Gothard and Wardle have done a good turn for common soldiers? Would the soldiers have dared to ask for such favours? That Arthur Wardle shook hands all round suggests that he was looking ahead to being part of the army. Thousands of soldiers had been gathering for the previous few days in the 'maltings', Burton's brewery buildings where labourers shovelled barley, but which were empty in summer. As so often that month, the men had to make the best of the basic conditions they were given. We can sense, therefore, that the soldiers enjoyed thumbing a lift, and being fussed over, and would have seen the humour in the rather prim civilian Clifford Gothard telling an officer to bring bags for them to sit on.

The first thing the army did with troops was to make them march. It filled the day, gave them stamina and hard feet, and weeded out the weak. In his memoir, Guy Paget made the wise and important point that only the young could stand the sheer physical fatigue, and sometimes hunger and thirst, of warfare: "However gallant the spirit may be, nature cannot be overtaxed when one is much over 40. The war proved it time after time." Similarly, soldiers who could get away with some disability in peacetime could not in wartime. A commander was only acting for the best for all his men if, like Sir Mark Sykes of the 5th Battalion, Alexandra Princess of Wales' Own Yorkshire Regiment, he set a higher standard than he would for his civilian workers. To take a 1909 example of a hard-working, well-meaning but deaf man called Edwards he proposed to get rid of:

> ... *suppose we have to mobilise with such a man as adjutant, it means getting another just at the moment when they will be impossible to find ... If Edwards were one's agent or employed it would be otherwise ...*

The army picked only the fit, because lives would depend on it.

III

Gothard had meant well. A couple of weeks later – it may have been significant that it was the day his mother went to Nottingham – Arthur Wardle and another man visited Gothard at home, and they 'talked for a long time about enlisting'. Still, it was only talk; and these were young men, the very sort that Kitchener was asking for.

11

Spectators on the Shore

... the mother country is now engaged in perhaps the most difficult struggle in her whole 1500 years of history.
Sydney Morning Herald editorial, August 6, 1914

I

"War, war, war, per mare, per terras, in short ubique in Europe. It is a horrible shame," wrote Denys Yonge, the vicar of the village of Boreham, near Chelmsford. As his fondness for Latin showed, Yonge was stuck in the past. He turned 78 in 1914 – 'mother would have been 109 today', he wrote on July 11 – and judging by his diary felt distant from, and perhaps indifferent to, events. As a vicar he still did some preaching, and held a place in local affairs. On August 4 he went to the meeting of the local board of guardians, which looked after the poor laws covering the sick, the aged and orphans, besides paupers. He had lunch with his fellow administrators: "All the people full of the war, as of course they would be." Yonge sounded detached, as any old man would be, who only followed events through *The Times*.

The clergy did what they could for their parishioners, holding 'intercession services' most evenings to pray for peace – presumably a peace won by Britain. Otherwise vicars, and their families, did their usual August rounds, of work and pleasure; such as mowing the grass in the churchyard, arranging the flowers in church, visits (Yonge reckoned he did 980 in 1914), music lessons and light sports. For example Dorothy Wright, the 19-year-old daughter of the vicar of Hemingborough in Yorkshire, wrote in her diary for August 4, the day war was declared, only that she, her mother, and her brother Charlie, a history student at Trinity College, Oxford, played in a tennis tournament at the club at Cliffe, the next village. ("Dad umpired.") She first mentioned the war on August 9, when Charlie cycled to nearby Selby in the afternoon for news. On the Tuesday morning, August 11, all the Wrights cycled to Selby: "Crowds of soldiers, 7000!" she wrote. "Played tennis in aft." Dorothy Wright did some war-related charity work; she went to 'Red Cross practice' later that day (and even later played croquet in the twilight and dark); wound wool for socks for soldiers and sailors; and held sewing meetings. Likewise her mother took the train to Pocklington on September 2, for a meeting of the Soldiers and Sailors' Families Association (SSFA), "and came back tired out and had to go to bed".

II

If the people of 1914 did one helpful thing, and otherwise left the war to others, they gave to charity. Reservists who left their jobs to join the army and navy, as they last did for the South African War of 1899 to 1902, might well have to leave their families out of pocket. At worst, as the Burton upon Trent branch of the SSFA found in 1899, a woman in a terraced house in the town would have been starving, but for the association's aid. In some ways the association was generous, in others not; in all cases, it set the rules; and the ones setting the rules were the traditional leading figures in a town and county. The Staffordshire president of the SSFA was Lady Dartmouth, Gerald Legge's mother; Lady Burton chaired the Burton meetings, as the wife of the brewer Michael Arthur Bass, first Baron of Burton. She looked into the cases of reservists' wives near her country home; she sent regular postal orders to her committee of ladies, who then gave out the charity, in cash, or groceries if the women were judged to be 'careless'. After the Boer War, Burton SSFA kept giving, to 'deserving cases'. That even included the wife and child of a soldier in prison for desertion; but not men who had left the army, because national policy reckoned that the men, if supported, would then not bother to look for work.

Such charity – whereby the ones giving the charity knew best – had ticked over for years, and began anew in August 1914. Lady Burton took the chair again. She told her committee, as was reported in the local press:

We must deal very gently and tenderly with these poor women whose husbands have been wrenched from them and who are feeling very sore and unhappy and as a result unequal to conform their lives to their altered circumstances. We must try and make them feel the help we are enabled to give them is not charity but freely offered of their more fortunate friends … a gift and a kindly thought to make up in a small way for their troubles and anxieties.

That sounded generous, except that, as working folk might have said, you couldn't spend it at the Co-op. People fallen on hard times, let alone those without a wage because the man of the house had left to serve his country, had no *right* to aid, only what charitable givers offered. Large employers, such as Burton's breweries, the post office and the railway companies, said they were giving the families of their workers called up as reservists about half the man's pay. Again, it sounded generous, but not if you only just made ends meet on your usual pay.

Worries about money ran through the letters of the reservist and Derby railwayman Arthur Bryan. As a King's Royal Rifleman, he found himself at Sheerness, on the mouth of the Thames in Kent, waiting to sail. In one undated letter in mid-August, he apologised for the handwriting, 'as I have had the butt of a rifle for a desk':

That ninepence a day I left to you will not start till we go out to Belgium so I am sending you five shillings. It's all I can spare as we are getting the princely sum of one and three a day and most of your food to buy out of that. There is a man in my tent that comes from Derby works at the carriage works MR [Midland Railway]; his wife tells him the company are allowing her something a week while he is away so if you hear anything about it you must go to Mary's and tell them about your change of address. Well sweetheart, don't worry about giving the house up as it doesn't bother me a bit as you know.

By that last line Bryan meant that his wife Louie and their baby daughter Doris might give up their house and move in with her mother, whether for the company or to save money. In a later letter while still in England, Bryan advised his wife on how to claim separation allowance, which with the ninepence a day from him would give his wife 14 shillings and sixpence a week, "so you will be able to manage and be sure to register your name for the relief fund as there is plenty for everyone I don't see why you should not have a share as well as anyone else". Like soldiers before and since, Bryan urged his wife not to worry about him; he assured her of his love and that he was well; and he longed to be home. "I should like to be chasing you up that garden walk again my love but never mind we shall laugh again shortly," he told her. Meanwhile, they had to make the best of it.

So too did the 'army wives' of officers, such as the newly wed Janey Brooke. A knock on the hotel bedroom door on the Monday night, August 3, had cut short her honeymoon, as a telegram from the War Office ordered Alan Brooke to be ready to leave for India from Southampton around August 11. Once at sea, Brooke wrote to his mother: "I was very surprised that they should be sending us back as I thought that they would be sure to give us a job at home." Like any ambitious army officer, Brooke wanted a job nearer rather than further from the fighting. Any officer, and any officer's wife, had to accept that duty came first: "We had to get up again and pack up at once so as to leave early the next morning," Brooke wrote. The Brookes crossed from Ireland on the Saturday night, August 8, and booked into a hotel in London. On the Monday, Brooke's last full day in England, his wife wrote her own letter to her mother-in-law. "My dearest mother," she began, in larger handwriting than her husband's:

> *Alan says I may call you that now I am writing to you for him as he is so very busy and had to go out at once after breakfast ... Life seems so to have changed for us in the last fortnight. We heard the first distant rumours of the war scare on our wedding day but we did not think that it would affect us so nearly and so very soon ...*

Brooke was leaving, probably, for Egypt, via Gibraltar and Malta, while Janey would stay with an aunt in Buckinghamshire, then make the return crossing to Ireland. "He is very well and quite splendid about it all as of course we know he would and he is the most perfect husband I am so very happy and these changes cannot alter that. Our time at Gweedore was just a paradise and it is so lovely to be able to look back on that now." Brooke, evidently having returned to the hotel after a day's errands, then finished the letter: "I did not gather much more today." As he did not know if the army would return him to India, or send him to Egypt, to guard against the (so far neutral) Turks, he did not know where to send himself money, nor whether his unit would bring any of his belongings from India. With 'great difficulty' at the military outfitters Cox and Co, where everyone else in the same fix as him was buying the same things, Brooke bought a uniform and such varied necessities as polo boots, haversack, water bottle, scabbard for sword, and waterproof: "But there was not a revolver or a Sam Browne belt to be got in town for love or money!"

Brooke, like many, was finding life awkward enough, trying to equip himself and do as he was told, without wanting to worry about his wife or the unsure future. At least Janey Brooke looked on the bright side; she cherished what she'd had, rather than cursed what she hadn't. Or as Brooke wrote to his mother, in yet another letter, while still on honeymoon, Janey was 'such a help, never a word about herself'. She, and he, in Brooke's words hoped 'it will all plan itself out in the end'. Janey Brooke understood the outbreak of war was *the* time to put her husband first, and not to fret about what was out of your hands anyway. Not so Lady Gwendoline Churchill, 'Goonie' to her husband John, the younger brother of Winston. She may have had several reasons, or none, for a crass and demanding stream of letters in the first days of the war. Maybe, parted from her husband, she felt 'dreadful blues', as she put it on August 5; maybe she suffered from an idle, self-obsessive life; she may even have been playing a deep game of torturing her husband; or maybe she was dim. Her second letter of August 5, from a holiday cottage near Cromer, was typical:

My darling Jack. I could think of nothing but you and what you are doing; I am dreadfully anxious to know your plans; I have the gloomiest thoughts and I cannot get out of my head the possibility of the Germans landing some soldiers while we are engaged fighting their navy on the high seas. In fact darling I am very unhappy being here and crying a lot though I do try and be brave and make myself believe that it is not all so bad and think you will be able to come here very soon. Do you think you will be able to get away after you have organised the squadron; you must let me know if I should go to Blenheim to be near you. I am torn in two about it, wanting to be near you, and not wanting to leave the children alone being here but it is of no use going on like this and I must pull myself together and be brave and sensible and not see things too black and after all if there is

a war in this country you may come out of it with medals
and clasps of which we will be both so proud of. Wire to me
please darling often and tell me what to do.

This was the letter of someone, as she said, 'torn' between responsibilities, though none of them added up to much. A nanny looked after her two sons; servants brought up children and did everything for the Churchills and their class. Winston Churchill's wife Clemmie, with young children, had visited, Goonie reported: "I have had to pack her poor French nurse off as she was in such a state and crying and having hysterics about her people in France." The hysterics might have been catching. Goonie might have felt she had not too many choices, but too few. She may genuinely have feared a German landing on the Norfolk coast. Writing to Clementine, Winston Churchill did admit to being 'a little anxious' that his wife was at Cromer: "It is 100 to one against a raid but still there is the chance and Cromer has a good landing place near." As a Churchill, though, married into the family of one of the ministers fighting the war, Goonie and Clementine alike had to set a public example. Did that explain why Goonie privately loaded her woes on her husband – as if he had time to spare, while preparing a cavalry unit for war? Evidently Jack Churchill did answer his wife's letters at once, because by August 7 she was writing back. "I am proud of you; but of course I am thinking of you all the time and longing to see you again." She sounded loving; in truth she only wanted her husband to satisfy her emotional demands. She went on: "I am in such a mortal terror of those dirty German swines and you are such a coco, such a sweet and I love you such a lot; you are my life and my being; ... it is always a person like you and loved like you that gets shot at." Did she have to remind her husband of that? Was she having a dig at him, or was she simply emotionally ignorant? She seemed to supply her own answer: "I am dreadfully silly but I am brave really and quite resigned." Clementine Churchill had arrived the night before: "Clemmie is full of stories and anecdotes and Cabinet secrets."

In another letter that day – having received another letter from her husband at the Churchill family seat of Blenheim Palace, and a telegram from Oxford – Goonie hoped that Clementine would stay, "but I am afraid she might want to return to Winston which is quite natural". Britain was in its third full day of war, and already Goonie Churchill was harping on to her absent husband! She did show signs of adapting: she and Clementine and other friends went into Cromer and told "the trades people not to put up their prices otherwise we would report them to the Board of Trade". Having something to do, ordering the lower classes around, seemed to help; she closed her letter cheerfully: "Bless you my Jacko your Goonie who is brave and happy." For the time being.

A couple of days later, after going to church, she had Sunday lunch with Clementine Churchill, "and she has just told us of the battle at Muhlhausen with advantage to the French but with appalling casualties, 20,000, 17,000, it is quite horrible; when do you think it will all end? I don't think the swines are coming out to fight our Navy; they are playing a dirty game; they have all their submarines out and are trying to sink our ships. Pray God they will not get any." As they had long planned, the French had launched infantry attacks into eastern France, gaining little and losing many men.

Goonie felt more settled – 'I am no more in a panic' – thanks to family gossip, the company of her father and others, and the sight of some defenders: "... we saw about 800 soldiers on the road and on the hill were the Light Horse; they had Essex written on their shoulders and they were Regulars; they looked like they could take on the Germans any day. It is a horrid day very windy and blustery and hot so the poor soldiers looked very hot and tired, but nevertheless it was very comforting to see them." The next day – 'Just received your wire from

Banbury' – Goonie told her husband more gossip, which made her one of the most informed people in the country. "Winston has just been on the telephone to Clemmie and he has told her about Muhlhausen been exaggerated also about the rumour of these swines threatening to cut the archbishop's throat at Liege unless the forts were surrendered." That correction did not, however, change her opinion of the Germans: "What barbarians and whole swines they are. I tremble to think what they would do if they ever got over here, the horrors."

Letter by letter she swang between extremes, just as she had to swing between roles, none of them made by her, but all in terms of other people – as a wife, a mother, and a Churchill who could out-bully over-charging tradesmen. She was on the same page a nervous and self-centred woman only ever allowed to be a spectator of life; and a swift retailer of the country's most important secret piece of war news, as told by Winston to Clementine Churchill to her: "... our expeditionary force had left yesterday morning and some more today. I hope our soldiers will not get killed."

Goonie went on with her holiday: "We sit on the beach and watch torpedo boats capture German tramps [other boats] which is most exciting and we play tennis."

12

Politics

There is no standing still in the world's history.
All is growth and development.

Germany and the Next War, by General Friedrich von
Bernhardi (1911)

I

Goonie Churchill's letters – simple and silly as some of
them were – did show Britain's thinking, a few days
into war. A fear lingered, and not only by the seaside,
that Germans would attack Britain, because the Germans were
so warlike; and had they not made such a fuss about their navy?
Britain thought first and most of war by her navy, to protect
the oceans that brought food and kept trade going; even the
army, if it sailed to France or anywhere, would need the navy
for a safe crossing.

Many spoke like Goonie of the Germans with hatred. At
best some, as in 1939, sought to excuse the German *people*
as oppressed or fooled, while the *ruler* Kaiser Wilhelm was
a despot, or insane. If anyone regretted war, and felt pity for
all, few said so, at least in public. An exception was the Rev T
F Jerwood during a short sermon for the Territorials leaving
Market Harborough on Thursday August 6. He asked everyone
to pray for the wounded of all sides, and to pray for loved ones
left behind, throughout Europe, and for 'our Father, yes the
father of all, even the kaiser, poor misguided man'. While it
took some nerve to feel charity for the kaiser, the most Jerwood
could do was suggest the German emperor was badly advised

– always the polite excuse when kings did wrong – or not right in the head. As a band led the town's reserve soldiers along the high street on the main Leicester road to Oadby – in the opposite direction to Germany, as each county's units gathered somewhere central – it was not the time to admit that the kaiser, and his countrymen, had as much right to their point of view as Britain. Only the artist George Rose made a leap of imagination, on Sunday September 6, during special prayers at church at home in Ongar: "I wondering at the time whether the German congregations were doing the same thing as we were." Even Rose was only querying war, not his country's right to take part in it. Rose conformed outwardly and probably only aired his doubts to his family, or his diary – or hid his feelings even more deeply. Rose's brother Frank joined the army on August 25; Rose's diary pages for the next few days were torn out.

In public, where politics happened, people had to decide where they stood. Who were they fighting for, and against? Why? What did they want, and how hard would they fight for it? The answers soon changed. If anyone remembered Servia, they forgot it; Germany, not Austria, was the enemy. Belgium was the cause, or small nations in general. That could include Servia, although as the country was so hard to reach and help, it was best left unsaid.

Why should Britain, with the world's biggest navy and empire, bother about small countries? Duty, and honour, said every public figure from Asquith down. Such words – so suspiciously widely agreed by the newspapers, and by Unionist and Liberal politicians – were abstract. You did something out of duty not because it suited you, but because if you did not, you would lose face or feel shame. The navy officer James Somerville in his diary for August 3 noted that his ship would have the 'honour' of leading the fleet into action:

It is a great compliment to our admiral and the ship but there is no doubt we shall suffer severely because as the fleets converge on one another the leading ships come into action first and have to stand the brunt of the attack; also after a short time the rest of our line will be shrouded in smoke and spray and we shall be the only clear target for the enemy to fire at so though we have the honour we shall also have the casualties.

In other words, honour could be bad for you. Britain seemed anxious to convince itself that it was going to war for moral reasons. That might be because Britain had doubts – could the Liberal Government have done more, sooner, to localise the war to Austria and Servia? – or simply because everyone wanted to feel they were in the right, doing something as wrong as war. As Rose's uncomfortable insight suggested, didn't the Germans, as civilised as the British, feel that God was with them? Would only victory prove who, if anyone, was right?

Another clergyman speaking to departing Territorials, Canon Ernest Morris in Ashbourne, told the men in the town hall that they could go with a 'clear conscience': '... in as much as the quarrel had not been our seeking, but we had been forced into this war by the actions of others'. The churchman – like the appropriate hymn Onward Christian Soldiers that they then sang – was telling the soldiers they had permission to do what was otherwise unlawful and unchristian: to try to kill other men. Morris, the father of an officer, and himself a reservist, used another moral term. Lord Dartmouth, presiding at a meeting in mid-August at Stafford, used the term too, and like Morris said the crisis had been 'forced upon them': "If ever any country went into a war with clean hands it was the British country today." His audience – including his wife, five other lords, and five members of parliament – applauded. The British wanted to believe they were blameless, although it begged the question of how long hands could stay clean, literally and metaphorically; if they ever were. If Britain had not chosen war (though strictly speaking, on that Tuesday,

August 4, it had), and had been forced into it, shouldn't the political leaders of so great a country as Britain have done rather better? Or, though it might hurt the national sense of worth, had the continental countries gone ahead with whatever they felt was in their interests, taking no notice of Britain? Because Britain was not as great in Europe as it thought it was? And was the fact that Britain deluded itself, with talk of duty and honour, part of the problem – that neighbours saw through it, and distrusted it?

II

At a distance, you might be short of news, but distance and that very shortage of news could make politics look clearer. Frank Balfour wrote to Irene Lawley on August 28: "One spends much time explaining the war, its causes and possible results to all and sundry – I've borrowed an Arabic map of Europe from the local school." Nearly all the sheikhs took a newspaper – unlike Balfour, who had cancelled his, as he had expected to be in Europe on leave by then. "One of the things that strikes them most is the sinking of the Ulster business (I suppose it has – but I'm rather in the dark.)"

Certainly the war was British politics' most pressing business of all. Public opinion would not allow anything else as a distraction. Suffragette organisers made the best of it and promised to stop their campaign, before they lost all sympathy. The Unionist and Nationalist sides in Ireland, and their English followers, each promised to support the war. Saying so in parliament was one thing; what they thought in private was another. Rallying against some outside threat did not solve Ireland's differences. At best, the Liberal Government would – as Lord St Aldwyn gossiped in a letter to his son Mickey on Friday August 21 – put the 'Irish and the Welsh Bills' into statute but not make them happen for 'possibly two years so that the next Parliament would be able to alter or repeal it'.

(The 'Welsh Bill' by the way was for the disestablishment of the church in Wales, also controversial, though not enough to make anyone do gun-running.) Two years would take it to 1916, and another general election. Either the Liberals would win then, and could start again, or they would lose and the Unionists could have the problem. St Aldwyn quibbled: "But the Irish Bill cannot be settled by mere delay; they will have I think to give up the six counties [of Ulster] or something like it as a result and then it will be a pretty good row if they do not."

As a former Unionist minister, St Aldwyn was still thinking as a party-politician. So was Lord Milner, who had tried, without much success, earlier in 1914 to set up committees across England against Home Rule. In a dictated letter Milner told an old friend, Philip Lyttelton Gell, on September 3 that he had no sympathy with the 'present speaking campaign', whereby Unionist, Liberal and even Labour politicians argued on the same platforms for the war and more recruits. Milner claimed he would like to forgive and forget at a time of national crisis. However Milner used recent history as a reason for not wanting to work with the Government and thus aid the Liberals:

At the time when speaking about the duty of National Service was still of some use because there was time to carry out a scheme of national defence the people who are now so eloquent were all engaged in crabbing and belittling and ridiculing the men who were prepared to face unpopularity in order to speak the truth. I should be prepared to forget all this if the government would even now have the courage to face the situation and adopt a measure of compulsion which is the only possible basis of an adequate military organisation and a great people in the modern world. As long as they themselves shrink from their plain duty in that respect it is detestable hypocrisy for them to appeal to the sense of national duty in others. I wonder how many more lessons we must have before they take the bull by the horns.

Milner preferred to be silent on the most important subject of the time, and leave the political ground to rivals, rather than stand with Liberals who talked of 'duty' but had, he felt, done the opposite of duty on Ireland and national defence. Milner, with reason, could claim he was serving his country; he was writing from 47 Duke Street in St James's – another politician with a central London address – while he let the local Yeomanry use his Kent property, Sturry House. Milner meanwhile was still the party-politician. He claimed that the Liberals could stay in office forever, for all he cared: "...in fact I should like to see them there if only they would do the right thing. It is easy for them. It would be almost impossible for the opposition if it came into power." Without saying so, Milner was admitting that the Unionists did not have the numbers in parliament to run the country; only the Liberals did. Hence the Liberals were running the war by themselves, and not inviting Unionists to become ministers; because they could. Likewise Milner thought only of the Unionists taking power, not sharing power if the Liberals fell. (Ironically, Milner did become a senior wartime minister under the next, Liberal prime minister, Lloyd George. Before then, much would happen.)

All Milner's letter was honest party politics, and Milner gave his very honesty as the reason for keeping such views to himself. He told Gell: "I should not like to say these things in public because at a time like this all public recriminations must be avoided but between you and me there is no room for humbug." By his public silence, however, Milner appeared to accept *national* humbug.

13

Business as Usual?

*The wag of the regiment, a cockney, who had just been
reading in the newspapers that the motto at home was 'business
as usual', brought out an old biscuit tin which he had put the
notice on and turned it towards the Germans as a hint that the
men were ready again.*

A story of Wiltshire Regiment men in France, from the
Bristol Times and Mirror,

September 4, 1914

I

"Our children talk much of the war," George Thorp, the
Hull architect, wrote in his diary on August 17,

*and Muriel's ideas as to its strictly just and ethical settlement
were very much to the point. 'Why,' she indignantly asked,
'do they send all these poor men to be killed, that have
nothing to do with it? Why don't King George and the
Emperor fight it out between them?' Then she paused: 'Well,
perhaps that wouldn't be quite fair, because our King is such
a little man!'*

*'My dear,' I said to her, 'your idea would settle all bloodshed
for if those who made this dreadful strife had in this and
other disputes to fight it out themselves there would be
precious little war.'*

We have no way of knowing how many felt the same as
the childlike Muriel Thorp; then or since. By contrast, there
are no end of examples of civilians and soldiers taking to heart
the sound idea that you ought to aim to win by marching into

*1. Patshull House, near Wolverhampton,
the home of the Earl of Dartmouth*

*2. A demonstration in Tipton by strikers, June 16, 1913;
note the men in the middle carrying brass instruments*

3. Much work in 1914 was heavy, hot and hard. Burton upon Trent was world-famous for brewing; Bass' steam cooperage made wooden barrels for beer

4. A pre-1914 photo of the bridge over the River Trent at Burton, looking from the Winshill side. Clifford Gothard would have come from Bearwood Hill Road to the right to go into town

13. Mobilisation of
Croydon Territorials,
August 5, 1914;
officers on horseback,
men march

14 Admiral Lord
Charles Beresford:
Conservative
politician, public
speaker, private bully

15. A French postcard from 1914 of English wounded

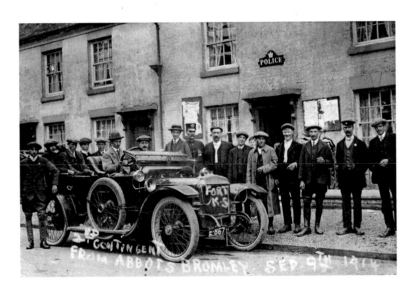

16. Second contingent of Army volunteers from the Staffordshire village of Abbot's Bromley, September 9, 1914

the enemy's capital. A month or two of war would show how unrealistic such ambitions were. In the meantime, 'À Berlin' was scrawled on the railway wagons taking the French conscripts to the front. J L Dent, a lieutenant in the 2nd battalion, South Staffordshire Regiment, felt low when the villagers who shouted in French 'À Berlin!' as his company marched into Belgium on Sunday August 23, murmured 'A Londres' as the men passed again in retreat, the next evening. Harold Cook in Clapham in south London posted a plain postcard around noon on Monday August 10, to tell a friend in Lincolnshire the good news. "I have been accepted today for the RAMC (Regulars) and received my first day's pay," he wrote. "I attend at Whitehall tomorrow for instructions. I will write to you from Berlin!!! Kindest regards." By 1915, Cook, in the medical corps in France, was complaining by letter to his friend of the monotony. In the meantime, whether in all seriousness or with some bravado, 'Berlin' was (with exclamation marks) a shorthand way of saying that you were throwing yourself into the fight. Most people settled into the war between the extremes of the girl-pacifist Muriel Thorp, and the likes of Dent of the British Expeditionary Force, who bumped into an army between them and Berlin.

Everyone had to ask, depending on their occupation, and wealth, how war affected them, if at all. Few stood with the socialists, at the best of times; even fewer stood with them against war. Men as different as the later secretary of the Communist Party of Great Britain Harry Pollitt (outside a barracks in Manchester) and Labour minister Herbert Morrison (on a Sunday morning on Hampstead Heath) each had meetings broken up by angry patriots. Judging by later memoirs, it seemed that you were nobody in the labour movement unless you were roughed up in August 1914 for telling the workers, in effect, that they were stupid, unless they agreed international war was not their business.

Ironically, some wealthy people took much the same view as the socialists, though the comparison would have insulted them. A common cry in August 1914 was 'business as usual'. Politicians, for example, had little to do, apart from the ministers who were crushingly busy with the army and navy, or with related matters, such as the railways and press censorship. Asquith adjourned parliament for two weeks on August 10, and MPs went on holiday; Richard Holt went to his family's usual retreat in Scotland. On his return on August 25, he admitted to his diary that MPs had 'nothing much doing' except emergency bills; and most of those in his opinion were not needed; but 'there is a passion for doing something'.

Donating money – and being seen to donate – was popular, because you could look generous, and newspapers took care to list who gave what. By the end of August the new Prince of Wales' Fund had £2m. A rare sceptic at this time, the writer Arnold Bennett, noted in the *Sheffield Daily Independent* on September 1 that some thought the sum marvellous. Compared with how much money people had to spare, and considering that the volunteers were leaving home to fight for the donors, Bennett called the amount 'miserable'. He dismissed the fund as 'machinery for enabling the income tax-paying classes to display their patriotism'. Another critic, Sheffield alderman George Senior, suggested a war tax, because while in his opinion aristocrats had 'nobly done their duty' by offering money and help, the upper middle class only did what they were made to do: "They are forced to pay rates and income tax; beyond that they do very little."

This question of how much people ought to give to society towards things for the good of all – roads, an army and navy – dated as far back as Caesar, to the dawn of civilisation, and such things as taxation. War only made the question more urgent.

At least donors had given something – or had said they would. In his August 21 letter to his son, Lord St Aldwyn wrote a postscript: " ... you and I have to give something to the county war fund – would you think £50 too much? I promised £100 but I have paid nothing yet ...". St Aldwyn was thinking of only paying half at first: "I might pay £50 for myself and £25 for you if you like when I find out where to pay it to."

Lord St Aldwyn would hardly miss £100; such a sum was a year or two's income for a worker. Charity, then, was hardly a fair way of drawing from people. Both the Liberal movement and Unionist aristocrats, however, believed strongly in the proverb of one volunteer being worth ten (or however many) pressed men. As they saw it, free people gave gladly, and would prevail over those told to do something by a kaiser. This cross-party feeling was under threat in the last few years before 1914, from socialists, and from Liberals such as Lloyd George who used the state to take money from some (in national insurance for example) and gave it to others (such as the old-age pension). The state would demand more in a war, from more people, than in peace; and would ask for more still, as the war went on and seemed ever harder to win. Whole towns would boom or bust, without seeing a German; some ports had more work, some less, because in a war against Germany, the enemy assumed by the Committee of Imperial Defence (CID) before 1914, North Sea ports could not run as normal, or at all. However, the state would not help those worse off as a result. A sub-committee of the CID, 'supplies in time of war', with Richard Holt among the members, said in 1911 that any 'inequities' (such as men out of work and starving families) could be left to 'economic laws' to put right, as soon as the emergency passed. During the emergency – presumably the days or weeks of change from peace to war – the state had enough to do, without looking for people to help. From the beginning, then, war made for coarser public affairs. If soldiers and sailors were dying, what did your suffering matter? And if you could not help the troops, why not help yourself?

When trade, jobs and food looked uncertain, and charity between classes was not nimble enough, or at all enough, to meet needs, society's principle of individual responsibility looked like something less moral: every man for himself. All this clashed with those public ideals of duty, and honour – which on the battlefield led to another abstraction: sacrifice.

II

Businesses could hardly carry on 'business as usual', if what had been their markets, or source of materials, were now enemy territory. Even in Sudan, Frank Balfour soon noticed that almost half the country's peacetime exports were gum, 'mostly taken by Germany'. As crippling, though more subtle, was the shaken confidence of businessmen; irrational, maybe, yet all the harder to put right. In mid-August the Hull architect George Thorp visited relations: "Auntie not well," he wrote. "Uncle pessimistic":

> ... was thinking an army of million men would be very useful in England to keep out the Germans, apparently thinks our fleet insufficient for the purpose, has discharged one of his assistants and cancelled his order for bulbs from Holland and yet had to confess that trade was normal and that they had to work very hard to keep up with the demand. To cheer him up told him a little story – a true one – the story had reference to the trenches being dug at Sutton – a resident there had one dug right across his lawn and flower beds; when he returned in the evening, his wife said to him, 'oh! Those poor men have been working so hard today, they looked so tired and dirty, so I had them in and made them a good tea!'

The trenches Thorp spoke of were between Hull and the sea, between the villages of Paull and Sutton. These precautions (also haystacks moved, and farm buildings pulled down, if they were in the way of these hurried defences) only fed the fear of invasion – last felt, as Thorp noted, in 1805, when the feared invader was Napoleon. Thorp's uncle, and many others, could not handle the unfamiliar sights, losses and unknowns of war: the commandeering of horses as mounts for officers and cavalrymen, and to pull wagons; and the 'streets full of soldiers', leaving as mysteriously as they marched in. Without confidence, businesses put up their prices not only because they could, but to hoard what *they* could, in case of even worse times, like any squirrel at the first sniff of autumn.

Given the trade troubles – holiday towns with cancelled bookings, hotels having to lay off staff and disappoint suppliers, who then could not pay their bills; and so on – you could understand the likes of Sophia Langmail, of Cardiff, who in a letter to the *Bristol Times* on September 2 asked: 'holiday or no holiday?' She reckoned that duty (that word again) for her and others like her lay 'in going forth fearlessly to the seaside or country apartments and in circulating our money as freely as possible in every legitimate way'. Even if well meant, she – like others – could be accused of making an excuse for doing what she was going to do anyway. It was suspicious that everyone found a good reason for carrying on whatever suited them. The *Newmarket Journal* for instance in its August 22 edition welcomed racing as usual at the town, in September:

> ... *it must not be forgotten that a great number of people are dependent for their livelihood upon racing and that the abandonment of race meetings would tend to produce unemployment and distress which would add to the economic difficulties which our country has to face.*

By contrast, Lord Derby, for one, asked the unmarried men in his Newmarket stable to volunteer for the army. If they did, they were promised their job after the war. If the army would not take them, they could keep their job. If they would not

129

volunteer, they were out of a job. Not surprisingly, nearly all the men so asked 'volunteered' for the army. Other landowners with servants did likewise. Lord St Aldwyn wrote to his son on September 1: "I have told the footman and the young men in the garden here that they must enlist and that I cannot keep them on unless they are rejected and I hear that three gardeners have been sent away from Hatherop," the next village.

By the end of August, then, the lords, as the leaders of society in the countryside and market towns at least, were, in St Aldwyn's words, 'getting excited' about recruiting. In fairness, the sons of these lords, like St Aldwyn's, were in uniform; the first were dead already.

III

Gentlemen were coming together for war, men who already knew one another through family ties, service in local government, fox hunts, and as Territorials – soldering and hunting often asked for the same skills. Francis Meynell of Hoar Cross Hall in Staffordshire was a lieutenant in one of the county's Royal Field Artillery batteries, which after coming together at Burton-on-Trent moved south. A fellow officer was Viscount Sandon. On August 29 – the day Gerald Legge was told to report to the depot of the South Staffordshire Regiment at Lichfield – Meynell wrote to his mother, on his usual headed notepaper, except that he crossed 'Hoar Cross' out and wrote 'Stopsley', near Luton, instead. By stages, the called-up Territorials were leaving home behind.

"You will have heard that Hoar Cross is waking up and that ten men are joining the Army," Meynell wrote. "I expect more will come by degrees; one must not expect them to think as quickly as those in the town." In fairness to men of the countryside, they might not have thought of the army because they were too busy bringing the harvest in, the most important work of the farming year. Some labourers may have been bound by contract, as apprentices were in towns. Farms could be short of harvest labour, at the best of times: J C White, the Somerset cricketer, had to stay on his farm at Stogumber, near Taunton, when Somerset hosted Yorkshire during Weston super Mare's 'week' of county cricket at the end of August. 'Farmer' White lived only 20 miles from Weston, almost in sight (except that he was on the other side of the Quantocks); he could not spare even the two days for the game, because some of his men were 'at the war'. As the cricket season was ending, cricketers could avoid any criticism of them, as could spectators – 2000 watched at Weston. George Thorp of Hull kept going to the nearby Kirkella cricket club each Saturday afternoon, where his brother played: "It seems rather anomalous to watch and play while such stupendous and tragic events are impending and happening in a near and friendly country," he admitted in his diary after the last but one game on August 22. It did not feel odd enough, however, to stop him going. As cricket ended, the football season started; professional clubs made the excuse that their players were under contract, and meanwhile went on taking money at the gate, from workers who did not go to war.

Hypocrisy was never far away in England in August 1914. One rule allowed 'business as usual', and another insisted that an employee went to war. Families could go on holiday, Lord Derby could race his horses at Newmarket; but young men could not go to the pictures, or play or watch sport, without someone resenting it, and saying so. Britain was dividing in two, between young and old: those fit to go to war, and those that could not.

Women, the too old, and the too young, could not enlist. If you were an Englishman aged 19 to 35, of five feet three inches or higher, of 34 inch chest or wider, and with good enough eyesight, teeth and everything else, Lord Kitchener wanted you in his army. Your country needed you.

14

Recruiting

I can understand a man opposing a war, but I cannot understand his waging a war with half a heart.
David Lloyd George from *The Prime Minister,* by Harold
Spender (1920)

I

Colonel Chichester, and all the other speakers at recruitment meetings, made the army sound so attractive. The colonel, 30 years a soldier, speaking in the open air at Godmanchester in Huntingdonshire, said that the pay after stoppages was 'a clear six shillings and sixpence a week'. What were the disadvantages? He answered his own question. 'There are none,' he said, to applause. Perhaps the audience did not notice, or out of politeness pretended not to notice, that the soldier's pay was about a third of a working man's. Then Chichester admitted there *was* one disadvantage: your job might not be open when you came back. Chichester hoped it would be; and anyway, those returning "would find plenty of work in the country to fill up gaps of the many poor fellows who might not return".

Was that not a disadvantage that Chichester had forgotten; you might get killed? If soldiering was as good as he reckoned, why was he and hundreds of other speakers trying so hard and often from the end of August to drum up recruits?

II

Judging public opinion is hard. A man's opinion could change. If you disagreed with something that someone powerful said, it was safest to keep quiet. Some men did respond to the recruiting appeals; 20 young men handed in their names that Monday evening, September 7, at Godmanchester. The meeting may have swayed them; they may have had half a mind already, else why did they attend? What of all the men that did not attend? As with the crowds at the outbreak of war in capital cities, supposedly enthusiastic for war, most people showed what they thought of recruiting by not being there. Some saw this, and deplored it. The local Huntingdonshire landowner, Lord Sandwich, early in September called the indifference in the villages of his county 'simply appalling'. Sandwich, so high in the social order that few would stand up to him, had a habit of making extreme statements; at a July public meeting about Home Rule for instance, he had spoken of his 'contempt' for Liberals. He seemed to expect people who did not have the time or energy to follow world affairs, to feel as strongly as him.

Some men volunteered because Sandwich and other lords had men in their power, literally or morally, and could tell them what to do. What of the rest? Depending on the standing of the man calling for recruits, his practice as a public speaker, and how subtle and strong was the pressure he could put on listeners, appeals had effects. Some volunteers would have gone willingly; some grudgingly, like a shop boy doing some thankless task after the doors shut for the night, or a wife running an errand for an ungrateful in-law. You 'volunteered', or else you got the sack, or a mouthful or worse from your husband later. Once a man gave his name, it did not matter why he did it: whether he cared about Belgium, fancied a change from small-town routine, or felt so niggled by the looks and remarks of workmates and neighbours that it was easier to give in. The recruiters had their man.

That said, cynicism can be a trap we can fall into, just as we might feel that the volunteers of August 1914 fell for speeches that meant nothing on the battlefield. It was true that the men giving the speeches never seemed to be the ones that did any fighting. However, the ones making the appeals, and the ones answering, might have enjoyed being part of a cause greater than any of them; greater than their understanding, even. Colchester-Wemyss, the chairman of Gloucestershire County Council, devoted one of his regular letters to the King of Siam to 'the wave of enthusiasm'. Shrewdly, Colchester-Wemyss suggested pride in the war so far was one reason; the more any country fought, the more invested in lives and effort, the more everyone would want to make it worthwhile. The more men enlisted, the more men left behind would feel the tug of brothers, workmates or others they knew. We forget how novel and thrilling Kitchener's appeal for 100,000 (and then another 300,000) men was. Whereas young men usually had to scrap for anything – a job, a sweetheart, a promotion, a place in the first eleven – the army was asking for them! All they had to do was accept! To refuse such an offer would take some opposing inner spirit – whether of socialist pacifism, working-class solidarity, or wife or parents begging you to stay at home.

On Tuesday September 1, Colchester-Wemyss wrote that a thousand men had enrolled in Gloucester since Saturday. "Let me give you a small personal experience."

I am chairman of the Stroud brewery company and yesterday afternoon I invited all the men, about 90, together to one of the stores and listen to me for half an hour; they came most of them in their shirt sleeves straight from work and I soon found I had struck oil and in ten minutes I had worked them and myself to a great urge of enthusiasm; I never felt nothing quite like it before, a sort of messianic influence seemed to pass through the whole of us and the result was that at the end of the meeting 29 men literally rushed forward and gave their names ...

What Colchester-Wemyss found more remarkable was that more than half of the 29 volunteers were married, "and their wives seem quite ready that they are going". Did it not seem to occur to Colchester-Wemyss – a widower, with a son in the army in India – that some men might have volunteered, to get away from their wives? Or that some wives would be glad to see the back of their husband? While the phrase 'struck oil' suggested an element of commerce – only the trade was in men, not goods – the 'enthusiasm' had much in common with religious preaching. Generally, more people went to churches after war broke out; but not every day, or everywhere. The Rev Denys Yonge wrote of large congregations in his Essex village, of 30 or 40; Robert Ramsey, the London solicitor, went to a special service of intercession at St Paul's, just after the declaration of war, and found 'the body of the cathedral was crowded'. They sang Rock of Ages and, after prayers, the national anthem. Ramsey wrote: "Voices seemed to pause slightly before the last line," namely, 'God save the king', "and gather tremendous force on the last line in a magnificently solemn and thrilling effect." Not for the last time in August 1914, the act of singing, and the beauty of the created sound, were comforts.

You suspect, however, that people still felt too shy to go inside a church or chapel building; for once you went in, you were at someone else's mercy. It's telling that a big religious success was the 10,000 people gathered on Sunday August 23 for afternoon and evening services in a Northampton park, arranged by the town's chapels before the war. William Thomas Pickbourne the diarist (and regular grumbler about small congregations) went to the open-air event after he took an afternoon service, "and amid an awestruck and most serious crowd listened, some grand singing and a most inspiring address from Mr J H Saxton," who was a Primitive Methodist. We have to take Pickbourne's word for it that the day was a 'great intercessory gathering', in other words a plea to God through prayer, and not a Methodist recruiting drive, or merely the best entertainment in Northampton on an otherwise sleepy sabbath.

Similarly, we can only sense what everyone had in mind when Robert Thornewill 'summoned' workmen at his engineering works in Burton-on-Trent on September 1. "We are all considering what we can do in this terrible war," he told them. "We are all anxious to help our country, and must each do so in our own way." And in our own time, he might have added, as he had summoned them in their dinner hour. Thornewill's way of helping his country was to tell the men, 'the youth and manhood of this great nation', to attend a recruiting meeting at the town hall. "I leave it in your hands ... consider how you can serve your country best in your hour of trial." The meeting closed with three cheers for the king – like singing, a significant way of binding everyone to whatever the gathering was about. If Thornewill said how *he* was helping the country – by making profits from selling metal goods? – the *Burton Gazette* did not report it. Thornewill could order his men to hear him, and lay hints as heavy as he liked, but he could not make the men do anything. That he had to resort to the meeting showed that his workmen were happy as they were. Was Thornewill's speech merely his way of doing his bit? Did he truly want many of his men to enlist – because how would he stay in business then? Again, if he promised to keep jobs open for the volunteers, the newspaper did not report it. Nor did the report give any clue to the men's reaction. Maybe they did not say anything. After a speech like Thornewill's, silence would be as loud, and as defiant, a reply as any.

III

Silence, or indifference, seldom makes news. As the last resort of the powerless, it seldom leaves a trace. Yet it deserves a history.

For all the thousands of words he wrote in his diaries, William Swift, the Churchdown old schoolmaster, did not give much away about his opinions. When he came home on the train from a morning's shopping in Gloucester at the end of July, and was in the same compartment as a man he knew 'full of socialistic views', he did not say if he approved of socialism or not. A rare clue to Swift's thinking came on August 11, after evensong – 'four there' – when the vicar told him of one of the three Gregorys in the village who went to war. His employer gave him seven shillings and sixpence as his wages owing. "He came home, took a farewell of his wife and youngsters, giving six and six of the seven and six to his wife and merely took one shilling and departed. Something pathetic about that," Swift wrote.

Three weeks later, the vicar took evensong early so he could attend the village's recruiting meeting. "I did not attend the meeting, nor Harry, read instead," Swift added. Harry, Swift's youngest son, a single carpenter and joiner in his late 30s, who painted in his spare time, still lived at home. Swift did care about the war; he followed it in the newspapers from the end of July; on August 21 he copied into his diary a list of all 48 Churchdown men serving in the forces; and he did not sleep much on the night of August 30, 'thinking about our country's threatened disaster', after the vicar had told him the British army was surrounded 'and nothing but a miracle can save them'. That left Swift 'instantly depressed', though the more cheerful news in the next day's *Daily Mail* reassured him. Still, Swift chose not to go to that week's recruiting meeting. Was it an act of resistance? Did Swift simply feel too old for such business?

The best guess might be that Swift felt too much for men he knew and had taught. On Saturday September 5, Ernest, his eldest son Reginald's eldest, visited to pick apples. "He has joined as a recruit to the forces and leaves on Monday. I could not help being affected at this," he wrote.

As the appeals for recruits became ever more urgent – because it dawned on the authorities that not enough men were coming forward – dissent seldom went public (assuming it was allowed a hearing). Rather, men dug in. After all, before August they never dreamt of giving up their jobs and families to shoot foreigners and get shot at, and they did not want to start now. The ones making all the noise were not the Swifts of this world, who stayed at home, but the busy-bodies, who leapt at the chance to tell other people what to do. When Colonel Chichester told the Godmanchester meeting there were no disadvantages to volunteering, he more truly might have said there were no disadvantages to telling men to volunteer. Take the bad and thankfully forgotten poetry of the day, such as a widely reprinted poem of early September by Harold Begbie. It had lines such as:

Is it football still and the picture show and the betting odds, when your brothers stand to the tyrant's blow and England's call is God's,

which at least tells us something about what was popular with young men. Every possible guilt was piled on men: they were lazy while their fellow men were fighting for good (and God), and 'if you sonny don't fall in, girls would cut you dead'. If you had a wife, your children would ask what you did 'in the war that kept men free', and burden you with more shame.

Would that really happen? Wouldn't women in fact be *more* glad to be with you, because fewer men were around? Would your children care in the least about a past war? Surely they would mind more if you were dead in Belgium. And as for keeping men free, if you were scratching a living down a mine or in a factory, breaking your back, black with dirt, did *you* feel that free? Where there was strength in numbers, as on coalfields, resisters to the calls for volunteers felt confident enough to air their disagreement in public. In a significant exchange of letters in early September in the *Cannock Advertiser*, a weekly covering a coal-mining part of Staffordshire, first an anonymous old soldier wished for a local branch of the 'white feather brigade'. He mocked young men, three or four in some families, he said, who were 'staying at home to keep mother'. The next week a Heath Hayes man called George Higgins mocked the old soldier back, saying he 'wears petticoats' – that is, wanted women to do his work. Evidently already women were handing 'white feathers' to men who they thought ought to be in uniform, seeking to shame them, by implying they were cowards. In Cannock at least, only the opponent of the 'white feather brigade' had the self-confidence to give his name.

That was how the 'white feather brigade' worked – they took it upon themselves to judge others, while they didn't have the courage to say who they were or to ask a man to explain himself – as he may have had reasons for not wearing a uniform. Miles Thomas, who went on to a distinguished business career, and indeed served his country well in both world wars, recalled in his autobiography how his Birmingham employer was happy that he stayed at work, making munitions; he had volunteered for a defence unit; and at 17 was too young for the army anyway. One evening on the corner of New Street and Hill Street in the city centre, 'a giggling chit of a girl' handed him a white feather:

The back of my neck and the whole of my face blushed scarlet as I hurriedly stuffed the beastly thing in my pocket. I was shocked beyond measure. I suddenly didn't want anyone to see me ...

Thomas walked to his digs 'burning with an anger that was fringed with shame' and soon left the city to become an armoured car driver. The white feather worked. What was the motive of that woman handing it out? A wish to help her country? Indignation that her love had gone, and not others? A bit of mischief? Or malice? Did women join the 'white feather brigade' for the same reason men volunteered for the war, and people crowded on seaside beaches each August – they wanted above all to do something right, because what everyone else was saying, or doing, had to be right? How can we explain Thomas' reaction – why did the silent accusation by a stranger cut him so? He felt he could not face society; even though he was the victim of a random, unjust, prank (did the girl hand out many others, or did the fun soon wear off?); and even though joining the army would make his mother cry. For the symbol of the feather to work, it did require Thomas to have a sense of shame, stirred by a woman.

Not everyone approved of such a trick. Early in September the *Harrow Observer* columnist 'Socrates' deplored anonymous postcards with words pasted out of newspapers, urging the 'loafers of England' to 'for God's sake play the man', and volunteer. Evidently two men (who had volunteered) sent their hate-mail to Socrates. Presumably the postcard-paster knew the men to send cards to, but felt unable to talk to them; or maybe he did, but felt he had to blackmail them as well. Interestingly Socrates throughout August wrote conventionally, describing the war as a test for the nation, urging young men not to be 'idling about', and so on. According to Socrates, men ought to know the proper thing to do, without nasty cards through the post.

The fact was, many men, maybe most, could not work out for themselves what was proper. Nothing in their lives told them how to react to a continental war. The men of affairs – the politicians of all main parties, the lords and generals – knew Britain faced a crisis. The rest had to be won over, whether by conviction, argument, the pressure of the herd, or most likely some of each. If you were inside Sheffield Artillery Drill Hall, for example, on Tuesday night, September 8, packed to hear Lord Charles Beresford, you were halfway to the army already. You were singing, over and over, songs popular with the troops such as It's A Long Way to Tipperary. The band of the local regiment, the Hallamshires, played patriotic tunes (shouldn't they have been at the war?). Listening to Beresford – in his khaki uniform – in such an intoxicating setting, the crowd around you clapping everything, it would take some gumption to spot Beresford's outright lies (he reckoned the authorities were running the war with 'faultless organisation'). As he came from near the centre of power in London – nearer than you ever were, at any rate – you had to take what he said on trust: those commanding the fleet were known to him. They could not be bettered; "Germany would be beaten and justly beaten but we must have men," and he appealed to the nuts, dandies and athletes.

If you believed Beresford, the men at the top were setting an example; the young, fashionable and sporty types ought to follow, and think of someone other than themselves for a change. In fairness to Beresford, if you listened closely, he did spell out what war would mean. They had to fight to the end, he said, whatever the sacrifice. And how much sacrifice? Beresford said the Empire was inexhaustible in men and almost inexhaustible in riches. "If we had time to do it the British Empire could put almost 20 million men into the field." Would victory over Germany, a country with more men than England, take 20 million? As Beresford was insisting on a fight to the end, would one side win only when the other – Germany, or England – exhausted its riches, in wealth, and men?

Cleverly the organisers did not give you chance to dwell on any questions; they made it easy for you to volunteer while you were still under the influence of the meeting. Buses waited outside to take you to the recruiting halls. Beresford turned up there, recruiting still, in what the *Sheffield Daily Independent* the next day called 'his usual breezy style'. Beresford told the men: "I like the look of you, and am glad indeed to see so many of you, but when the enemy see you they won't like the look of you. Every man jack in the country will be proud of you."

15

United?

England, said Henry VIII in words echoed by Shakespeare in King John, can never be conquered so long as it remained united.

Wolsey, by A F Pollard, 1953 edition

I

Beresford did good work that night in Sheffield: some 125 men took the oath, and who could say how many more thought harder about volunteering afterwards? The thousands in the meeting who were too old, or too female to join the army, would add to the climate of opinion that men who could go, should go. As Beresford, the 'white feather brigade' and their followers took care to impress on everyone, right was on their side, even if it meant sacrifice.

Of all Beresford's remarks, the most relaxed ones – and therefore most significant – came after the proper meeting, in the more intimate setting of the recruitment hall. As the men there had heeded him, he no longer had to win them over; he only had to wish them good luck. *Every man in the country will be proud of you*, Beresford told them. How did he know? Beresford and his kind, based in London and dashing from meeting to meeting, had no way to gauge public opinion. It merely suited them to claim that the country was united. If it was, why did only 125 men come forward that night? Surely that meant most of the men had gone home ignoring him, at least for the time being, or had not turned up at all? And if the country was so keen to fight, why were Beresford and others like him having to convince people to volunteer?

II

The recruitment rallies began one month after Britain began the war, not because recruitment was flagging, but because that was as fast as politics could go. News reached people weekly, at most daily in papers; at best a town or city paper would bring out several editions over several hours as the very latest news came in. Meetings would come together, speakers and venues arranged, by letters through the post, at the very fastest fixed over the telephone or by telegram. News of such meetings, again, would reach people through the papers, or on posters. Labour and trade union speakers, if ignored by unfriendly newspapers, might have to advertise their gatherings by chalk, on pavements. Word of mouth would take over. Likewise, newspaper buyers passed their paper to a neighbour or workmate. Newspapers reached many more readers than copies sold; but far from everyone, all the time.

Robert Blakeby for instance, the London draper's employee, according to his diary like many people heard about the 'threatened European war' by buying a newspaper. On July 29 he wrote: "Mr Burgess (advert department) said he would give me his Daily News and Leader every night instead of throwing it away." For the first time on August 13, walking after work to his mother's to eat dinner, Blakeby 'read Selfridges war news on the way', evidently displayed in the Oxford Street department store's windows to draw customers. While on a week-and-a-half's holiday at the end of August Blakeby bought his own newspaper, and on August 31 – the day he went by train to Skegness and back – he bought two. Besides learning the news, the act of reading a newspaper gave readers a shared experience. Meetings, as in peacetime, were the way men of power explained the news without the newspaper's slant, and gave their own message, whether party-political or religious. Beresford and the rest were making the first effort of wartime to tell people what they should do.

Some, speakers and listeners alike, welcomed the unity that war brought, as a contrast from the conflicts of peacetime. At a meeting in Stafford on Monday August 31, Lord Dartmouth said what others did on other stages. "They did not," he said, according to the *Stafford Newsletter*, "forget that six weeks ago we were at each other's throats over questions of politics; there was no party now. There were no classes now. Today we were all Britons united in a common cause to face a common danger." As at many meetings, songs were a way of binding people. At Stafford, the meeting began with the national anthem, and then the anthem of their French allies, the Marseillaise, 'which was not a success' as the *Newsletter* put it politely.

Assuming Dartmouth was correct, the change over six weeks from national conflict to unity came in stages. Before any thought of war, the trade union leader Ben Tillett could dismiss talk of war as imperialism, the work of the army and navy and their cheer-leaders, with nothing in it for the workers. Tillett told a meeting in Walsall in June: "If the working man had any sense at all, he would be only too glad to see the Germans invade their country." Once war came, the likes of Tillett had to change their tune, shut up, or face being called a friend of the enemy. Because as the Hull MP Sir Mark Sykes put it in a letter dated (probably) Thursday July 30 – the night he set off from London to command his Yorkshire battalion on exercise in north Wales – "this has put an entirely new complexion on affairs":

> the Nationalists are behaving vilely and also the Radicals and Labour Party – the Nationalists boast that they will not have a united front without Home Rule on the statute book – in this they are very foolish – I believe the Ulster

volunteers will volunteer to serve us – this should smash the
Irish because they are avowedly against us now – if it comes
to war, the Government have got to face coalition with us,
as the extremists intend to vote against them, all this if it
comes out will tend to help us toward National solidarity.

Sir Mark was thinking of uniting with the Liberals, but judging by his tone, only Liberals who thought like him; he did not feel as welcoming towards socialists, Irish nationalists or peace-preferring Liberals ('Radicals'). Once Germany invaded Belgium, and Britain went to war, men who had sincerely stood against war had second thoughts. The trade unionist and Labour MP for Derby, J H (Jimmy) Thomas, by September was sitting on the same platform as his political and social opposite, the Duke of Devonshire, lord lieutenant of Derbyshire. As Thomas said at the time, and in his end of career memoir (a point worth making, because public figures are not always as consistent), the war was not a question of political parties, nor between capitalists (who made workers do all the killing); the war was between nations, and between, so Thomas insisted, 'might and right'. Thomas still took care to defend his own kind; he asked that employers look after workers, so that volunteers for the army could look after their families.

The socialist Robin Page Arnot, in London again in August, had few visitors at the Fabian Research Department off The Strand, after he, other Fabians and socialists debated the end of capitalism in the Lake District. According to him, first the war bewildered people, then caught them in what he called a 'patriotic wave': "and most of them were to be swept into the torrent". Labour politicians J H Thomas and Arthur Henderson, who spoke up for the war, were scorned by purists like Arnot, as somehow weak enough to be caught by the 'tide' of feeling for war. It's at least as fair to say that Thomas and Henderson were sticking up (as best they could) for their country, and against the older enemy – capitalists at home or abroad who wanted to screw more out of workers for less. The likes of J H Thomas were already having to defend the principle of voluntary service against the imperialists, who even before the war had wanted conscription (like Germany, which nearly everyone agreed was so wicked). Forcing men to join the army, and knuckle under generally, would mean even less power for working men. In short, wartime Britain had the same divides, whichever way you described it, between rich and poor; capitalist and wage-earner; educated white-collar and ignorant and dirty (or no) collar. Some did believe in unity, and found it remarkable; such as M W Colchester-Wemyss, chairman of Gloucestershire county council, who (in a fine example of local government) set up a general committee. He wrote to the King of Siam about its first meeting on August 19:

All sorts and conditions of men and women were there, all distinctions of class or politics or religion were forgotten. One moment I would be talking to a duke, the next perhaps to a trade union leader then perhaps to the wife of an earl and directly afterwards to the daughter of a butcher then to the bishop of the diocese, a minute afterwards to a nonconformist minister but with one and all the case was the same; all differences of class religion and politics were forgotten ... and they did me the compliment of accepting almost without alteration the scheme I had prepared.

Colchester-Wemyss had the usual charitable and sometimes vague ideas, such as women to make garments for the troops; and do-gooders in each district to care for the wounded and to help soldiers' families in distress. Without doubting that Colchester-Wemyss meant well, as did the 180 people he invited (and nearly all turned up): after they left the room, was anything different? The war had given the country a common enemy. That did not mean that anyone felt more like trusting men of other parties and opposing interests who (as Dartmouth and others admitted) had been 'at each other's throats'. Men did not suddenly change character; or if they did, goodwill could wane. It's telling that even at the very start of the war, when you might have expected fellow-feeling to be strongest, few spoke like the *Yorkshire Telegraph and Star* did on August 7: "This is a People's War," its editorial ended. Few people said it, because few believed it. Britain was no more 'one people at war, all pulling together', than it had ever been in peacetime.

III

Besides, the war divided Britain in new ways, showing people as the good and bad characters they were. We have already met the Conservative MP Lord Charles Beresford who loved the sound of his own voice. He went too far in the hall of the Carlton Club on the Thursday evening, August 27, in the hearing of several members; we know because one of them, the Conservative MP Arthur Lee, told on him.

Winston Churchill sent a letter to Beresford on August 30 that he had heard Beresford was in the habit of talking 'in a rash and loose way about the First Sea Lord', Prince Louis Battenberg. Churchill, as the politician in charge at the Admiralty, made this his business. The prince was a lifelong Royal Navy man; he married a granddaughter of Queen Victoria. King George V likewise was a grandson of Victoria, who had married Prince Albert, a German; Battenberg, too, had come from Germany. In short, when Beresford said (as Lee insisted he did) that all Germans should leave the country, including highly placed ones, and Prince Louis ought to resign, Beresford had to watch out: it might have sounded like a threat to the king.

Beresford understood the danger he was in, and like the bully he was, or because he sensed attack was the best form of defence, he went after the tell-tale, not the more powerful minister. Lee wrote to Churchill on the Saturday, August 29, from his weekend home in the Chilterns, Chequers Court: "I have just been called up on the telephone by Beresford who has assailed me with a torrent of violent abuse in consequence of a letter which he says he has received from you." Lee was not the first or the last to learn how thankless it is to be a snitch. Beresford, according to Lee, called the report 'a malicious libel and a foul untruth'; in other words, Beresford was threatening Lee.

The ins and outs we have to guess, because in his letter of August 30 Churchill said he considered the incident closed. Churchill had warned Beresford to watch his mouth; the only man left unhappy was Lee. In another letter to Churchill, from his Mayfair address on Monday August 31, Lee noted that Beresford was also complaining,

> *however absurdly, that I had violated club law or the decencies of social intercourse by repeating a private conversation. It takes some time for even the most sensible people to realise what being at war means and they are apt to cling to social shibboleths even when the enemy is at the gates!*

Beresford had made another stab at Lee, accusing him of 'ungentlemanlike conduct'. Certainly Lee felt threatened, because he begged Churchill for the Admiralty's protection, by adding his name 'even in the most honorary capacity of any one of the numerous committees that you must have at work'. While Churchill had a war to run, and Beresford was the one going after Lee for crossing him, you have to fault Churchill – like so many in authority – for not looking after a well-meaning man who blew the whistle on a wrong-doer. What had Beresford said, exactly? According to Lee, Beresford said: "Feeling is very strong in the service about his being First Sea Lord, it is strongly resented." When Lee had expressed surprise, Beresford had added: "I am entitled to speak for the service, I know the opinion of my brother officers on the subject. It is very strong. If things went badly at sea, as they may, there would be a howl in the country and the mob would attack Prince Louis' house and break his windows."

Was Beresford only repeating what others thought – which was not the same, or as bad, as giving it as his own opinion? As with any loudmouth, or a criminal, if they are caught once, you always have the suspicion they are doing the same thing, or worse, many other times without being caught. This story shows the unwritten rule that men of affairs could say one thing in their members' clubs, and suppress it or deny it, and say another thing in public. (Surely Beresford's threat of libel was a bluff; would he want any of it aired in court?)

Quite likely Beresford felt jealous that he did not have an Admiralty job. If he was losing his temper so early in the war, what would he and his kind be like, once things went badly?

IV

Working people were used to things – life in general – going against them. They had their own agreed ways to make themselves feel better. They sang; and nothing serious or uplifting such as the national anthem. When 74 reservists left Gresley in south Derbyshire on Thursday August 6, to march their first ten miles to Derby, they sang such popular (and risqué?) songs as 'Hello, hello, who's your lady friend' and 'Everybody's doing it'. When someone shouted, 'shall we be beaten?' they roared, 'no!'.

The more common cry and answering shout, as made by the men in the motor buses taking them from Beresford's meeting at Sheffield to the recruiting halls, was 'are we down-hearted?' and 'no!'. Men, even from different factories or neighbourhoods, plainly knew it and responded to it. As the first half of the phrase admitted, you *might* feel down-hearted, on the football field, at work or on strike, or leaving home for war. The group denial, the united voice, gave the individual new strength to carry on; or at least made it harder for him then to give up. Here, among the soldiers and sailors, was a sort of unity, a rapidly deepening comradeship against a common danger. While (if only the soldiers knew it) Beresford ranted against the First Sea Lord (behind his back) and gave a deceitful speech a few days later, the soldiers and sailors were risking their lives. Not that Beresford cared about the men; he only spoke of 'things' going badly at sea. When Beresford repeated in speeches that the country was united, behind the soldiers, he was profoundly wrong. Simply by joining the fight, by going abroad, the volunteers separated themselves from the rest of the country and went through experiences that the civilians left behind could not go through, and maybe would even not want to know about. This lack of sympathy for the fighting men began early, at or even before recruitment. Across the country – in Manchester, Sheffield, Derby, though some places reported it more than others – men had to queue for hours to enlist. They had to give up, exhausted, or miss meals, or go back to work because they had taken time off. (And remember, the 'white feather brigade' was on the streets!)

It did not make sense; why did it take so long – too few doctors to test recruits, was one excuse – to join the army, while the newspapers were demanding volunteers? The army and government had not expected to have to recruit such a big army; the authorities had enough of a job looking after the British Expeditionary Force. More sinisterly, the army evidently took the attitude that anything was good enough for recruits. They wanted to join? They could wait; they had to learn to do as they were told in the army, anyway. If the army had so little regard for men even as they queued to volunteer, what would it be like on the battlefield?

16

Food and Other Secrets

*Who doubts that if we all did our duty as faithfully as the
soldier does his, the world would be a better place?*
Charles Dickens as The Uncommercial Traveller, in *All
The Year Round*, April 21, 1860

I

The war knocked on William Thomas Pickbourne's door on
August 28.

*A billeting officer came around on Friday and asked us
how many we could do with. My good wife remembering
she has a son who is a Territorial said we could do four.
Accordingly four was chalked up on our door. They came
yesterday (Sunday!) and with them many more, 36 in all.
Just at tea time, about 430, we were roused from our teas
by the tramp, tramp of a number of soldiers going down the
street. They passed our door and we thought they had gone
elsewhere but at the bottom they turned sharply and came
back halting just outside our door! An officer stepped forward
and presented a note to me signed by Captain Hazeldine
asking that we should prepare a meal consisting of meat
potatoes etc and tea for the whole of them (36) at 7 o'clock!
We were astounded and Mrs P almost collapsed. But one
soldier brought us a huge joint of meat, another brought
potatoes in, another two tea and sugar and dumped them
down on our little scullery! The officer in charge apologised
for the trouble he was causing us and they decamped
promising to return for 7 to 7.30!*

So many exclamation marks show how Pickbourne was torn many ways: between Christian charity, respect for authority, and outrage at having his day of rest (and not someone else's) upset. His wife Kate had the grace to see that these young men were someone's sons, and their son Frank (in camp at Derby race course, then Houghton Regis near Dunstable) might be glad of a good deed by someone like them. The fact was, however, that the Pickbournes had three hours to prepare a meal for 36.

Well there was nothing for it but to make the best of it. And so with the help of Mrs Swann next door and a young fellow who said he was to help us cook we set to work. I took off my coat and commenced cutting slices from the huge piece of beef and mamma cut up some onions. Wilfred and the 'cook' cut up potatoes. Mrs Swann took some meat to cook in her kitchen and so we were all at it. Am glad to say we got the whole thing cooked lovely for 715 and about 730 the soldier lads trooped down the street, stood outside our door in single file, came in one by one to receive their ration of meat, potatoes and tea till all were served. And this was on Sunday! Such an experience we have never had and do not want repeating. Still we felt a certain pleasure in doing it. For were we not helping our soldier lads who are going if need be to lay down their lives to defend us. Most of them are from Carlisle and Cumberland.

The Cumbrians were fed in that Northamptonshire village of Upton that Sunday evening not because the whole country was united behind the troops. As it happened, Pickbourne knew Cumberland; he had visited the small town of Brampton only in July, to preach as a guest of his former Methodist minister, Henry Scott. The meal was possible because all classes were used to preparing and eating the same few basic ingredients, cooked or cold. Food had to be cheap, easy to prepare and carry, and had to fit you for heavy work or exercise. An unnamed horseman in the Leicestershire Yeomanry, living in a field at

Diss in Norfolk by early September, wrote that he ate 'bread and bacon for breakfast, stew for dinner, and bread and jam for tea, and my word, we can eat it!'. Then as now, such simple food suited masses of people. It was good enough then for the well-off, too: vicar's daughter and diarist Dorothy Wright and her mother ate bread and cheese on a moors walk from Whitby during their Easter 1914 holiday.

Of all the diary-keepers of 1914, William Swift in Churchdown went into most detail about his meals, perhaps because food was relatively more important in the old man's life, or because as a widower he did his own cooking, unless his neighbour Mrs Phelps 'sent in' a meal. Swift recorded an apple tart from her for Sunday lunch on August 9. Swift had to leave the morning church service early, 'during the singing of the Benedictus as in Harry's absence there was no dinner unless I cooked it and which I had to do'. On August 12, Mrs Phelps sent 'R Mutt, cabb, potatoes, apple tart'. The next meal Swift described from Mrs Phelps a week later was the same, mutton with vegetables, apart from 'K beans' for cabbage. On one of Mrs Phelps' 'off days', Swift cooked nearly the same for himself: potatoes, tomatoes and bacon; the apple tart he had for afters may have been a piece of Mrs Phelps'. The diet may have been healthy, but heavy and unvaried. On a visit to Cheltenham on August 20 – for tea to mark his relative Walter Hambling's silver wedding anniversary – Rose Hambling was having indigestion; Swift recommended 'Savoury and Moore's absorbent lozenges'. He used to buy them on occasional shopping trips to Gloucester, one and fivepence a box from Boots. Swift did not say whether he sucked the lozenges as a luxury, or to treat another effect of a stodgy diet: wind. On August 26, he admitted that he took an afternoon walk, 'very slowly for I had flatulence badly, but afterwards felt all the better for the exertion,' as he put it.

A typical meal of his was roast meat or chops, potatoes and green vegetables, and sago pudding. According to his diary he was growing several rows of potatoes; Brussels sprouts, broad beans, cauliflowers, Savoy cabbages, beets and onions; and had raspberry and currant bushes. Unless it was raining, the upkeep of his garden took some hours each day, with help sometimes from visiting sons and grandsons. Despite the drudgery of cutting a hedge, tidying the road in front of your house, and the like, gardening was valuable and gave you a place in the give and take of village society. Swift's family regularly left with windfall apples, and fruit, to eat themselves or to sell: Annie Swift on August 21 for example 'took 20lb of Victoria plums kept for her to make into jam'. Sharing produce was an excuse to visit other gardeners. On August 11 Swift 'went to Henry Morris for carrots' and inside saw 'Mrs Morris who was sitting in the settle and with her Mrs Seborne her near neighbour who is very kind to her and goes in several times in the course of each day and with whom I had a pleasant chat'. On the way home, presumably, Swift 'fell in with Mr Merrell who hawks fruit &c, bought a couple of cucumbers from him'.

The labour that went into growing, and preparing food for the plate, meant that better-off people might well leave such work to servants (besides washing, dusting and so on). Swift did his own housework, but was occasionally a spectator in the homes of people who did have servants, as on August 16 when invited to Sunday tea by a Miss Court. She was renting Green Hayes, from John Jones, one of the leading figures in the village. Swift reported that Emily Prince was Miss Court's domestic, possibly a girl he knew from teaching her. In a matter of fact way that may have hid his amusement at people not like himself, Swift wrote: "Miss Court complained of the obtuseness of Mr J H Jones' domestic in not turning on the water for her drinking purposes from Barrow Hill, Mr J H Jones' residence ... Emily P was dispatched to see to it. Then the next upset was Emily had not got the kettle boiled for our tea; she Miss C had to put fir cones on to hasten the matter." Swift and Miss Court talked about Abergavenny, the corner of Wales that Swift had taught in as a young man before bringing his family back to Gloucestershire.

Miss Court may have wanted to excuse the late tea; she may have enjoyed an audience to hear her grumble about servants; or the old schoolmaster Swift may have looked like a wise and trustworthy listener that people could speak freely to, and even share secrets with. The humbler sort of villager came to Swift, as someone who had taught their children (and maybe themselves). He could help with the occasional legal business or serious letter that was beyond some. In mid-August, after his Aunt Sarah Pick was given notice to quit, she was posting on her landlord's letters to Swift for him to write her appeal to stay. In July Swift read a woman's will, made a clean copy of it, and with his son Harry witnessed it.

Swift's family told him some secrets, maybe not for advice, but on the principle of a problem shared is a problem halved. Walter Hambling called on Monday August 17:

… he told me how he was entangled with Charles Hambling's two daughters, one of whom had married a sergeant in the Army and had started a market gardening business in Hayden, bordering on Staverton and in order to do so had borrowed nearly £100 from him and an additional sum from Mr and Mrs Carter, Annie Hambling, and seemed in no hurry to refund. And he was afraid it was a bad go.

If Swift gave Hambling advice, he did not say so; it sounded like the age-old story of a family stuck with an in-law who abused their trust. Hambling may simply have wanted to unburden himself to someone who understood. Mr Walker, who visited Swift on July 13 and September 7 and twice in August, may have felt the same. His married daughter was in a lunatic asylum at Binstead in Surrey and the son-in-law had sent his son to an asylum in Germany, seemingly to get rid of him. Mr Walker was unsurprisingly depressed after visiting his daughter, who was sane enough to be 'discontented with her surroundings ie the other patients who made unearthly noises crowing like a cock, grabbing at her victuals on her plate &c'. What must have made it worse for Walker was his 'wife's nervous state and her reproaches', because Mr Walker could not free their daughter. Whether because Walker asked too much, or Swift had had his fill of it all, even Swift ran out of goodwill: "He several times spoke quite in heat and I felt bound to check him and to tell the truth I was glad at his departure."

II

Besides public business, the stuff of newspapers, meetings, and commerce, beyond even the unremarkable dealings of family and friends, that seldom left a trace, there were the private matters of every man and woman, intimate or even shameful things seldom admitted, even in diaries. Even the notes made by a diarist may be beyond understanding now, such as the circle and cross each month in Dorothy Wright's diary, a week or two apart (the start and end of her periods?). Things that people took for granted, such as food, or baths, were not thought worth noting. That makes it hard to say anything in general about people's habits. At the back of Robert Blakeby's 1914 diary were dates 'when I had a bath during the year', and 'how was the water'. He had his first on January 9 ('cold') and nine by April 9, but only one more, with a question mark against it, on August 7 ('water nice and hot') before the eleventh and last in November. Did Blakeby go months without a bath? If so, did he wash himself in other ways? In midsummer, did he smell? How typical was he?

If people were shy of writing intimately about themselves in the most intimate place possible, a diary, how much more shy they were about airing such things in public; and not only the physical details of their toilet, but the inner workings of their mind. People in 1914 were as curious as in any other era about others, and above all about extremes – murders, and divorces. Many other things affected lives, without quite ever becoming the business of some institution and making the public record: a child deemed insane, or neglected, an animal treated cruelly, an in-law who took a loan and never paid it back. Some people had strange, unseen streams running through their life, that usually they chose to hide, for the sake of a quiet life. M W Colchester-Wemyss revealed one case in his July 1914 letter to the King of Siam. Perhaps because he was short of a topic of proper news, he gave his letter over to a near-miss he had, with a neighbour in Westbury-on-Severn. He described Miss Day, the tenant of Westbury Court, as a 'distinguished lady of about 40 … violet coloured eyes and perfectly white hair'. Whether Colchester-Wemyss liked the woman, or her wealth, or both, they agreed to marry. Miss Day said she had a fortune, but kept making excuses about where it was and why she didn't have it to hand. Maybe Miss Day was trying to keep what was hers from her husband-to-be; she may have been pretending that she was more of a catch than she was, to trick someone well-off into marriage; or, her fortune was in her head and she wasn't sane – or at least not sane enough to marry. Colchester-Wemyss decided that Miss Day's fortune was imaginary, and he broke off their engagement. It was a rare and intriguing glimpse of how, in a generally plain and earthy society, with pungent smells to match, not everything was as met the eye.

17

Rumours

Untruth did not begin with us; nor will it end with us.
The last line of *August 1914*,
a novel by Alexander Solzhenitsyn

I

The last phenomena of August 1914 – little remembered, as they showed British civilians as gullible or stupid – were the absurd rumours of a Russian army in transit through Britain. This was however only the final fairy-story or unnecessary panic of the month, that began on the outbreak of war, when selfish but jittery householders hoarded food, or anything they could afford. As Goonie Churchill did in Cromer, in places the traders or local civic leaders (who quite often were tradesmen) informally enforced rational shopping, telling traders not to sell to strangers, or give any customer too much. Similarly at a bank – where people afraid for their deposits might take out all their money and cause the crash they feared – other customers and bank staff could police behaviour, and shame the worriers out of withdrawing unnatural amounts of money. Newspapers, also, could ask their readers to behave. For example the *Willesden Chronicle* of Friday August 14 noted the market in food was 'almost normal again':

Panic mongers would now appear to have diverted their attention from the food market into an equally foolish channel, for throughout the week remarkable rumours have been afloat as to houses having been raided in Willesden and found to be in occupation of hostile foreigners who have

stored there innumerable bombs, rifles and ammunition ...
there is not the slightest foundation for such wild stories ...

A house had artillery, ready for invaders to fire, according
to one story; in another house, foreigners had made poisons. As
the north London weekly spotted, the original 'panic mongers'
hoarding food were turning to rumours, one after another, to
voice their witless fears. Poisons were a favourite, because they
were hard to disprove, and yet could be anywhere. George
Thorp, the Hull architect, likewise understood that rumours
were symptoms, passed on by the fearful and received by the
willing. In his diary, when noting the first battles of August 24
and 25 by British troops, he wrote of 'foolish rumours' of spies
poisoning springs and water:

> *I can see that it wants very little to put this population into
> a panic, they or a section of them believe anything. Our
> ex-Mayor's youngest son aged 22 was shot by a sentry at
> Saltburn last Friday at midnight, he was with his brother
> in a motorcycle, and did not hear or heed the repeated
> challenge – verdict 'accidently shot'. This makes the fifth
> innocent person killed by sentries since the war began.*

In the summer of 1940, too, guards on roads in case of
enemy invasion shot dead civilians, without punishment.

As in 1940, unknown people (never ones to give interviews
to newspapers, write memoirs or leave their diaries to public
archives) were spreading tales, that respectable-seeming
figures were, in fact, German. Their motives may have been
commercial jealousy, or spite. In mid-August, for instance, a
motor engineer with the English-enough sounding name of
George Lakeman put a notice in the *Newmarket Journal*, to
deny 'malicious rumours' that he was a German. Clearly stung,
he said his father was from Cornwall, and his mother from
Berkshire; he was born in Derbyshire, and had always lived
in England. Whoever started that story might have resented
Lakeman as an incomer; or may genuinely (though ignorantly)

have doubted that such a man, maybe with an out-of-town accent, was truly one of them.

Rumours flourished where they sounded believable. Thus the seaside town of Clacton, according to the *Essex County Standard* in mid-August, deplored 'wild stories' of the beach and visitor attractions closed, the pier destroyed by bombs, and the place near-deserted. That was bad for business, but unless you saw the town for yourself, you had no way of knowing the truth.

August 1914 lacked one panic that the summer of 1940 had: only in 1940 did villages, even small towns, mobilise after false alarms of a German landing. All 1914 had were the likes of the homeless 'aged labourer' Henry Oakden, stopped on an Ashbourne road by a police constable Pell on Wednesday August 19. Oakden was waving a stick and shouting 'the Germans are coming'. When PC Pell spoke to him, Oakden said 'be careful, or they will have both of us'. The town's magistrates a week later laughed; and fined Oakden for being drunk.

II

That little story shows that the gap between rich and poor, the respectable and rough, was often also one of intellect – maybe the widest gap of all and thus the most cherished by some; the educated were able to look down on the stupid and credulous. However, the rumour of a Russian army in Britain found many learned people wanting.

One of its earliest sightings came in George Thorp's diary on August 28:

> *A very curious and persistent rumour has been circulated in Hull, coming from numerous very reliable people, none of whom however have it at first hand, that bodies of Russian troops had landed in Scotland for the purpose of*

proceeding to the Belgian frontier by way of Boulogne. Most circumstantial accounts have been given as to ordinary trains have been side tracked, while unheard of quantities of Russian troops in from anything from 36 to 16 trains have passed by.

Thorp named four people 'who knew it for certain', but noted that the official press bureau called it a 'pure fabrication'. As shrewd – though admittedly it was in his memoir well after the event – was Sir Almeric Fitzroy, the permanent head of Liberal minister Lord Morley's department (at least until Morley resigned because of the war). Sir Almeric noted the Russians had 'appeared' as far apart as Bath, Reading and Southampton; or rather, no-one *saw* the Russians inside the trains, because their carriages had drawn blinds. To the believers, this was proof; the movement of troops was a *secret*. Sir Almeric wrote: "I very nearly forfeited Lord Haversham's good opinion by venturing to doubt the grounds of his confidence ... the paucity of authentic news is perhaps responsible for the avidity with which fiction is devoured," he added wisely.

Another lord fell for it. Writing from Wiltshire on August 29, St Aldwyn told his son: "... what a splendid stroke it is to have got Russians around this way, it seems to be true and it will be a nice surprise to those barbarians of Germans to meet them unexpectedly." So it went on. In Essex at the end of August, the Burnham-on-Crouch shopkeeper Robert Bull wrote in his diary that 70 train-loads of Russians went through the county town of Chelmsford in the previous week, from Aberdeen on their way to the Continent. The story persisted, or cropped up in different regions later, because in his letter to the King of Siam on September 11, the Gloucestershire civic leader M W Colchester-Wemyss said the rumour had been 'on everyone's lips for some days'. He had asked scores of people about it, but had not found anybody who had seen Russians. A lord said he had asked a cabinet minister, who said it was untrue. The lord then asked another lord, who said it was true. Colchester-Wemyss came down on the side of believing it: "If it is not true it is a remarkable incident of how an invented story can obtain widespread belief." That, at least, was correct.

The question plainly gripped Britain in late August 1914. We can no more get to the bottom of it than the diarists at the time could. Where and when did the story start? How did it spread – did many people have the same idea at once, or only one? The French, even more than the English, willed the Russians to come; as an English holiday-maker, a Miss Laura Partridge, a girls' school teacher from Brondesbury, told her local north London paper on her return from Interlaken. Changing trains at Montgaris before Paris, and seeking news, an excited Frenchman in a blue smock told her: "Tout va bien, et ils viennens les Russes."

All was going well, the Russians were coming. It might be more than coincidence that the British rumour seems to have begun in the days of the first news of the BEF on the Continent; which only left people anxious for more news. Indeed, after Lord St Aldwyn wrote of the Russians, he next fretted about the British losses. Imagining Russians – 80,000 according to Colchester-Wemyss – was the most a gossiper could do, to help the BEF. It was, besides, wishful thinking; that the Russians would share the fighting (and the deaths) in western Europe. This reflected a deeper, geopolitical hope among the rulers of Britain and France, that Russia would do some, maybe much, of the hard work of beating the Germans, just as Russia from 1812 had broken Napoleon.

As for the truth of the rumour, it was a beauty. The rumour-makers and spreaders could impress people with what they knew. However you tried to disprove it, the gossipers could give an answer. If Britain's ally was sending thousands of troops, why didn't the government give out this good news, or ask people to welcome the visitors? Because (as St Aldwyn spotted) it was to be a *surprise* for the Germans. Yet could thousands of foreigners cross hundreds of miles from Aberdeen (and Hull and other ports, according to Colchester-Wemyss) and not stop *once*, not speak to *someone*? Stop for a smoke and something to eat? Wouldn't someone – a locomotive driver, a liaison officer – have a story to tell? As with the persistent stories that Germans *did* land on the English coast in 1940, but were thrown back – burned by a secret weapon, some said – and all traces removed, you had to ask in the end: where were the photographs? Some evidence?

The fact that Russians did not show in France was proof; eventually. Meanwhile, you had to manage with argument: *why* would Russia send soldiers abroad – when presumably it wanted every man it had on its own frontiers? Wasn't the story as unlikely as Britain and France sending an army to Russia? If anyone knew of a Russian shipment, it was Winston Churchill at the Admiralty, whose navy would have to escort the ships to British ports. In a letter to the Minister of War, Lord Kitchener, on August 28, Churchill did have that very idea: a Russian corps going from Archangel to Ostend, "though I dare say it would not greatly commend itself to the Russians", he added. As so often in life, if you wanted something done, you had to do it yourself.

18

First Returns

The population of this country had been schooled in the glories of the British Empire and the deeds of her victorious armies, and, of course, the British Navy, the greatest navy of all time .... Oh! What a shock we got! Oh God! What a shock we got!

Years of Change: Autobiography of a Hackney Shoemaker, by
Arthur Newton (1974)

I

A s the *Bristol Times* daily put it mildly enough on September 3, the country would welcome news from the front; 'practically none has come'. As the newspaper was sharp enough to suggest, it might not be that the authorities were keeping news from the people; maybe the War Office had no news, either?

The previous day, the first returners – wounded from the port of Southampton – arrived at Bristol Temple Meads station. Hundreds of wounded went north, to London, Birmingham and Sheffield, generally cheered on arrival, fed and waved at, and taken to hospitals. On the railway platforms, and later on wards, newspaper reporters (with official permission) sought the soldiers' stories.

This was a first in British history; witnesses of a battle asked for and giving their accounts, fresh from the battlefield. Some had made what must have been a bewildering round trip: one unnamed artilleryman from the Totterdown district of Bristol left home, was wounded in France, and returned to the city within ten days. In previous centuries, a free press (or any printing press), and a literate mass market for news, had not existed. After the last war, in 1902, men took weeks or months to come home from South Africa; by that time memories (and newspaper readers' interest) had faded.

We remember the soldiers of the 1914-18 war (if at all) as men who suffered doubly: first, because of what they went through; then, once home, civilians did not want to hear about what the soldiers suffered. August 1914 was the exception, if only because it was early days, before anyone could become disillusioned; and before the authorities enforced censorship, in case anything bad disheartened the public. Newspapers printed what the wounded told them, and carried the plentiful letters (few enough compared with the 100,000 men in the BEF, but plentiful compared with later years of the war) sent by men on the road to the front line, and after the first shock of battle. In later years, soldiers might no more want to put upsetting things on paper than people at home wanted to read about it. In 1914 as in any war, a soldier might want to shield his wife or mother from the worst. "There were some awful sights to be seen, things you will never hear of in the papers, I cannot describe them in a letter ..." wrote William Thomas Simpson, to his family in Ashbourne from Netley Hospital near Southampton. An artilleryman, he was wounded on Monday August 24, the second day of fighting. Simpson indeed did not go into details; some similarly wounded men did, and their families passed the letters to their local newspapers, which printed them.

Just as some men plainly felt a need to get their experiences out of their system and onto paper, so families, and newspapers on behalf of society generally, had curiosity about war. After all, as the papers kept repeating, the 200-mile, two-million-man battlefront of northern France was the greatest in history, by far – greater than any in the wars against Napoleon, the American Civil War, the 1870-1 war between France and Prussia, even the 1904-5 war between Russia and Japan. (That Russia and Austria and Germany might put even more men into the battlefields on their side of Europe went unsaid.)

To sum up, the newspaper reports of soldier testimony of August 1914 – from interviews, and letters home passed to the papers – are a rare and full source, for the 1914-18 or indeed any war. Decades later, a new generation of oral historians asked the veterans, in old age, for their stories; they asked too late for many of the men of August 1914, dead long before then.

II

Not that the men off the train at Temple Meads were much help. To be fair to them, they had not come home to bear witness, but to have their bodies repaired. "All the men told practically the same story, which differs little if at all from the accounts of the battle that have already appeared in the newspapers," the *Bristol Times* reported. Possibly the wounded, having a few days on their journey to compare experiences, unconsciously trimmed their stories so that nothing sounded too out of the ordinary, or unpatriotic; maybe they, too, had read the first accounts in newspapers, and did not want to sound peculiar.

Some news from the front arrived even more direct – on dirty scraps of paper, to a Colonel Lang in Wiltshire from his son, dated August 30, and read by Lang to a recruiting meeting at Pewsey on September 2. The younger Lang, presumably, handed it to a wounded man on his way to England – and so avoided any army censorship or other delays. Even this most authentic account, written or spoken, gave an ant's view; whether of the most junior, or a slightly more senior, ant. The weapons of war had come on but the British soldier at Mons was the same as his forefather at Waterloo, or indeed at

Hastings; he only knew about the 200 yards (or 20) of battle-line that he could see and influence, besides any chance news (maybe out of date, misheard in the stress of battle, or jumbled by tired minds) learned from comrades bumped into. Few had the data to give them the larger landscape; perhaps even the commander could not grasp the whole battle.

The returning wounded at least had time to order their thoughts, about the most extreme experience of their lives (worse than anything in South Africa, the veterans of the Boer War agreed). While they did not want to talk themselves into trouble, they felt above all a duty to their comrades, still in battle. It's striking how many of the wounded men spoke of wanting to go back, as soon as they could. Their listeners may have wanted to hear something as patriotic as that. Yet men in other wars said the same; that they felt they had to help their mates; they felt guilty for being out of danger. The least they could do was to be true to themselves, and their fellows, by saying what the battle was like.

The army did not let this honesty last long. The fighting men soon felt the censor, and not only at the front. Officially, according to the Field Service Pocket Book, printed by the War Office in 1914, censorship was a 'necessity', criticism 'forbidden'. The book detailed what military things you could not write about. G C Harper, a cadet who left Devonport on the brink of war for *HMS Endymion*, summed up censorship, when told about it, on August 7:

> *We were not to mention in our letters the name of any ship not even the one we were in. We were not to mention war or anything about it, nor anything about the navy. We were not to mention our ranks or anybody else's or any place we had been in or were going to … so the letters were restricted to about two lines, a date and a signature.*

That made sense, as any facts if captured might help the enemy. It made less sense far away in Sudan. There, as early as

August 11, Frank Balfour wrote to the woman in England he was trying to woo, Irene Lawley: "It would be a charity if you wrote some of the home gossip – bearing in mind that it will probably be read by the censor in Cairo – as also this – I raise my hat to him." Balfour's warning, and his droll acknowledgement of the unknown censor, were elegant. In plainer English, but just as effective, was the undated letter from Dick Wallis in camp in Essex to 'Mother and Dad' in Leek: "They will not allow any of us to go home unless there is some one ill, so when I want to come I will let you know and you can send a wire to say someone very ill, come at once. But do not send until I tell you." This letter's envelope, unlike other letters he sent home, did not have a red 'passed by censor' envelope. Wallis had evidently put the letter about his dodge in a civilian postbox (not available to sailors at sea).

The Field Service Pocket Book said nothing about it, but evidently the army read all the letters it could, to watch out for any wrong-doing or rebellion. After the rush simply to put an army into the field in August 1914, and clothe and arm the recruits, the army enforced its discipline; and civilians learned to obey. For the time being, plenty of newspapers – presumably in ignorance rather than seeking to defy the army – printed the forbidden ranks, names of places passed through, and the shocking, bloody stories, of what happened after men marched out of town and sight.

III

Whether in England or even further from the battlefield, the first casualty totals from the continent, even if sketchy or sensationalised, told everyone what war meant. In his letter to his son on August 29, Lord St Aldwyn quoted an estimate of 12,000 British casualties, "and even half that number is frightful and so dreadful for people waiting to hear of their relations; I think it is a good move to arrange for some public meetings to explain the reason for the war etc." In other words, once people heard that war killed people, they would need more convincing that war was worth the cost. Writing from Sudan on August 28, Frank Balfour felt once more far from the centre of affairs: "It's pretty rotten reading of British losses of 2000, knowing that one will see no names for three weeks at least." Sure enough, not until September 21 did the casualty list dated September 3 arrive with the mail, 'and it makes unhappy reading'. What was the nature of this war, taking so many lives so soon? And what was it like for the soldiers in the middle of it?

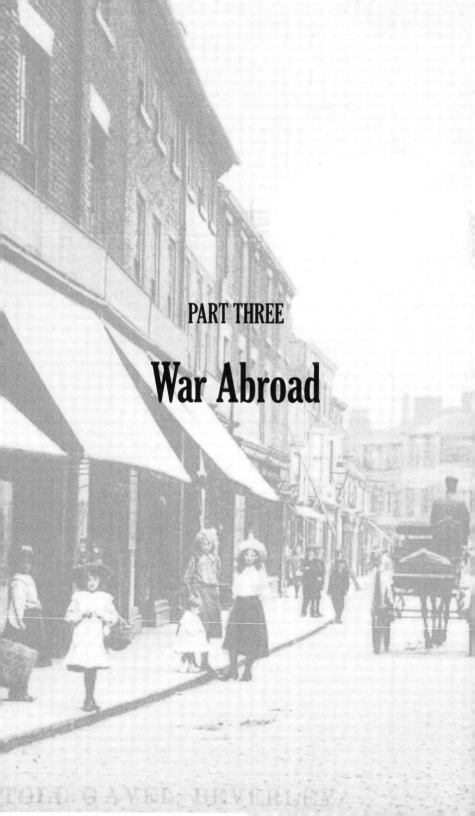

PART THREE

War Abroad

19

Going

It is impossible now after the bitter experience of two world wars to recapture the spirit of this country in August, 1914. As I marched through those cheering crowds I felt like a king among men.

A Full Life, by Lieutenant-General Sir Brian Horrocks (1960)

W e have already been sceptical about the cheering crowds in London and other capitals at the outbreak of war; we can be kinder towards the well-wishers waving off the then 18-year-old Lieutenant Horrocks from Chatham, with 95 men of the Middlesex Regiment. Towns such as Chatham with a military tradition would want to do right by such men. Even if you knew none of the men leaving, the march to war was the event of the year, like an overturned tram or a factory fire; and cheering, like gawping, was free. For anyone who did know the men marching away, marchers and watchers alike would want to put on a brave face. Any farewell tears were best cried in private, before the procession, or after your son or brother left. Besides, even if they might not have wanted to upset family by admitting it, some departing young men, like Albert Batty, enjoyed the prospect of something more thrilling than everyday life:

I was proud to think that I was a fully trained Saturday afternoon soldier in the Horse Transport section of a divisional field ambulance, as I had trained assiduously and attended three annual two week camps.

Batty, and four Salford friends, had joined the Territorials from the same church and cricket club. Whereas at work and in their leisure such young men were junior to their elders, with little to look forward to except becoming elders themselves, Batty's memoir (based on his diary of the time) shows how he relished what the Territorials gave him, even before a war: responsibility for a wagon and horses, a small but guaranteed part in something big, and hard work for your country. 'Never had a more excited time', he wrote on August 8, though later in the month he admitted it was 'graft on no food and no sleep'. Batty reported for duty at 9am on August 5 – the depot had turned him away, the evening before – and was soon a victim of stupid army discipline. He went home to sleep on August 6 because there was nowhere to lie down, and next day was told he was under arrest. It meant little, however, while the unit was busy taking in civilian horses and equipment of all shapes and sizes, the only available: "mineral water carts with a high dicky seat, parcel vans which served as ambulances and large butts on wheels with which the corporation watered the streets to keep the dust down", Batty recalled. Three weeks later, as the British retreated from Belgium, the German captain and novelist Walter Bloem misunderstood the abandoned commercial vehicles he passed, 'from apparently every big town in England … England obviously regarded this war as a business undertaking'. It did not occur to Bloem that the British army had scraped together any transport it could.

Bloem saw motors with burst tyres or broken axles; horse-drawn transport brought its own troubles. On August 19, as Batty's unit took to the road, his horses took fright, until he pulled them up only feet short of a ditch. Understandably, noise from well-wishers made animals bolt. In Bristol on August 10, two Territorial battalions of the Gloucestershire regiment left their drill hall and marched, separately, down to the city centre. Two horses pulling a wagon of baggage, leaving first, became restive and galloped out of control; down steep Park Street they swerved and hit a wagonette standing outside Newcombe's, a carver and gilder at number 73. The wagonette turned over and crushed an old lady inside a parked horse and trap. She died later. One of the two horses, with a broken leg, was shot where it lay; all this watched by the crowd, until a cart took the carcass away.

The Glosters got on trains in the city. The picture we might like to have in our mind's eye of the departing troops – a band leading them, hundreds cheering in the market place – is true enough. What we don't imagine so readily is what happened after the last townsman accompanying them out of town turned back, and a turn in the road or a watershed hid their last view of home, and the marchers were left with themselves: the sun in their face or on their neck, the clump of boots, and the 70lbs of kit on their back. As two days' rations they might have had a 2lb loaf. Some units had further to walk than others, but terrain and weather made a march feel longer, not only the number of miles. Ashbourne's 50 Territorials set off on the Buxton road on Wednesday August 5, crossed the Derbyshire dales to Matlock by evening, and arrived at Chesterfield the next day, a good 20 miles in all. The 5th North Staffs took two days to march the 30 or so miles from the Potteries to Burton-on-Trent, in mid-August, resting overnight at Uttoxeter; at times the weather was 'almost tropical', according to the Uttoxeter paper. Newark Territorials had a similar journey, to Derby, stopping halfway at Radcliffe-on-Trent.

For whatever reason – the still familiar surroundings, their relative freshness, the euphoria of the extraordinary, the goodwill of householders offering tea from the roadside, and perhaps more – some men had yet to knuckle down. Aubrey Moore was a young lieutenant (he would celebrate his 21st birthday on August 30 with a bottle of champagne in a Luton hotel) of the Hinckley company of the Leicestershire Territorials. He recalled in old age how he arrived in Hinckley on Wednesday morning, August 5, to find it had gone 'mad': "By midday the pubs were running short and men were crowding into the drill hall to sign on for enlistment with us, being quite prepared to take on the whole German army single handed." Moore was one of the few memoir writers of August 1914 to admit the part played by beer. His men had about 20 miles to walk, to Loughborough, resting overnight at Groby outside Leicester. On that first day, Moore recalled that 'a contingent of ladies followed us from Hinckley on cycles who proved to be a bit of a menace', by 'luring' the men from their Groby billets into a park. Why, Moore (the son of a clergyman) did not say. The rest of the month saw the Leicestershires in Belper for a few days, before a march to Derby and another train (through Loughborough) to Luton in Northamptonshire.

Gradually the army put its stamp on man and beast – literally, as blacksmiths stamped a number on horses' hooves, and men wore an aluminium disc stamped with their name, number, company and regiment. The further the men went, the fainter the contact with home and the more the army took over their lives. Letters were hard enough to write, if you never held a pencil from one month to the next in peacetime; visitors were even more the exception. 'An Old Newarker' described in the *Newark Advertiser* how he saw men of the town among the thousands leaving Derby on Saturday August 15. "All seemed in a jovial mood as they marched on to the ground, sometimes whistling, sometimes singing national airs and ragtime but all in high spirits." While the men waited at Osmaston Park sidings for their train, wives and mothers of railway workers living nearby offered 'large washstand jugs of hot tea'. Grocers, showing more enterprise than charity, sold bananas, pears and tomatoes. Troops tucked the fruit away in kitbags for the journey. 'Newarker' spotted that the soldiers still had unmilitary mementos of home: "Many men carried their pet mascots, teddy bears, dummy dogs and dolls tied on their knapsacks whilst one private had a live black kitten with red ribbon tied around its neck."

Officers had more freedom to roam thanks to money and, if they ran a car, transport, except that command tied them to a place as surely as discipline bound their men. Francis Meynell of Hoar Cross Hall began the war with his battery in Stafford and was able to nip home to his estate at night. He may well have passed within sight of it on the way to his next base, Burton-on-Trent, where he was in charge of an advance party. He was tempted to commute the six miles to sleep at home, rather than in the 'little anteroom off the town hall' he wrote to his mother about on August 12. "It is very tantalising being here on my own, yet not being able to leave for fear the telephone may ring." He like many Territorials, let alone the new recruits, had to get used to waiting to be told where to go next. At the end of August Meynell told his mother from Northamptonshire that he was starting 16 weeks of training 'and then shall be supposed (?) competent to go into the field abroad'.

More impatient were Oliver Lyttleton and his friends, whether because they were young (Lyttleton was 21; his friend 'Bobbety', Viscount Cranborne, turned 21 in August 1914) or because as aristocrats they expected to get their own way. In August Lyttleton was on guard duty on the nervous East Anglian coast: "Sometimes a sentry on the shore fires a shot and then you rush out with a revolver and find that a bathing machine is riddled with bullets. Officer after admonition returns to his tent," he told his mother with dry humour in an undated letter. He was doing an officer's work, but he and his friends did not have the all-important commission:

Though the War Office gazetted six officers all complete outsiders yesterday to the regiment, none of us. The regiment is furious because they loathe having outsiders in them ....

*six fellows of a sort they do not like and no doubt it will do
the battalions a lot of harm after the war because they will
not get the right people from the country. However Lord
Salisbury has been to the WO and has raised hell I believe
so I may yet be well.*

As ever, a private word was the way to smooth someone's
path; Lord Salisbury was the son of the former Tory prime
minister, and father of 'Bobbety'.

It seemed that regular army officers were fretting that the
need for a far bigger army, to beat the Germans, would lower
the tone. In fairness, the snobs had a point. Every war had an
ending; armies were usually at peace. If a war made 'outsiders'
into soldiers, the upset would last for years after the war, just
as if a business took on too many staff in a boom time, the
staff already there would resent the change to their quiet life,
and might be out of a job altogether when trade went back to
normal. Lord Kitchener, as war minister, was taking as long a
perspective, albeit as a military statesman rather than the army
equivalent of a trade unionist.

In *The Times* on August 15, under the headline 'The policy
of Pitt – Preparing to see the struggle through', the newspaper's
military correspondent, Colonel Charles Repington, set out
Kitchener's plan. (Though not one word of Kitchener's was
inside speech marks, by the conventions of journalism of the
day this was as plain a statement of policy as Kitchener, or
anyone in power, made that month.)

Kitchener made the reasonable point – though allies might
have seen it as selfish – that Britain's 'voice in the terms' of
peace would be equal to 'the weight of our sword'. Kitchener
was not to know that four years of trench warfare would so
cripple Britain (and France) that they dared not stand up to
Hitler, or Mussolini or anyone, a generation later. Two weeks
into the war, before the BEF had seen a German, Kitchener had
in mind the need for a big army, as big as France's or anyone's,

not only so that Britain would be on the winning side, but so Britain could bargain with its allies for a better deal. As Britain was 'dreadfully in arrears' of everything military, organisation, men, arms and equipment, so Kitchener put it, he was having to start from scratch. This would take time; this assumed the war would last well beyond 1914.

Kitchener was proved right. Not that being right ever does anyone any good. Liberal ministers resented that Kitchener had shown up their pre-war 'callous indifference to defence', as Repington put it in the article. Gossips at the time and historians since have argued whether Kitchener was out of his depth as war minister from 1914, or as skilled a schemer as any politician. Surely it's more to the point that as the lone military man in cabinet, surrounded by civilians, he had enough to do without making enemies, or worse enemies. Repington had his scoop, but – a warning to every journalist managing his contacts – it was the death of his relationship with the scoop-giver. Lord Kitchener told Repington it was 'as much as his life was worth' to see him again. (Had Kitchener, the newcomer to cabinet government, broken the unwritten rules of politics by speaking plainly through Repington, and was bullied into not doing it again? Or had Kitchener had his say and had no more use for Repington?)

Leaving aside the squabbles at the very top, Kitchener was proposing a wholly new army. As the 'New Army' had no history, it did not appeal to the Oliver Lyttletons of this world. "We are angry because it seems possible that we may be gazetted to K's army," he told his mother. A 'New Army' meant that whatever was already around – the Territorials – did not matter so much. Kitchener, so he told Repington, proposed to divide the Territorials in two: those willing and able to serve abroad, and those not.

Given the choice, whether because they did not feel they belonged truly to the army, or because they only wanted to do what they had signed for – home defence – a fair few Territorials did *not* volunteer to go abroad. The 4th battalion the Lincolnshire regiment, for instance, set off by train from Lincoln on August 11 with 1020 men; four officers and 432 ranks who had not volunteered, or were not passed fit for foreign service returned home on September 4. Though Repington reported Kitchener's view that Britain needed both kinds of Territorials – because the stay-at-homes freed somebody else to go abroad – some got bullied for taking the less warlike option. Some 270 Newark Territorials came home on Saturday September 5, half unfit, half by choice. After a Sunday church service, they formed up in Newark Market Place for their depot commander, Colonel G S Foljambe, to tell them he was ashamed of the number of young unmarried men who came back to the town. Not surprisingly, the next day some 'volunteered' for foreign service.

II

The country waited for news of the men who had marched away, and who did not come back unfit, or who were not sending postcards from camps in the shires. Where had the British army gone? The newspapers of mid-August did not say, or even speculate about the most newsworthy question in the biggest news story of the century.

For a clue, as faint as the wind on the Wiltshire downs at dawn, you had to read the inquest into two airmen, pilot Robin Skene and his mechanic passenger Raymond Barlow. They and their 3 Squadron, Royal Flying Corps (RFC), were at Netheravon airfield. Above the Avon valley, a few miles from Stonehenge, it was one of the first homes of British military aviation – though flying was still in its early days, and in an emergency any flat field would do to land in. On the morning of August 12, Skene took off, with full petrol tank, tools and other gear. At 150 feet the machine turned to the left, lost speed, and dived vertically, killing both men. Was the aeroplane over-loaded? So the court asked. Other aircraft had taken off loaded as much, it heard.

Even if you saw the case, which only made the local papers, it would take some deducing. Why were the aeroplanes flying so dangerously heavy? It could only be, because the squadron was moving. Where? To the war.

III

Much later – wars later, in 1952 – one of the men taking off from Netheravon that morning, Philip Joubert, recalled the crash in his memoir The Fated Sky. The aircraft had stalled when taking off – always the most dangerous part of a flight, besides landing. Joubert called the crashed Bleriot monoplane his 'old friend'; he used to fly it.

Like the other young men of the RFC, Joubert shrugged off death, as something that happened to other people. What else could they do? They had chosen the newest military tool since man had tamed the horse. They learned to fly the same as they had learned to ride a horse; they stayed on or fell off, except that an aeroplane usually fell from a fatal height. Everything the pilots tried was new: flying upside down; flying in the dark (and landing); taking photographs from the air (an interest of Joubert's). What they could do changed by the year, as aeroplanes flew faster and longer. Joubert's squadron's 140-mile hop from Netheravon to Dover was a day's work in August 1914; in 1908, it would have set a world distance record. Could the aeroplane become an army's eye in the sky, to spot the enemy, and return with warning, many times faster than the cavalry that every army had relied on for the last few thousand years? The airmen – and the enemy airmen – would find out soon what (if anything) an aeroplane was *for*.

Aeroplanes were still fragile, untrustworthy things; engines could stop, pieces could break. Few of the airmen, setting off for France the next morning, had ever crossed sea before. Some had flown to Ireland (and back), but only by the shortest crossing, the 16 miles from Stranraer. Anything more was risky. Joubert and the pilots leaving Dover early on August 13 – before the inquest at Netheravon would open – were each given a motor-car tyre inner tube, 'which we were instructed to blow up and wear around our middles', Joubert recalled, 'in case we fell into the 'Drink' on our way to France'. One pilot tried to drop his like a quoit on the lighthouse at Cap Gris Nez.

20

Forward

He was at the age of hope, and something within him, which did not represent mere youthful illusion, supported his courage in the face of calculations such as would have damped sober experience.

The House of Cobwebs, by George Gissing

Even to see the sea was a novelty for some, to the condescending amusement of others. While at Dovercourt, guarding the ports of Harwich and Felixstowe, Oliver Lyttleton ended a letter to his mother: "I hear a sentry behind me saying to a pal watching a school of porpoises, 'look at that bloody great fish'. Local colour OL."

A sea voyage was even more exotic if you had never been beyond the seaside, or the horizon. Not that the soldiers had a good view, or any view. John Harding, a private in the Queen's West Surrey regiment, recalled the next month how men were packed on their ship 'like sardines in a tin', some crowded on deck, some below, some even crammed in the lifeboats. Neither they nor the crew knew where they were going.

A fuller account of a crossing came from the brothers Harry and Will Woodin, who did at least hear that they were heading for France. In peacetime they each drove motor omnibuses between Alfreton and Derby; each had joined the Army Service Corps as drivers. "We had a fine-send off from Liverpool," they told their parents in a joint letter. "All the ships in the river cheered us as we passed with their whistles. We could not hear ourselves speak when they were all on at

once. There were hundreds of people on the banks cheering us, and the ships were signalling 'good luck' with their flags."
After they set off at 11am, on Saturday August 15, they did not have much to write home about, apart from a Saturday night concert, and an 'exciting few minutes' on the Sunday afternoon when they saw a 'big battleship making straight towards us':

We began to wonder whether it was a German. Our ship ran up a lot of signal flags. It still made right towards us, till we could see it plainly. It had four funnels. It turned out to be an American battle cruiser ...

On Monday they did nothing except sleep between meals, 'which were: cheese and biscuits for breakfast, bully beef and biscuits for dinner, and jam and biscuits for tea'. By the Monday evening they were sailing up a French river, so they thought:

The French people at the villages on each shore of the river were cheering and waving flags. A lot of them came out in boats and got on the ship, and gave flowers all round.

On the Tuesday they landed, in Rouen; they had come up the Seine:

The place is packed with soldiers of all sorts. The French soldiers look very funny in their uniforms. There must be thousands of soldiers here. I keep seeing whole regiments marching off to the front. There are eight or nine ships unloading soldiers at once. As fast as one ship goes another comes to its place. I have discovered a post office. With best love from Harry and Will.

If the Woodins knew what censorship was yet, they had broken it. Plainly they were still thinking like civilians; understandably, as they were doing the same work as at home. As their local weekly, the *Alfreton Journal*, did not print the letter for a couple of weeks, by that time the world knew where the British Expeditionary Force had gone. The government censor allowed the papers to break what *The Times* on August 18 called a 'conspiracy of silence', and the country heard the BEF had landed in France, without a casualty.

There were a few casualties soon after landing, who only had themselves to blame. The 'right royal welcome' as Private John Harding put it stuck in the memory of many that month: "It was one of the finest times in our lives," he recalled a few weeks later, with a smile, to a reporter of the *Essex County Standard*. "As we marched along, the roads were lined with people holding tobacco, cigarettes, jugs of wine and baskets of fruit. The men had only to put out their hands to help themselves." J L Dent, a lieutenant in the 2nd battalion, South Staffordshire Regiment, left Aldershot on August 11 and landed at Le Havre on August 13. "The town was en fete, flags and banners welcoming les braves anglais were displayed on all sides," he wrote in his diary: "... we had been to some pains in teaching the men the Marseillaise and there were a good many mouth organs among the company so that when we struck up there was a tremendous burst of enthusiasm ..." Unfortunately, after two sleepless nights of travel, and little food, of the hard biscuit variety as endured by the Woodins, the march out of town to a camp was enough to exhaust some of the South Staffs. Well-meaning French people poured wines and liqueurs down the flagging soldiers' throats. "Many fell out," Dent recorded. "These were increased when the men in the ranks passed those who had fallen out and saw them being fanned, bathed with eau de cologne and revived with brandy by pretty French girls."

A rail journey, and days on the march followed, "in the hot sun, along the dusty, stony roads," as Harding recollected: "the nights were just as cold as the days were hot". Whether because the French would only risk sending trains so far towards the enemy, or because you could always rely on the soldier, the Tommy, to walk, the soldier walked. The intoxicating welcome to a foreign country – at Le Havre 'civilians fairly hugged us' recalled a Royal Engineer corporal, Charles Wallbank, later – was only a break in the deadening limbo of travel. Wallbank described his train to train to Landrecies in northern France as 'tedious and miserable'. It all created an air of unreality which Wallbank was one of the few to note afterwards. "Hardly a soul imagined that we were really going to fight, not at all serious," he wrote.

On the march, no longer with women around their necks, they went back to soldiering at its most basic, no different from the armies of Wellington, or King Alfred for that matter. Men carried what they needed, heading (they assumed) for the enemy, who was doing the same. Weapons, true, had changed with the times. The BEF wore khaki, as the fashion for red-coats to scare the enemy had passed. Now you were not supposed to advertise where you were; you found cover, a hedge or wall, or made your own, a 'fire trench' dug three feet deep or more, and waited to shoot the enemy off the battlefield. *If* you knew where the enemy was; and if your feet lasted long enough to take you there.

II

Private Dixon, a postman from Pudsey, had a rupture. "We pressed on and on, night and day, with a load of 80lbs on our backs, and from 100 to 500 rounds of ammunition." Dixon, and everyone, was carrying the equivalent of a small person on his back. "We had very little time for meals. Men who were in South Africa say they never suffered so much. I stuck it until I dropped by the road, and was picked up by a Scottish regiment." Dixon was serving in the Munster Fusiliers. "I bandaged myself as best I could with a puttee," the long strip of cloth with a Hindi name that the soldiers had to wind from their ankles to their knees, as support, "and was placed in the ambulance."

We can hardly expect such men to remember, or care, where they were or which day it was. From now on the wounded, or the incapacitated like Private Dixon, offer the best stories, as their time on the campaign was cut short. Or occasional civilian witnesses offer a different point of view: such as an English couple, the Taylors, living in Quievrain a few miles inside Belgium, halfway between Valenciennes in France and the Belgian mining town of Mons. British troops began arriving on Saturday August 22. As a sign that the clash was expected, Mrs Taylor had to tell the Quievrain villagers that the soldiers were British, not German. Besides feeding hundreds, so she told the *Loughborough Echo* after fleeing to England, she was much in demand to translate:

> *The British soldiers were all enchanted with their reception in France and Belgium and many said they wanted for nothing as the inhabitants came out with food and drink which they freely distributed among the troops ... I saw several of the men carrying French children as they marched along while their mothers walked at their sides.*

By later on Saturday, Mr Taylor was concerned, so he said later, whether they were in front of, or behind, the armies:

> *All Saturday night troops poured in and on Sunday we distinctly heard the firing of guns but could not distinguish the exact locality. Airplanes were soaring over at a great height over the village during Sunday afternoon and towards evening one of the English soldiers told me that they had to harness up immediately. I went into the village and saw a great deal of activity, horses and artillery being prepared for evident departure. The staff officers were also on the move ... several of the soldiers told us they thought we ought to have been already gone several days. About 11.30pm the tocsin bell which is rung at the churches in case of a national calamity such as war began to ring and I was told that volunteers were wanted to dig trenches*

around the district and it was then that I finally decided to start for England.

III

Private Thomas Cross of the 2nd South Staffords, a veteran of South Africa, was among the first to fight and the first to be wounded, in front of Mons on Sunday August 23. "The Germans were like bees on honey. As fast as we shot one down others came up in rows. After about 20 minutes of this the order came to retire and as we were doing so I was knocked in the right side by a shell from a big gun which luckily for me failed to explode. It knocked me down and for a time I was unconscious. I got back with the regiment and didn't know I was so badly hurt."

Private John Jennings was an old soldier called up from the loco department of the Midland Railway Company – or rather, he re-joined the Royal Irish regiment before the call-up papers reached his Derby home. "I expect you have heard about the battle of Mons," he wrote a couple of weeks later, in hospital at Netley. "We had enough to do, but I can tell you we gave them something, though there were thousands of them, and they kept coming." Another wounded reservist, Bombardier William Simpson, told an *Ashbourne Telegraph* reporter that the German fire at Mons 'defied description':

> *He did not think there was a man amongst them who believed he would get out of the battle alive, but thanks to the skilful tactics of their officers the retiring movements were carried out most satisfactorily. The English guns were hopelessly outnumbered, but it was evident that the Germans were surprised and angry at the stubbornness and pluck with which the English fought.*

We can query how Simpson could tell what the Germans were feeling. He may have felt he had to sound knowledgeable to the newspaper reporter. He was the town's first returned hero, welcomed off the train by the same band that sent off the Territorials the month before, and carried to his parents' house by two men on their shoulders. He had every reason to praise his side (and hence himself). Yet however he tried to hide it, the Germans were too many and too strong; the British had fallen back. Or rather, as that did not sound heroic enough, the British made 'retiring movements', leaving Mons in flames. (Mons was the first town they reached in the country they had gone to war to save; the BEF was back in France and the Belgians were on their own.)

Already the pattern was set, whether you bumped into the enemy or he bumped into you, or a little of both, as happened to Harry Mason, a cyclist of the 2nd South Staffords, from Walsall. He, too, was one of the very first British units to fight. He rode all through Saturday night, August 22, he wrote to friends from hospital, and at daybreak on Sunday ran up against uhlans, German cavalry with lances.

We were only about 180 strong and the job we had in front of us was a very hard one. We occupied rather a good position and caused the enemy to open out but after scrapping for about nine hours they got their artillery up and then I experienced the hottest time in my life. After being shelled for about half an hour we had the order to retire and then the fun began. Knowing we were part cyclists and that we could only get away by the road they had the range already eyed, so when we began to get away they simply dropped shell after shell after us. I think when we got to the next rise we only had about 70 men left.

Here Mason got his wound, in retreat down a hill: "I was riding by the side of one of the hussars. This poor chap was killed by the shells that were sent after us as also was the horse, the poor thing taking the best part of a shrapnel shell. It fell on the top of me and at the rate we were going you could guess what a nasty spill I had." Picked up unconscious, he came to in a Belgian nunnery. Here was the pattern: the British, infantry or cavalry (or cyclists, a sort of mechanical mix of both) could fight other infantry or cavalry well enough. Another Walsall man, 19-year-old Private Charles Broadhurst, spoke of 'ten hours' continuous scrapping' at Mons. He saw a captain's head blown off, had a bullet pass through his cloth cap, and but for the kit he carried, would have had a bullet in his back; yet they 'revelled in their work, and those who were unfortunate enough to get wounded', like Broadhurst in the thigh, 'were as bright and jolly as those who were more fortunate'. Man firing at man (on foot or on top of a horse or bicycle) was reasonable enough 'work', if you like Broadhurst, Mason and the rest were under cover, killing German after German until their rifles became hot – too hot to work, even. The battle became 'hotter', in the soldiers' slang, when the Germans fired something heavier, artillery shells, from guns you probably could not even see. You either ducked, until the shells hit you and killed you, or the Germans stopped firing, or fired at someone else; or you fled; and by showing yourself you put yourself in even more danger until you were beyond the shells and out of sight or under better cover; as Mason found.

The battle of Mons, and the first battles of August 1914, are supposed to hark back to previous wars, the battle of Waterloo, even, while the rest of the First World War dragged on in trenches, until a few more open months at the end. In truth the British were digging from the very start, as they were trained and for their own good, the same as they did in the Second World War. Private Charles Dudley Moore of the Yorkshire Light Infantry was wounded within half an hour at Mons:

The shrapnel shells of the Germans were bursting over the trenches where we were lying and I was struck in the foot with a piece of shell which took the heel of my boot clean off. Five minutes later when I was trying to help a fellow near me who had been hit in the shoulder, I was struck in

*the right thigh by a pellet from a shrapnel shell. This was
my first experience of actual fighting, and I can tell you it
is a funny sensation at first to see the shells bursting near
and around you, to hear the bullets whistling by you, and
to see men being killed and wounded near you, but you soon
get used to it all.*

Or as Charles Wallbank of the Royal Engineers put it, with
a few words that hinted at the agony of suspense and then the
shock of violence: "My God, to think of that first day."

The British understood well that the killing power on
the battlefield had become so great; they had seen what their
firepower had done to the Zulus, Sudanese and enough others.
Now that the British faced firepower like their own, they
knew they had to burrow, to have more chance of survival.
The problem – and the failure to get around the problem
would be counted in deaths – only became plain later, when
the front line settled and the British and French found they
had the task of pushing the invaders scores of miles back
to Germany (let alone as far as Berlin). Until then, the first
wounded returning to England in early September agreed:
the German infantry couldn't 'shoot for toffee', they shot from
the hip and didn't take aim; you were quite safe from it at
100 yards. But their artillery! Men called it 'simply terrible'.
Some did not like to admit it, and claimed even the German
artillery couldn't shoot. "It's numbers that does it, nothing
else," said one wounded man. But more men were killed
and wounded by the artillery than anything else. Either the
Germans had more or bigger guns, and machine guns, than
the British, or they made better use of them. Private J R Tait,
of the 2nd Essex regiment, wounded at Mons, spoke for many:
"Their rifle shooting is rotten; I don't believe they could hit
a haystack at 100 yards. Their field artillery is good, and we
don't like their shrapnel."

IV

To put across the sights and sounds of their first battle, to people who would never go near a war, the soldiers fell back on what they did know: the natural world. Private Frederick Bruce of the Suffolk regiment, wounded in the shoulder by a shell, told his parents in Cambridge the German artillery was 'worse than being in a hailstorm'. Charging British hussars cut Germans down 'like chaff', an easy comparison to make if the cavalry rode across fields. Private C E McLoughlin of the Coldstream Guards spoke of shooting Germans, caught on barbed wire in a village one night, 'as easily as shelling peas'. Other infantry spoke of shooting Germans 'like rabbits', whether because at a distance the men looked smaller or because some of the shooters were used to shooting rabbits (whether legally like Clifford Gothard, or as poachers). If Germans on the attack lost heart, they 'ran like rabbits', someone invalided home told *The Times* on August 31. When the British in their hastily dug trenches shot gaps in the packed lines of attackers, the Germans filled the gaps 'like marionettes'. It sounded as if men in battle saw the enemy – and any civilians in the way – as less than human. Private Shepherd of the 1st Lincs spoke of 'being compelled' to open fire on old men and women in front of him, 'mown down like so many sheep' – 'the occasion was not one for squeamishness'.

Another vocabulary to explain the battlefield came from religion. Sgt Crockett, a gardener and Royal Welsh Fusiliers reservist, the first wounded man home to Burton-on-Trent, called the artillery 'hellish'. Likewise to Private Thomas Cross 'it was like opening the lid of hell when the first shots came upon us'. Bombardier William Simpson went even further: "It was worse than hell, if it could be expressed that way," he wrote home to his parents; and he only went through the first two days.

21

Back

Retirements in face of the enemy must be conducted
with the greatest circumspection.
Infantry Training, War Office manual, 1914

I

That Infantry Training manual, helpfully printed on August 10, 1914 – and so official that any other training was 'forbidden' – had chapter after chapter about drill; plenty to say about attack, and defence; but barely a page about 'retirements'. British soldiers were evidently not allowed to go backwards on the battlefield; it was altogether best not to think about it. Yet after a couple of days at Mons, the British were ... retiring.

Retirement did rather suggest that that you thought you were not winning. And as the manual was quick to point out, in case anyone was too dim to spot it, a 'hurried retreat' not only might panic your side, but gave 'a great encouragement to the enemy'. You were giving the enemy the impression that he was winning.

II

Like all things, a retirement (or withdrawal, or whatever you wanted to call it) could be worse, or better. How far you retired, and how fast, would affect how well your army managed, because no matter how strong your will, and young and fit your body, you could only take so much for so long. Lieutenant J L Dent and the South Staffords began marching back too on the Monday night, August 24, after they had been shelled, but before they had fired a shot. Joseph Dent found that bad for morale. So began days of marching, and nights of entrenching:

> *I shall never forget the march, the terrible heat, the feeling of disaster which one scarcely dared admit even to oneself, the struggle to maintain march discipline and keep the men going at all and the terrible sight of the villagers crying and rushing to pack their belongings, realising what our retirement meant.*

By the Tuesday night, Dent was making himself stay on his feet, 'to avoid falling off to sleep'. Even so, several times he fell asleep standing 'and crashed to the ground'. By then the order had come for men to leave their packs, so they could walk with less load, and Dent 'lost' his 'useless' sword. Tiredness may have dulled Dent to the physical discomforts. His last night under a roof had been on the Saturday, August 22. The nights were cold enough to leave a nip in the air and dew on the ground by early morning, which men would feel in the open as they had thrown away their bedding. Or, discomforts may have depressed an already tired man, no longer able to think straight, so that he felt the confusion and the shame of retreat all the more. In a diary entry for Thursday August 27, he wrote:

> *.... it must be remembered that since the beginning of the battle of Mons we knew absolutely nothing, operational orders were unknown and we were never told anything ... we were undergoing the most terrible privations and fatigue, without sleep, completely in the dark and without being permitted to turn and show fight. That the Army survived such a terrible test of morale is a marvel.*

On Friday August 28, they reached La Fere, 60 miles south of Mons as the crow flies. (Another 60 miles would take them to the River Marne, level with Paris.) "General French came around and personally addressed each unit. He told us that he had never been prouder of a British soldier and that the Army had saved the French from annihilation after having undergone the most terrible test an Army can experience." Dent and his men cheered, 'and everyone felt much better'.

III

Even assuming that a few words from the commander of the British Expeditionary Force, General Sir John French, made the suffering feel worthwhile, was the general right? Was anything (let alone everything) better, after days of retreat?

Even while the going was good, the BEF seemed to be living off the land and the goodwill of the locals. Once in battle, every man and unit had to fend for themselves. True, the Germans were having as hard a time, if you believed the captured ones. At least the Germans, by going forward, might find food left behind by Belgian and French civilians, now refugees, and the British. Lieutenant R Macleod of the Royal Field Artillery began retiring on the Monday evening: "They outnumbered us about five to one," he told a public meeting in the village of Waterbeach outside Cambridge a couple of weeks later. "On Tuesday our transport ran into the Germans and they had to burn it so we got no breakfast. The inhabitants were very kind and gave us bread and eggs and fruit. We had a 30 mile march and I don't think any of us would have lasted it if it had not been for this." The German captain Walter Bloem, to his mind in pursuit of a defeated enemy, likewise came across abandoned heaps of tins of Fray Bentos corned beef, burned to deny it to enemies like him. Setting it on fire merely cooked the meat in the tins, however: "It was excellent!" Bloem added.

If you lost your unit, through exhaustion or battle, you were even more on your own. Sgt Bird and Private Woolgar of the

4th Dragoon Guards, for example, had their horses shot under them, and took shelter in a hen house, with a German sentry outside the door, because the Germans made the adjoining building into a headquarters. They joked afterwards: "So that we could say we dined with the German generals that night, the only difference being that they were inside and we were outside; they were having wines and we had swedes and no &c." The men escaped the hen house, and travelled south-west with the sun as their guide, dodging German troops, and trusting to the kindness of Belgian people.

Airmen were above it all. If they saw any enemy planes, they were finding it difficult to do much damage to them; even L A Strange, who had had the idea of fitting a Lewis machine-gun to his aeroplane. More danger came from his own artillery, which he noted 'had a nasty habit of firing at every aeroplane they saw ...'

In his diary for Friday August 28, he called the retreat 'hasty but orderly':

... many stragglers and some confusion along the line of retirement but perfect discipline and order extending back to the fighting line which is very difficult to define as so many little separate battles are going on in isolated spots, some so forlorn that they are obviously only desperate last stands.

Here lay the reason a 'retirement' could lead to catastrophe, and you did not need a training manual to tell you why. In retreat, you had all the problems of an advance, of one unit not tripping over another; plus, you had to go faster than the enemy, or the enemy caught up with you and made you fight, when and where he chose, maybe before you dug a hole or even knew he was there. The more you retreated, the more men got lost and found themselves in hen houses; the more could go wrong, until the army didn't look like one any more.

One story that made the newspapers was of a wounded man, an unnamed sergeant in the Inniskillings, who was shot in the shoulder after an all-night march on the Tuesday, August 25. He had his wound dressed at a French farm. When he set off again, Germans were nearby, and nearly captured him. He found himself in a village with a couple of hundred men, from mixed units, which was always a bad sign of confusion. These 200 stragglers did not know that the main British force had retreated further; in ignorance likewise, the Germans thought the British had left the village:

> *There was a lot of dead lying about too, men who had been carried there and had died on the way. When they were doing the charge one German shouted to us in broken English to surrender. We never spoke, but let them come on, and when they were within about ten yards we let them have it with the rifle. A few of them got up close enough to bayonet about two or three of our fellows, but they were only slight wounds. One fellow got a bayonet through the neck. Then we beat them off.*

The British, so nearly over-run, took the chance to slip out of the village: "We had to leave our transport behind us, but we filled our bandoliers with ammunition." The soldiers were learning that ammunition was most important to carry, more important even than food; and living was most important of all, more important than burying your dead. The life of one mattered less than the lives of many. Later, when these stragglers were sheltering in a wood, the man on guard was captured by two German cavalrymen: "... we saw them taking him away, and they were prodding him with their lances." The British officers would not let their men shoot; not, you suspect, in case they shot their captured comrade, but so they stayed hidden and safe. They kept marching by night until they found their division again. The Royal Engineer Charles Wallbank, 'like heaps of fellows' got lost, all the way back to Le Havre.

Such was the BEF's retreat; not a neat campaign, of orders given one day and carried out the next, as according to

197

the commanders' memoirs, and historians' maps. The hunter chased the hunted, with never a word from a general, let alone a hot meal, or a letter from home. Every day the men became more exhausted, more likely to make mistakes. Private C E McLoughlin, 'a fine, upstanding Irishman, and a typical Guardsman', according to the *Burton Evening Gazette*, was digging trenches at Mons on the Sunday night, August 23. All Monday night, his Coldstream Guards retreated, without sleep. Time was so short, officers and men alike ate turnips from the fields.

It may have been on the Tuesday, August 25, that McLoughlin found himself at Landrecies, an important road junction 25 miles south of Mons:

> *About half past eight that evening, my company, numbering about 120, were ordered on outpost duty. It was raining dismally at the time, and shortly afterwards a thunderstorm burst. A party was seen advancing not far away, but in reply to our sentry's challenge no reply was received. A French officer then challenged the oncomers, and the reply, 'We are French', came from the advancing party's commander. The latter walked up to our sentry, his left hand extended in friendly greeting. The next instant a sword flashed in the commander's right hand, and the unsuspecting sentry's head was severed at a stroke. One of our men, unable to control himself, rushed madly at the treacherous German—for such he proved to be—and flooring him commenced a violent struggle on the ground. Our boys were now getting ready to fire, and the man struggling with the German was ordered back to the ranks. As he was returning, however, the officer rose to his knees and brought our man down with his revolver. I need not tell you that when we received the word to fire, more than one of us had reserved our first shots for that German traitor ... The advance guard retreated bellowing and screaming like madmen. The wounded also*

shrieked horribly; it was more nerve-racking to hear them than it was fighting.

The longer the soldiers lasted, the more they learned about war. Let us assume that all of McLoughlin's vivid story was true, and not pieced together with others', and not (in parts at least) unknowingly altered by his mind, suffering as it was on a third night (or more) short of sleep. Who or what had the German been a 'traitor' to, by tricking the defenders into thinking he was friendly? Was it unfair, that the German killed the sentry, to give his side the advantage of surprise? In the end, were McLoughlin and his fellow guardsmen any less fair towards their enemy, shooting them and leaving them to shriek?

The troops were learning morally, and practically. The Germans were using what some soldiers called 'searchlights'; a sort of shell fired at night, that lit the battlefield like day. If this German flare caught you moving, bullets or shells could follow. Soldiers on all sides were learning to be hard. They did show some feelings for suffering civilians, who did not belong on the battlefield. Bugler Tom Reeves of the 9th Lancers was yet another man hurt by a bursting shell ('I shall probably have to lose one or two of my fingers') who wrote from hospital: "It is a lot different to what most of us expected. Women and children leaving their homes with their belongings. Then all of a sudden their houses would be in ashes – blown to the ground." Sgt Crockett was one of many to claim that the Germans used women and children as a shield to advance behind: "It nearly broke some of our boys' hearts to have to keep on firing, but we had to do so to preserve ourselves." The Germans denied the crime, and we can ask besides, how or why would the Germans have pushed Belgians (who, whether French or Flemish speaking, would not understand German) in front of them? Would that not have been more trouble than it was worth? More likely, Crockett was seeing civilians simply caught between the warring sides and running wildly, like rabbits in a harvested field with nowhere to go – except the waiting guns of sporting shooters such as Clifford Gothard.

As soldiers on both sides were absorbing the shock of their first close combat, they learned to be indifferent to others. Lance Corporal Ball, from Walsall, stood his ground with his fellow Grenadier Guards when Germans made a bayonet charge: "I don't know how many I accounted for, I lost count, but it was a terrible slaughter." A day or two later, while he and the Grenadiers were in reserve, he saw a British cavalry charge:

> *The spectacle of the horses thundering down on them and the men with their lances ready was too much for them. Some began to run as fast as they could go, others went down on their knees and held their hands up for mercy, and another lot made a rush for a neighbouring haystack. The way they scrambled up the side of that stack was the most comical thing of the lot. We absolutely roared with laughter.*

Men were learning to laugh at absurdity of war when they could, even during the act of killing and being killed, because of another cruelty: the man doing the killing one day could be killed the next. Were their *commanders*, who normally were spared all this, harder and wiser too? If they had blundered into a fight with far too large a part of the German army, were they learning from the experience, of fighting the first European enemy in their working lives? At the time, and afterwards, the closest observers thought not.

IV

> *The lesson is: don't be too senior at the beginning of a war!*
> *The Path to Leadership*, by Field Marshal the Viscount
> Montgomery of Alamein (1961)

We can make an even more general point than Lieutenant Bernard Montgomery, as he was in 1914. It's a risk to be the first to do anything, whether looping the loop in an aeroplane, or (as by the time Montgomery was writing in retirement) riding the first rocket into space. Other people, maybe not as good as you, learn from *your* mistakes and you, the one who had the harder job, never get the credit. Just as the campaign of August 1914 had echoes of 1815, so it had the seeds of the blitzkrieg, over some of the same country, of May 1940. The Germans of 1914 had the blitzkrieg spirit: to first put themselves where the enemy did not expect them, or want them to be, and then to pin the enemy, cut off his retreat, and make him give up or kill him. The Germans in August 1914 had many of the ingredients of May 1940. What Sgt Crockett, the Welsh reservist, said he went through would have sounded familiar to men of the second BEF, 26 years later:

> *Their aeroplane service was also very effective. When we were lying in the trenches we were fired at from aerial craft. Almost as soon as an aeroplane hovered above us the aviator would drop a signal to let the enemy know our approximate position, and they would immediately direct their hellish artillery upon us.*

What the Germans of 1914 lacked were tanks, which were artillery moved by motor, rather than horses. Tanks made a difference not so much because of the armour protecting the men inside, because enemy tanks would have the same armour and more or less the same guns to pierce that armour, but because the engine gave the tank speed, making it ten times as fast as a man or a horse. In 1940, the second BEF retreated to the beaches of Dunkirk and barely had time to sail home. For a while, the Germans of 1914 seemed to produce a similar effect, without tanks: had J L Dent retreated not 60 miles south from Mons, but east, he would have been well on the way to Dunkirk, and well within the May 1940 rate of retreat. In 1914 as in 1940, the Germans upset their enemy not only physically, but *psychologically*. Both times the British did not help themselves, by being so surprised by the Germans' tempo. Take the staff officer Sidney Clive, head of the British missions at French general headquarters, where he arrived on Tuesday August 18. He had a 'quiet' first couple of days, and a relaxing enough Saturday August 22, to have time to visit Rheims cathedral. After Mons and the days of retreat, his next Saturday was quite different; he met the BEF deputy chief of staff Henry Wilson at Compeigne (about two-thirds of the way from Mons to Paris, as the crow flies). Clive wrote in his diary: "Much dismayed at Hy information that we must go to Havre and home."

By 'we' Henry Wilson ('Hy') meant the BEF. Now it might have been natural to wish for a break in a hard fight, even though probably impossible; but to say so was foolish and would only provoke alarm. Nor was this an exception. In a telegram to Kitchener, on August 24, Sir John French suggested 'immediate attention' to the defence of Havre. Did the BEF commanders think that the French would lay on trains? Perhaps the French would have liked to return home, too, and let Paris defend itself? What would the Infantry Training manual-writer have made of the British army leaving a war after one week? In between the two Saturdays, besides the clash at Mons and the start of the retreat, had come the battle of Le Cateau, on the Wednesday, August 26. How the battle had to be fought was both cause and effect of the British breakdown.

Half of the BEF, Douglas Haig's I Corps, carried on retreating from Landrecies after the Tuesday night fight. That left Horace Smith-Dorrien's II Corps alone at Le Cateau. General French's headquarters was then at Saint Quentin, a good 20 miles further south of either. As a British official document of 1933 ahead of a tour of the battlefield put it, under the title 'lessons' (always the polite way of saying 'this is what went wrong') St Quentin was too far away; the headquarters gave orders to its two corps without knowing where they

202

were. It was only through headquarters that I and II Corps knew where each other were. HQ had told Smith-Dorrien to carry on retreating and did not know (and nor did Haig) that Smith-Dorrien had decided to stand at Le Cateau for the day. Smith-Dorrien in the middle of Tuesday night decided he had no choice as his men were, as the 1933 document put it, 'already thoroughly exhausted'. More to the point, so were the cavalry that would have to cover any more retreat. Not that the brigades of Smith-Dorrien's brigades heard of the decision to stand, until dawn, if they ever did (let alone the battalions, companies and the men at the very front about to do the fighting).

One reason for the fouled communications, that meant thousands died where they did, was the impossible job of the motorcyclists carrying messages, such as J K Stevens. His equivalent at the battle of Waterloo rode a horse; but only took a few miles to go from one end of the battle to the other. The messenger of 1815 and 1914 alike was shot at, shelled, and outdoors in all weathers. Stevens told his local *Cambridge Daily News*: "We were soaked to the skin when we reached Le Cateau and wet as we were we were glad to get a couple of hours' sleep on the top of wet corn sheaves. The worst of being a motorcyclist was that even after settling down for a sleep we were invariably called up to take a message." Around this time – Stevens may have muddled his story by the time he told it, a few weeks later – a piece of shell had chipped his motorcycle's petrol tank; a farrier patched it with some solder. Another time, while Stevens had to make another repair to his machine, he lost his brigade. Once he reached St Quentin, he took a message for a field ambulance, until five miles out of town he skidded and buckled his front wheel. He put his motorcycle on a passing horse-drawn wagon and rather than add himself to the load he walked alongside the convoy, 'as the horses were done up':

Never shall I forget the trek along that road. There were the stragglers of the army who had fought at Mons. Men who had not shaved for a week, men footsore and weary with nothing but their uniforms. Many had lost their caps and most of them had discarded their equipment. Some had cut the heels from their shoes on account of soreness. Every few hundred yards was a dead horse while I counted no fewer than 15 motor lorries abandoned by the roadside. Boxes of ammunition, sacks of flour, tins of meat, Cardigan waistcoats, caps, rifles, broken bicycles were scattered along this long, straight road. Here and there a few men had stopped to make a fire to boil tea, others gathered apples from the gardens of deserted cottages.

This part of the British army, at least, sounded beaten; it did not sound like an army at all. After the Germans mauled half of the BEF at Le Cateau, the BEF made sure to retreat until they had outrun the Germans. From Le Cateau on August 24, the RFC moved airfields ten times in the next 11 days. Stevens walked 20 miles with the convoy as far as La Fere, where he had his machine repaired again. Stranded again, he went a dozen miles more, to Laon, where – maybe because he had in ignorance strayed away from the rest of the BEF –gendarmes held him for two days until an English officer freed him. His war for the time being was over.

V

In his great novel August 1914 Alexander Solzhenitsyn sends his main character, Colonel Vorotyntsev, into and around the battlefields of the Masurian Lakes to show how badly the brave and faithful Russian soldiers were led, so that the more agile Germans first exhausted them, then surrounded them – as the Germans in the west would have done to the British, given more of a chance. As Montgomery said, it was a 'wise

decision' of Sir John French's to retreat from Mons (though would it not have been even wiser not to have gone there in the first place?). In the climax to the book, Vorotyntsev tells his story to the commander in chief, the czar's uncle, Grand-Duke Nicholas, in front of the failed and guilty headquarters staff, with the hope that the truth will lead to change for the better. Vorotyntsev fails; he is asking too much for the system to reform itself. Solzhenitysn and his readers knew well what followed; the fall of the czar, and a much worse, soviet, tyranny. Yet would a real, British Vorotyntsev have done any better? The nearest equivalent – a piece of journalism from a roving reporter, not a staff officer – suggests not.

Though a necessary character as a thread through the novel, Vorotyntsev is believable, as a man with permission to rush from battlefield to commander's table. Journalists, from neutral countries, or allies, or even following their own troops, were not welcome on any battlefield. This was, partly, for their own good. In any war, before and since, strangers or foreigners asking questions were suspect. Reporters could easily find themselves under arrest, as spies. The British authorities, as much as their French hosts, did not want journalists finding out things for themselves, in case what they printed gave the enemy clues, or encouragement. No news was good news. In mid-August *The Times* noted that they had heard very little from Russia since its mobilisation began in July 30; it had to suppose that the 'grim silence of Russia means much'. The silence was ignorance; and the ignorance a sign of incompetence. In Solzhenitysn's novel and in reality Russian officials said little about the battle of Masurian Lakes, the crushing of their invasion of East Prussia, and instead talked up a lesser, flawed, victory over the hardly more competent Austrians.

Hence *The Times'* news of a 'broken' and 'beaten' British army in one of their special Sunday editions on August 30 was so shocking, both unexpected and as an outbreak of truth; an

unwelcome shock, to the Liberal government. In the House of Commons the day after, Asquith commended the 'patriotic readiness of the whole of the press from the beginning of the war', with the 'very regrettable exception' of the Times on an 'alleged disaster' to the British army. By the formal standards of the day, the prime minister was condemning *The Times*. What proved to be the single piece of news nearest the truth – the setback to an army that everyone, then and since, took for granted as the best that ever left Britain – was deplored, for rocking the boat.

Why then had the censor, the Unionist politician F E Smith, allowed the article – and, bizarrely, even added a few lines, to urge readers to join the army? With more honesty, Asquith did admit that the country was 'entitled to more prompt and efficient information' from the war. With that line he might have been – again, without rocking the boat – putting pressure on the army to tell the people (including the politicians) what was going on. In his war memoir Lloyd George recalled how the cabinet at this time had no news of the BEF for days, and was 'bewildered by the scrappy and incoherent reports given to it each morning by Kitchener'.

If the most junior Guards officers, like Oliver Lyttleton, felt so opposed to 'outsiders' joining them, we can imagine how the army would resent journalists scratching around for news. Newspapers, so the generals and politicians liked to think, ought to know their place like everyone else – for newspapers did have a place: printing what rulers chose to tell them. Thus for example, the day before *The Times* made its stink, Lady French, the wife of the BEF commander, sent an appeal to the newspaper, "for knitted socks &c for our troops. It is indeed a crying need as the War Office allowance is only three pairs for each man and a long day's march will wear socks into holes." Local newspapers widely picked this up from *The Times*. Similarly, a few days later in Staffordshire newspapers

Lord Dartmouth appealed for 'comforts' for the troops: "Socks, Coloured Pocket Handkerchiefs, Shirt Collar Studs, Towels, Soap, Tooth Brushes, Pipes, Tobacco, and later on Woollen Helmets and Warm Underclothing." As that list suggested, the authorities by now were expecting the war to run into winter. As with the families left behind by the soldiers, it was taken for granted that charity (collected by a small committee of ladies, Dartmouth suggested) would make good hardships. Yet was it not asking too much of the state, to give enough socks? The state did give a soldier a rifle and a uniform (a reservist had his old uniform which, hopefully, he had not grown out of). Did the War Office not know that a soldier might march for days?

Who was responsible? The administrators, or the ministers of either main political party, in and out of office every few years? The king and his family? Because King George V and his relatives, even the more German-sounding ones, such as Louis Battenberg, took particular interest in the military, because it was one of the few jobs fit for them, and the army was the ultimate institution that kept a monarch in power (or not, as the German kaiser and Russian czar would soon find out). Did the politicians keep the army so short of money, that it could not afford more socks, or was there a lack of sympathy, a sense that three pairs of socks were plenty for the common man? As for the officers, a sword had long been no good as a weapon or as protection against bullets; so why carry one? These small things mattered on the retreat, as men's feet ached and every unnecessary load rankled. Such institutional shortcomings – being set in their ways, always preparing for the war they had last fought, or not preparing at all because a quiet life was easier – were hardly only Britain's, though only Britain had the cheek to call itself 'great'. If you rocked the boat by asking questions, of any institution, you rocked them all.

That was why so many people did not like Winston Churchill. He was a boat-rocker. A grandson of a Duke of Marlborough, the son of the Unionist politician Lord Randolph Churchill, he was in rather too much of a hurry, too obviously ambitious, for some tastes. He made a name for himself, first, in the army and as a war correspondent, and then in his father's footsteps in parliament – only to rather spoil it, by switching from the Unionists to the Liberals. Churchill had a way of getting on by 'being Winston', energetic and sure of himself, not by attracting a following – which was as well, judging by the diary of Richard Holt, the businessman turned Liberal MP. Holt seldom made comments on politicians; he made an exception for Churchill, who clearly riled him. "I don't like the clever Home Secretary Winston Churchill. He has a bad face," Holt wrote in May 1911. To Holt, someone 'clever' seemed suspect, for in July 1911 he called F E Smith 'clever', 'too clever, and unprincipled; a nice pair with his friend Churchill'. Soon after, Churchill switched to the Admiralty, and nettled more people; or the same people, in new ways. Ben Tillett in speeches in 1914 singled out Churchill as an imperialist, for wanting to build more battleships while families had to do without food or chairs.

Why did Churchill get up the noses of such different people, without, it seemed, even trying? Neither Holt nor anyone else might mind a clever person; it was what Churchill *did*, or tried to do, that annoyed people, whether he was proved wrong or right. By August 1914, not quite 40, he was one of the leading, rising Liberal politicians; much of the dislike he provoked may have been envy. Some would have liked his job, or would have been glad to see him out of his job.

VII

The trouble for Churchill by later August 1914 was that his job – any job, except the very top job in British politics – was not enough for him. The British army reached France safely; the German navy was not showing fight. The Admiralty warned the home fleets on August 12 to beware that the 'extraordinary silence and inertia of enemy' might be hiding an attempt at invasion; as days passed, the silence looked simply like inertia.

G C Harper, the cadet, started the war well, on the cruiser *HMS Endymion*; on August 26 the captain raised him to midshipman, and Harper proudly added home-made patches of rank to his uniform. On August 31 he reviewed the month of patrolling. Like many on land and at sea, he always felt tired: "Every third day you get a day's work of 24 hours with three hours sleep, ie from midnight to midnight, sleeping from four to seven in the morning. But the other two days you can get seven hours with good luck." After four weeks of the same breakfast – 'porridge, brown sugar, kippers, bacon and eggs, uneatable butter, bread and marmalade' – he was sick of it, though he said he did not want to grumble (or grumbling to himself in his diary made him feel better). Otherwise, the sheer routine, domestic nature of his diary – and as he admitted, no real hardship – suggested he was having an uneventful time:

The main trouble is that you cannot get enough water either to drink, wash in or wash your clothes. I am speaking of the gun room of course. We have been at dinner without anything to drink. We often could not get a bath in the mornings; it was the utmost luxury to get a third of a can of warm water to bathe or wash in. It was very difficult to get people to wash clothes but I must say they did their best in spite of the lack of water and no drying arrangements. Of course starching and ironing was unknown. My collars are still holding out but when our collars run out we wear

209

them soft ... as to food they make the great mistake of trying to keep up appearances and we have proper meals in style instead of giving us plenty of plain food. A typical dinner consists of one small fish, a perfectly microscopic helping of beef and potatoes and one sardine (as savoury). Perhaps some beastly dried fruit takes the place of the sardine and on a great occasion a small cup of nasty coffee follows. Now see how much more satisfactory dinner would be if it was an unlimited supply of good bread, eatable butter and jam with plenty of good coffee. Yet that would not be a proper dinner you see with the regulation courses. The butter is generally uneatably disgusting, there is no milk but the rest of the food (what there is of it) is good.

The navy did have a small battle, off Heligoland, in late August. It gave Oliver Lyttleton, still guarding the coast at Dovercourt on the north tip of Essex, something to write home to his mother about. It made a change from his own news ('still no commission!'), his friends ('Bobbety insists upon making the most infernal row on a mouth organ which is rather distracting') and the war news from France ('isn't it awful!'). Lyttleton and his fellows visited the destroyers from the battle at Harwich, 'the most thrilling thing I have ever done'. Lyttleton and friends went on the *Laertes*, 'or rather were dragged on board', by 'a red bearded young naval officer'. He showed the shell holes on the ship, 'one which went through three cabins and then burst'. British destroyers had attacked German destroyers to bring out the German cruisers, but for a while the British destroyers had to fight the bigger German cruisers. A 'mouldy' (a torpedo) disabled the *Laertes*; the disabled ship tried to hitch a hawser to another destroyer, the *Laurel*, but it broke. Men on the *Laurel* cheered; the naval officer telling the story to Lyttelton had shaken his fist at them and cursed. Just as German battle cruisers came out of the mist, and it seemed that the *Laertes* had a minute before destruction, "boom whroo-oo-oo zip the Crecy let off a broadside and one funnel was all that was left on the cruiser's deck. 'God I cried like a child,'" the naval story-teller said, "and upon my word he nearly wept again at the mere description of it," Lyttleton added.

Otherwise, the threats to the navy were unglamorous: the floating mine and the submarine. An early loss was the *Amphion*, blown up in the North Sea by a mine, a German tactic Lady Goonie Churchill deplored in a letter to her husband Jack as 'a low, base game'. The most junior of the *Amphion*'s four wireless operators, William Cash, at home on leave a few days later in Walsall, told the Wolverhampton daily paper the *Express & Star* on August 15: "I had been off duty for two hours and was asleep on the mess desk at the time the explosion occurred." The reporter may have tidied his English. "The uproar was terrific and the first thing I remember was that I was going up in the air." That Cash came out without a mark appeared miraculous, the reporter said to him. Cash laughed, as if he realised that civilians hadn't a clue about war and what he had been through. "The first thing I did was to get out," he said. That was obvious. What was of interest was the way that military drill had taken hold of the men, as they understood that a panic to save yourself would only make it worse for everyone. "Everyone was right quiet and the people behaved just as though they were at exercise in harbour. There was no rushing about and we were transferred to other boats in a few minutes." Also foreshadowing what men home from the BEF would say soon, Cash said that he already felt anxious to go back: "We are all eagerly awaiting the chance to go back to have a pot." Churchill, too, wanted a pot at the Germans.

22

An Outing to Ostend

... and another thing that appealed to us was that we would be travelling overseas and would be able to see what the other part of the world was like.
A Fortunate Life, by Albert Facey (1981)

I

After it was all over, the expedition by Royal Marines to Ostend made excellent photos in *The Graphic* of September 5; the port and Belgian seaside resort hardly looked as if it were at war. It helped that readers who had journeyed to the Continent had quite likely passed through Ostend – and from there taken the train to more historic and beautiful places than the rather plain towns in northern France that the BEF was having to march forward and back through. One photo showed the Marines marching past the 'Royal Yacht Hotel'. Ostend had that in-between feel – not England but not quite Belgium either – that, you suspect, satisfied neither the locals nor visitors.

Churchill had sent the Marines there, 'for reasons which seemed sufficient to the Government and the military authorities', he had told the House of Commons airily. Another picture showed Marines following the horse-drawn coffins of policemen, killed defending the town against German cavalry raiders. Evidently the war had come as far as this corner of Belgium, 60 miles from England. Yet the war was not raging enough to keep a large crowd, mainly of men, from the funeral;

and clearly the Marines could spare men for the ceremony. The very fact that the newspapers had pictures suggested this was not the front line; or did the British have a reason for allowing publicity?

II

George Aston had had a busier August 1914 than many. He began the month as the second commandant at the Royal Marines barracks at Eastney, along the prom from Portsmouth. He was in his early 50s; the Marines had been his life. He had gone into staff-work at the Admiralty, and written some naval books. On Sunday August 2, after helping the called-up Marines reservists find uniforms that fitted, a telegram ordered him to the Admiralty the next morning. He left from the nearest station, Fratton, at 8.20pm and arrived at London Waterloo late, finding excited crowds cheering naval reservists. He checked in at the Grand Hotel. Next day he found himself a member of a special committee of the Committee of Imperial Defence to look into 'oversea attack' and moving and escorting British troops by sea. Fourteen-hour days followed, of conferences that wore him out, 'but intensely interesting'.

At 6.30pm on Tuesday August 25, he was asked whether he had any uniform, because he had to command a Royal Marine brigade off Ostend, at once. Aston said that he had a brigadier-general's uniform, at his tailor's. He left at once, to collect it; then went to the home of a friend, Lady Tryous, to put it on. He had moved out of the hotel, to be a guest of George Tryous. He returned to the Admiralty, for 'a hasty meal in my room and instructions from First Lord followed by official orders in writing signed by secretary at 9.20pm'. Aston caught the 10pm train from London Victoria for Chatham, to meet his new command. Aston was qualified, available, dressed for the part, and away within three and a half hours. But why Ostend? Why then? And why the hurry?

This was Churchill's way, with what forces he had under his control, of taking part in the land battle. News from France was 'disappointing', as he put it in an Admiralty message on August 24. He warned that the Germans might 'control Calais and the French coast'. In fairness, this was Royal Navy business. Ostend sounded even more at risk, judging from a *Daily Mail* reporter, who returned to England from the port on August 25 and rang the Admiralty with news at 8.30pm. (The press had its uses.)

The correspondent had left Ostend that day, as German troops were approaching. Ostend's garrison of 4000 had gone along the coast to Antwerp the previous Friday, August 21, leaving only 200 gendarmes. They had seen off the 300 German cavalrymen. "The gendarmes suffered about 45 casualties and having defended the honour of the town now intend to surrender when larger forces of Germans arrive," the Admiralty noted from the *Mail* reporter. Whether you thought the Belgians ought to try rather harder, or that the outnumbered defenders had done all they could, this did not sound promising territory to enter. "First Lord informed who decided to make no change to orders." Churchill had indeed already told Aston to occupy Ostend, and to send cyclists on reconnaissance to the towns of Bruges, Thorout and Dixmunde, each about a dozen miles away. Churchill was asking Aston to create a diversion, 'favourable to the Belgians who are advancing from Antwerp', although the latest news had suggested the Belgians were doing exactly the opposite, and to threaten the western flank of the German southward advance. "It should therefore be ostentatious."

The Admiralty would supply details about the enemy (such as: were they waiting for him to land?). "The object in view would be fully attained if a considerable force of the enemy were attracted to the coast. You will be re-embarked as soon as this is accomplished," his orders ran.

Aston reached his command at Chatham at 1.30am on the Wednesday, August 26. On the way the Admiralty had sent him another telegram, which already made a dangerously vague and contradictory mission worse. If, on arrival at Ostend, he found the enemy, 'you must act according to circumstances and their strength, endeavouring to avoid bringing calamity upon the town for the sake of a minor operation'. Some of that was contradicted by yet another message on the way to Belgium; if the enemy were in Ostend, Aston was to land somewhere else, and turn them out (and never mind the townspeople?). Aston had an impossible job. As he wrote later, putting the best face on it, the hope "was that my little force would be looked upon as the advance guard of a strong British army and have some moral effect. Failing that if it drew down upon it a strong enemy force that would otherwise be launched into the decisive battle in France it might be considered to achieve a strategic effect." Put less kindly, he was bait. If the Germans took no notice, he was wasting his time; if he succeeded, and made the Germans think he was a threat, they would smash him, and Ostend.

Aston arrived off Ostend on the Wednesday night. The admiral carrying him was against landing the Marines in a choppy sea in the dark. Aston did not have any staff, 'not even a servant to look after my kit'. He landed at 3.30am on the Thursday, August 27, and began preparing for his 3200 men and 300 tons of stores, 'designed mostly for the defence of Scapa Flow'. He had besides to deal with the mayor of a town of 25,000 people 'in a state of panic', the Belgian military, and the British embassy at Antwerp, as the Germans had marched into Brussels days before. "Then ended the longest and heaviest day I have ever spent," Aston recalled. "But ended with men on the approaches to the town and entrenched." For that he had to thank his 'magnificent men', mostly old reservists, who however were not trained to work in battalions; nor were there many officers to go around. Aston set up 3000 men on a seven-mile perimeter, thin by the standards of war, and which as he wrote would have 'sufficed to keep off a cavalry raid', but nothing more serious. The month ended with Aston ordered to return to England 'at your earliest convenience'. That meant fetching all the 300 tons of stores, including many tons at a barracks a mile from the quay. "Well," said a doubtless by now thoroughly weary Aston, "the men rose to the occasion magnificently. Men who had lain on outposts all night came in marching order also carrying WP [waterproof] sheets, blankets and boxes of ammunition. Then did fatigue work on the quay." All 300 tons went back the way they had come, and the Marines embarked in the dark, 'cheered by the town as they cheered the British in', Aston noted cynically. Ostend had been a town 'that did not want us', because they did not want the war to hurt them or their property. So much for Britain going to war to save them.

III

Aston landed at Portsmouth and took the train to London, returning to the Admiralty one week after he left. What had he – and his hard-working men – achieved?

They had not fought any Germans, which Aston implied was as well, because his brigade of four battalions was 'not really battalions but just herds of old reservists', and 'recruits who had never fired their rifles'. "The main difficulty," Aston summed up, as if men too rusty or untrained to be any good were not difficulties enough, "is that no-one will explain to the First Lord what a battalion or a brigade is and what it requires in the way of officers, organisation and equipment to make it a mobile unit in the field." Churchill, the First Lord of the Admiralty, was only ever interested in being a commander, issuing commands; he had been born into an aristocratic family that had been telling other people what to do for centuries. How to make

Churchill's commands work was for lower ranks to fix; or not, as Aston found out, and as others would find out later.

IV

In London again by the end of August, Lady Gwendoline Churchill kept up twice-daily letters to her husband Jack, still asking him to write to her and console her. Not that she was doing a very good job of consoling her husband, who was the one who faced the prospect of going to war. She wrote to him on September 1 after lunch at the Admiralty, with news about him, from Kitchener, via her brother-in-law Winston; Jack's yeomanry would train for three or four months, then go to war: "I am not happy as you may imagine as that means you will go face to face with those swines of Germans who by that time will be more savage and desperate than ever," she wrote, tactlessly. She did however do an excellent job, passing on gossip. In another letter that day after a visit from Winston's wife Clemmie she reported that Winston was too tired to motor to see Jack: "W had only three hours sleep last night; there was something critical, I don't know what ..."

The next day, she called the war news 'pretty grim': "Do you think we will be able to hold the Germans long enough to give the Russians time to march on to Berlin, I doubt it very much." Again, we see that faith in Russia to do the hard work, sooner or later to be disappointed. She shuddered at the long list of missing troops in the newspapers, and yet again in a self-obsessed way urged her husband to visit her and give her courage to bear it all (but wasn't her husband the one in need of comfort?). In the afternoon she was 'so miserable', still haunted by list of missing men, but cheered by her biggest piece of gossip yet; from Winston and Asquith. She marked this letter 'secret':

The PM was at lunch and he told me that our Army is the best, better than the Germans and better than the French. The German individually are rotten, cannot face steel, cannot shoot, but their headquarter staffs is splendid, organisation and strategy.

Was Asquith unconsciously projecting his dissatisfaction with the panicky, dumb British headquarters on the Germans?!

August 1914 ended with many men where they had not started the month. Alan Brooke was in Cairo. He saw the sights, such as the well where Potiphar was supposed to have imprisoned Joseph, and (more likely genuine, and more likely to interest Brooke the artilleryman) the marks made by Napoleon's guns on the city gate and nearby mosques more than a century before. On August 30 he took a trip to the Sphinx and then the Great Pyramid:

...and went right up to the King's chamber in the very centre. It was desperately hot and stuffy inside and stank of bats but I would not have missed going inside for a lot. We then climbed on to the top and were well repaid by the magnificent view from the top. I felt I could have stopped all day on top looking around. On our way back we dropped into the zoo and had tea there ...

For many, in the same place as ever, life went on as ever. Frank Balfour in Sudan was 'wrestling very inadequately', so he told his friend Irene Lawley, 'with one of the plagues of Egypt': locusts. Working out of a steamer along 20 miles of both banks of the Nile, his weapons against the pests were paraffin and arsenic:

A swarm of locusts is a thing to wonder at. The eggs from which these have hatched may have been laid years ago – as soon as there are good rains and food for the young crawling locusts they hatch out. As we have them now they are bright green-yellow and an advancing swarm looks as if the ground was all on the boil. Later they will go black

and shed their skins – after that they can flie – the object
is to kill them all before that happens. It's a brutal business
– you drive hundreds of thousands into a clump of bushes,
surround it with dry stuff – pour paraffin on top and apply
the match – or else you lay poisoned grass on the ground,
let them eat that.

On August 31 William Swift's daughter-in-law Annie called on him in Churchdown. Her son Reginald, who had joined the army's commissariat (food supply) branch in mid-August, had left the Bristol port of Avonmouth for abroad. "He has sent his photograph. He is a nice looking lad. Annie will get a dozen taken from it. He is in uniform, looks well. She took a bag of apples back with her and brought me a bottle of jam." The next day Swift rose early as usual, just before 6am. As a man in his 70s, he was asking a lot of himself by working five hours in the garden: "Had two or three swoons perhaps the effect of the heat and of my hurrying to get the potatoes out while the fine weather lasts." A letter from his Aunt Sarah asked him to tell Mr Hooper, her landlord – who wanted to move into her house – that she would not leave until the proper time, April 1916. That may have seemed a way off to a man like Swift, who might have sensed he was near the end of his time, and who was anxious for the young men of his family heading for danger.

Shadowy as the first battles in Europe were, it was dawning on some that war between two of the most powerful nations ever would be on a scale not seen before. As Donald Weir, the army officer in India, wrote to his mother on August 27, having heard the first news of the BEF: "The war will no doubt last a very long time and the losses will be enormous on both sides before any final result is attained."

23

To the End of the World

The world has indeed never been the same again,
and never will be.

Antony, *A Record of Youth*, by his father, the Earl of
Lytton (1935)

The same amateurism that made a shambles of the
Ostend expedition at the end of August 1914 had
already doomed the Gallipoli campaign by the time
Gerald Legge landed in July 1915. Even on the battlefield, he
could not help telling his father, Lord Dartmouth, about the
wildlife – 'some topping birds' – with a difference; he was no
longer the lone hunter: "No big birds ... which surprises me as
they would get lots of cheap meals here now."

He kept his hunter's instinct and curiosity. He wrote of
'wandering about the front line' for two days before he led
his company of South Staffords there for the first time. "I am
enjoying myself hugely at present," he said, "it is only the smell
and flies I object to." All he left unsaid was *what* was making
the stink and so many flies, and what vultures, if there had been
any, could feed on. The locals, too, seemed to evoke his travels in
Sudan the year before. "Their snipers are very accurate and very
quick and I respect them. They, the Turks, are real gentlemen
and fight as such. They could shell our hospitals and hospital
ships for certain but never yet have they fired at either." It did
not seem to occur to Legge that the Turkish defenders were
saving their guns for the men they had not hurt yet.

From a friend of a friend, Legge had heard how the attack,
meant to capture the Turkish capital Constantinople and

change the war, had gone wrong before it even began: "…if only the fleet had not come fooling around before the Army was ready we could have gone straight through with little trouble." Three months on, the campaign had stalled, and what Legge called 'this old hill Achi Baba', a commanding point on the Gallipoli peninsula, was a long way off yet. He summed up: "Now we have many thousands of men here and can move but very slowly with thousands of lives lost. It seems like a baddish bit of self-advertisement by someone."

A letter to a friend dated August 5, after nine days in the trenches, had much the same tone; and if you sensed any faltering in his good cheer, any wistfulness, and brooding on death, you may have been reading too much into his words, written on very small sheets of (unusually for him) plain paper.

It was most interesting and in spite of flies, heat and stinks I was completely and entirely happy there. It seems odd that there are people who can be happy with all that noise and suffering going on all round and I am rather ashamed of it in a way but still I am sure a contented and happy man in command of a company is an asset even if he is a damned bad soldier. The Turks are gentlemen and fight as such; their snipers are sportsmen and I respect them. I had an exciting bout with one, one night I went out to stalk him but he knew his job too well, which was to lie still while I had to move the result was he located me before I located him and he put two or three all round me so I gave him best and crawled back to the trench with my tail down …

Again, despite the suffering due to the extreme climate of the Mediterranean midsummer, let alone the fighting, Legge credited the Turks as gentlemen, and likened war to sport. He went on:

… it is extraordinary how one can carry on with very little sleep for a long time and how fit one feels on it but I expect it tells after a time. I wish we could get done with this old

war all the same; I long for the old life again but I suppose it can never be the same with all those good fellows away. Did you see that Woosham was killed out here. That is the greatest loss I have had in this war. After all he and I have been through together it seems hard for him to go out like that. I wish I could tell you all that I believe we are going to do today I hope it is going to have a big effect out here but I am sworn to secrecy. Write and tell me anything cheerful you can. Yours ever Gerald Legge.

Four days later he and his company left their trenches to attack machine-guns, and snipers who seemed to aim at leaders. Legge was dressed conspicuously in shorts, puttees and light boots with rubber soles. One of his men, Private Apdale, wrote later that he bandaged the wounded Legge's arm and leg. "The most marvellous thing about all this, how I was not riddled with bullets I shall never understand if I live to be a thousand. God alone knows why I was spared … the only reason I can give that I was not riddled with bullets is that the Turks seeing me dressing wounded may have refrained from firing at me." He wrote clumsily, like a man not used to putting his words on paper, and trying to make sense of something as inhuman as battle. Apdale told how Legge's servant, Private Walters, came to them, with a wounded wrist, and Legge was hit again. Legge supposedly told Apdale to find stretcher bearers. 'Shall I take my equipment?' Apdale claimed he asked.

No, he says, so I took my rifle and bayonet bandolier water bottle and made a dart across the open, back to find any stretcher bearers, the snipers firing at me as I ran. I ultimately found the stretcher bearers but they informed me that it was a certain death to venture up as far as the hole where Captain Legge was. Anyhow I tried several times to get someone to go back with me but they appeared to have plenty of work in looking after wounded who had managed to come out of the battle towards more safety.

Then, according to Apdale, came the order to retire. Stumbling on ungrammatically, but doing his best, Apdale went on:

Now your lordship is what most certainly happened because I saw it, the ground where Captain Legge lay and also the rest of the wounded was set in flames by the Turks and I very much regret to inform your lordship that the wounded was burned. It may console your lordship when I say that in my opinion Captain Legge was either unconscious or dead before the ground was on fire as he was wounded four times while I was there his servant Walters no doubt dead by him.

Apdale ended this account for Lord Dartmouth of the death of his son: "I hope you will excuse my rather illiterate way of explaining what happened but of course you will understand."

Other letters reached Lord Dartmouth with different stories; one said that when all was quiet that night, Legge was buried with respect and a small cross put on his grave. Several wrote of Legge, while wounded, urging his men on, with the shout 'get on Staffords'. But as one man admitted, men circulated stories that others knew to be untrue. Apdale may have felt a need to explain away why he left Legge dead or dying, to be burned. Surely, even if the Turks were wicked enough to burn their enemies alive, it made no sense for them to set fire to the attackers' ground, because any smoke would hide the busted attack and aid the retreat. More likely the shooting had set things alight, one more mishap in a failed and pointless attack.

It says something about the power of an aristocrat, and something about the humanity of the surviving South Staffordshire soldiers, once miners, shop workers and labourers, that although about half their fellows were killed in those few minutes, some took the trouble to write letters to Legge's father, in the simple, only way they knew. A Sgt Cooke wrote to his wife, who forwarded the letter to Lord Dartmouth, that Legge 'used to expose himself so much, didn't know what fear was d-d it':

> *He was my ideal type of an English officer and gentleman, I got on splendidly with him. We were talking together all night on the 7ᵗʰ, he was telling me about the travels in different parts of the world. He used to go all over the world, collecting or something of that sort. It is a pity but I somehow felt he would get knocked out. I cannot explain the feeling but there it was, he had an exaggerated idea of the Turk, he used to say the Turk was a gent and fought like one.*

Some of the Characters After 1914

Robin Page Arnot (1890-1986) wrote such Communist works as Fascist Agents Exposed in the Moscow Trials (1938) and, less dubiously, a multi-volume history of British miners.

Soon after Ostend *George Aston* (1861-1938) commanded a similar expedition to Dunkirk. He retired in 1917 with the rank of major general. He wrote several books, mainly on the navy, or fishing.

Frank Balfour worked in the Middle East during and after the 1914-18 war and in 1920 married ... not Irene Lawley, but another Honourable; Phyllis Goschen. For the Balfour family tree see The Letters of Arthur Balfour and Lady Elcho 1885-1917, edited by Jane Ridley and Clayre Percy (1992).

Eric Bennett served in France in the artillery. In April 1918 he won the Military Cross for bringing six wagons of ammunition to safety despite artillery fire. He lived to old age in Staffordshire; two of his brothers were killed in the war, one invalided out.

As for the men linked by the outburst by *Lord Charles Beresford* (1846-1919) at the Carlton Club on August 27, 1914: the anti-German campaign worked. *Prince Louis Battenberg* (1854-1921) resigned as First Sea Lord in November 1914 and left public life. In 1917 Battenberg translated his name to Mountbatten, as King George V asked his relatives to un-German their surnames. A few months before Prince Louis died, he became an admiral of the fleet on the retired list thanks to the First Lord of the Admiralty – *Arthur Lee* (1868-1947), by then Lord Lee of Fareham. Lee donated his home, Chequers, on the edge of the Chilterns, to the state as a weekend retreat for the prime minister. *Winston Churchill* had to resign in 1915 over the failed Gallipoli campaign and was out of office for not quite a couple of years.

Possibly as it was the only way to stay in his job, *Robert Blakeby* put his name in for the 'training corps' at his employer, the London West End draper's Peter Robinson, at the end of September 1914. He kept a diary until at least the 1940s.

Alan Brooke was in France by the end of 1914. He was the driver of a car in which his wife Janey died in an accident in 1925. By the Second World War he rose to become Churchill's CIGS (Chief of the Imperial General Staff). For more, see War Diaries 1939-1945 Field Marshal Lord Alanbrooke, edited by Alex Danchev and Daniel Todman (2001).

The Derby railwayman and reservist *Arthur Bryan* was in France by the end of October 1914 and killed at Givenchy on March 10, 1915.

A T Daniel retired after 22 years as Uttoxeter Grammar School headmaster in December 1923. He had taken leave after the armistice to do 'education work with the troops in France and Germany, a task for which his wide interests and continental experience were most valuable', according to school historian and old boy W G Torrance.

Clifford Gothard (1893-1979) ended 1914 as he began it, shooting; and lunched on venison he had shot. He gained a BSc in mechanical engineering in July 1915. He served in the heavy artillery in France. He became an accountant and company director and a leading Conservative in Burton-on-Trent and was knighted. My father as a railway signalman in one of the town's many railway signalboxes in the 1950s sometimes saw him arrive at an office: "He used to come in an old Rover. If anybody was in the box, I used to say, watch him. He would go in and come out again because he had left his attaché case; he did it every time." Sir Clifford married in 1961 and was childless.

G C (Geoffrey Coleridge) *Harper* (1894-1962) survived the First World War, retired from the Royal Navy in 1931, went into teaching, and joined the navy again in the 1939-45 war.

Richard Holt (1862-1941) was the Liberal MP for Hexham until 1918. His shipping company flourished in wartime, but he argued in vain for Liberal principle and against conscription. On that, he wrote in his journal in 1916: "The betrayal has been cruel; war seems to arouse so many bad passions that Liberalism cannot live in its atmosphere. Let us have peace as soon as possible."

Horatio, *Lord Kitchener*, was tall, 'lithe, straight-limbed', according to a reporter who saw him become a viscount in the House of Lords in July 1914. Minister for War from August 1914, he gave 'inspired if unorthodox leadership', in the words of one War Office official, Major-General Sir CE Caldwell. Kitchener sailed for Russia in 1916 and his ship sank on the way.

Gerald Legge was killed in action on August 9, 1915, aged 33. He has no known grave; his name is one of 21,000 on the Helles memorial on the tip of the Gallipoli peninsula. There is a memorial chapel to him in the long-shut Patshull Church, near Wolverhampton; and his name is on the roll of honour at Lord's cricket ground as a member of MCC.

In October 1915, replying to a letter of condolence, his father *Lord Dartmouth* wrote: "I am grateful to you for your kindly reference to my son. This is not a time however to give way to private sorrow and we have much to console us in our loss. It is a help to have plenty of work to do." He died in 1936. Among his many public roles, he was president of the Territorial Army Association from its beginning in 1908; and president of I Zingari cricket club. The Dartmouth seat, Patshull House, is now a hotel and golf club.

Gerald Legge's brother in law *Francis Meynell* (1889-1941) served in the artillery, first near Ypres in 1915, was wounded home in 1917, and ended the war as a lieutenant colonel. He returned to Hoar Cross and died in 1941.

Oliver Lyttleton (1893-1972) did make it into the Guards, and reached the rank of brigade major. He was a member of Churchill's war cabinet and became Viscount Chandos in 1954.

Guy Paget found himself over-worked and under-equipped training Northamptonshire recruits from September 1914, who were part of the British Army's first large attack from the trenches, at Loos in September 1915. Then, according to his memoir, 'three-quarters of this magnificent division was just thrown away by the incompetence of the Staff from Division upwards'. He ended the war in Beirut. His son Reginald was Labour MP for Northampton 1945-74.

William Pickbourne (1860-1932) and his wife returned to their native Nottinghamshire in March 1918. Of their four sons in uniform, Wilfred worked in the Army Pay Corps in Salisbury; Stewart survived Gallipoli but was killed at Gaza in April 1917; Frank, a private in the Machine Gun Corps, died of pneumonia at Alexandria in October 1918; and Arthur, the youngest, was wounded at Messines in 1917. Pickbourne wrote characteristically after his final loss: "It was with a very heavy and sad heart I set out to preach the gospel but again as so often before while watering others I myself was watered and helped."

The solicitor *Robert Ramsey* (1861-1951) took the train on Saturday August 22, 1914 from London – 'Peterborough Cathedral stood up white against a thunder cloud with a startlingly beautiful effect' – and changed at Darlington for a holiday in Teesdale. "We seem here in a kind of backwater far removed from the war and all its terrors and excitements," he wrote in his full, but very hard to read, diary.

Arthur Ross left Beverley on August 24 to join the 5th Yorks Regiment at Darlington, commanded by Colonel Sir Mark Sykes MP. He had his last home leave in April 1915, 'before going on Foreign Service in our just cause'. He was wounded in France in March 1916. He rose in the Royal Naval Division to the rank of lieutenant and was killed on October 8, 1918, at Cambrai.

Lord St Aldwyn (1837-1916), as plain Sir Michael Edward Hicks-Beach, twice a Unionist chancellor of the exchequer, took up an offer of late 1914 to become first Earl St Aldwyn of Coln St Mary. He has a memorial in Gloucester Cathedral.

William Swift (1842-1915) ended his diary, after 55 years, in mid-sentence on February 5, 1915. He died on February 10 and was buried in Churchdown. His grandson Ernest Swift died on the Somme on July 3, 1916, aged 21, and is buried there.

Donald Weir served in France from 1914, then Mesopotamia, and France again, ending the war as a battalion commander. He returned to India via Malta, having in June 1919 received a bar to his Distinguished Service Order at Buckingham Palace. He died of cholera in India in 1921.

Dorothy Wright (1895-1993) saw her older brother Charlie off from Selby railway station in September 1914 as a volunteer. After the war he finished his history degree at Trinity College, Oxford, and became a schoolmaster. He married in 1922, she in 1955. Both were childless.

Background Reading

'What 10,000 pities I didn't keep a diary in 1914 and 1915 – such vital years: the war for one thing.' So Mrs Henry Dudeney the novelist opened her 1916 diary (edited by Diana Crook, 1998; the original is in East Sussex record office in Lewes). Mrs Dudeney was right; they were vital years for the country, and for her, as she gave up her lover (eventually) and went back to living with her husband. Might that be why she did not keep a diary?

In a way it's not a pity, but a relief, as it means one fewer possible source. Like everything, diaries and newspaper reports have their pros and cons. Some diarists and newspapers were more insightful than others; all make an alternative to the usual tired printed sources. Few knew what war had been like and made the effort to be true to it, such as Captain J C Dunn in *The War The Infantry Knew 1914-1919: A Chronicle of Service in France and Belgium* (1987 edition), who covered August 1914 from pages 1-41. Even he told of August 1914, knowing of the years of stalemate next; only sources from the time can have the freshness, and innocence of ignorance, that marked that month. August 1914 offered a change from everyday life, drudgery if you were poor, boredom if you were rich; gradually the war became another, much deadlier, sort of everyday life.

The number of books about August 1914 are legion; let alone the books with a bearing on that month. Take the people who later became famous, who had something to say about going to war, such as George Orwell, whose first published work was a poem 'Awake! Young Men of England', as juvenile as its title, on page 36 of Bernard Crick's *George Orwell: A Life* (1980). Or, the already famous people who were to become yet more famous, such as the philosopher Bertrand Russell. Never short of a word, he was against the war from the first:

see Ray Monk's biography (1996), pages 367-70. Monk describes Russell as 'against the multitude', and indeed as he shows, most literary and public figures came out for the war. Yet beyond their central London and literate world, no end of common people that Russell did not know (and presumably did not want to) were *indifferent* to the war. Most great events, done by and for the ruling class, were distant from the mass of people; intellectually, and geographically. Someone ought to write a history of *indifference*.

Truthful reporting was more possible in August 1914 than later in the war, when all sides were at work to force everyone – men of fighting age especially – to conform. The longer the war went on, the less indifferent you could feel to it. There were more signs of it. Books about the war came out at once, meeting the market for them. W Stanley Macbean Knight, 'assisted by eminent naval and military experts' (are there any other sort?) finished volume one of his *The History of the Great European War* in September 1914, and only got as far as August 2. You could even argue that writing books about the war from your side's point of view was part of the fight, to keep the public satisfied and to win neutrals over, such as the United States. Hence Winston Churchill's interview with an American reporter, widely carried in the British press at the very end of August. There's always however at least another point of view.

Some memoirs from the German side touching on August 1914 include *The Dark Invader*, by Captain Franz von Rintelen (first printed 1933, 12th impression 1942), pages 17-34; and *Surgeon with the Kaiser's Army*, by Stephen Westman (1968), pages 30-49, who were at the German Admiralty in Berlin and at the front respectively.

On the British side, equivalents include *Old Men Forget: The Autobiography of Duff Cooper, Viscount Norwich* (1955 edition), pages 36-7; *The Memoirs of Field Marshal the Viscount Montgomery of Alamein* (1958), pages 27-8; *The Memoirs of*

General the Lord Ismay (1960), page 28, who had even less to say of his 1914-18 years, serving in Somaliland; and *A Fortunate Life*, by Bert Facey (1981), an early Australian volunteer, pages 233-4. William Robertson went with the BEF to France as quartermaster-general, and covered the month in pages 197-212 of his memoir *From Private to Field-Marshal* (1921; the 2005 facsimile edition by the University Press of the Pacific has 'Marshall' on the cover).

Some books, by leading historians then, have become historical documents, such as George Macaulay Trevelyan's *British History in the 19th century and After 1782-1919* (edition with 1941 postscript). Winston Churchill covered Sir John French, Kaiser Wilhelm, King George V and Herbert Asquith among others in his *Great Contemporaries* (1937). In *Winston Churchill as I Knew Him* (1966 edition), Asquith's daughter Violet Bonham Carter quoted her father's diary on the Ostend expedition, pages 328-9.

To give just two books on the politics of the day: *The Prime Minister*, by Harold Spender (1920), pages 177-81; and on the crisis leading to Britain declaring war on Germany, volume two of Randolph S Churchill's biography of his father, *Young Statesman 1901-14* (1967), pages 707-22.

The outbreak of war on the Continent did show who holidayed where. The Alps, Rhineland, France and the Low Countries, future enemy, ally and neutral, were all popular: see D H Lawrence's *Twilight in Italy* (first published 1916) for his – how can we put it? – *individual*, Alpine viewpoint. Also evoking the era and mood: *Memoirs of a Fox-Hunting Man*, from the *Complete Memoirs of George Sherston* by Siegfried Sassoon (1937 edition). Shooting, like hunting, equipped men mentally and physically for war. See *A G's Book of the Rifle*, by A G Banks, (first edition 1940; fourth edition reprinted 1958), that hailed the British Army regulars of 1914 on pages 18-19. As that book's printing history suggests, the teaching of 'musketry' by rifle club enthusiasts, and the peacetime emphasis in Army training on rifle fire (as detailed in the War Office manual Infantry Training 1914), cast a long shadow, to the Home Guard of the Second World War.

Long-serving men were able to place August 1914 in their working lives, such as the early 'air correspondent' Harry Harper, in his *Man's Conquest of the Air* (1942), page 126; the university servant Fred Bickerton, in *Fred of Oxford* (1953); and the spy Bernard Newman as in his memoir *Spy* (18th edition, 1947), pages 14-16. On the retreat from Mons' place in the 1914-18 war, see Basil Liddell Hart's *History of the First World War*, which suggests that the Marines at Ostend and even the false rumour of Russians in transit through England, rattled the Germans crucially (page 81, 1972 edition). On warfare more generally, read *The Profession of Arms*, by General Sir John Hackett (1983), around page 153. On the fighting in France, *The Marne 1914: The Opening of World War I and the Battle that Changed the World*, by Holger H Herwig (2011), and more briefly *Opening Moves: August 1914*, by John Keegan (1973 edition). That must have been one of the first books I ever read, as I coloured in some of the drawings with pencils and felt tips.

The chapter 'ways to die', by showing just how harsh and short life could be, also suggests that many people were too occupied by surviving to heed the war. The second edition of *The Edwardians: The Re-making of British Society*, by Paul Thompson (1992) goes into such topics as war as sport, and game-shooting. An oral history more rooted in home and neighbourhood was Elizabeth Roberts' *A Woman's Place* (1984). For London, see *Rothschild Buildings: Life in an East End Tenement Block 1887-1920*, by Jerry White (1980), especially pages 83-5. For Wigton in Cumbria, *Speak for England*, by Melvyn Bragg (1976), includes a veteran's point on page 61 that war was only a 'bit bigger risk' than going down a pit. Carl

Chinn's *Poverty Amidst Prosperity: The Urban Poor in England 1834-1914* (1995) shows just how hard life was.

Quid pro quo, the English equivalent of the Australian ideal of everyone having a 'fair go', was becoming institutionalised around this time, as shown by Keith Middlemas in his *Politics in Industrial Society: The Experience of the British System Since 1911* (paperback edition, 1980).

Britain was never as united as those in power insisted. What if Britain had not gone to war in 1914? So Niall Ferguson asked in the collection of 'alternatives and counterfactuals' he edited as *Virtual History* (1997). See also 'The What Ifs of 1914' by Robert Cowley, editor of *What If? Military Historians Imagine What Might Have Been* (2001).

The origins of war in 1914 have a huge literature; the most concise guide is by Ruth, now Baroness, Henig. By discussing 'deterrence', *The Games of July: Explaining the Great War*, by Frank C Zagare (2011) also asks questions of the nuclear, twenty-first century. For the pig's ear that Britain made of foreign relations, see *The Policy of the Entente: Essays on the Determinants of British Foreign Policy, 1904-1914*, by Keith M Wilson (1985).

As the watershed between a largely peaceful previous few decades and a pair of world wars and a potential third, August 1914 provoked many reminisces and soul-searching about what it did to Europe. Two examples from different eras are *World War: Its Cause and Cure*, by Lionel Curtis (1945), and the inaugural lecture by Prof A G Lehmann at the University of Hull, published as a pamphlet *The Unities of Europe* (1979). A book I grew up with, about the town I grew up in, *County Borough: History of Burton upon Trent, Part One*, by Denis Stuart (1974) has its own poignancy, drawing on ageing townspeople's memories of former things such as trams, temperance and pawnbrokers. Part Two (1977) has a pen-portrait of Clifford Gothard on page 218. For the Meynell family see the evocative

Hoar Cross Hall Staffordshire: Portrait of a Victorian Country House, by Gareth Evans (1994); for A T 'Dan' Daniel's years as headmaster, see W G Torrance's *The History of Alleyne's Grammar School Uttoxeter 1558-1958,* (1958), pages 59-66.

You can walk down long Ella Street in Hull as the architect and diarist George Thorp did, and I have been inside Clifford Gothard's old house at the top of Bearwood Hill Road in Burton, now a retirement home. Anyone can pay to go in Francis Meynell's Hoar Cross Hall, now a spa. You can walk as Arthur Ross must have done from his home, then on the outskirts of Beverley at 101 Grove Hill Road, into town, over the railway crossing, and to his workplace, county hall. Any sense of 1914 anywhere is, however, elusive. Likewise in my cricket book *The Victory Tests,* about matches between England and an Australian Services XI in 1945, it struck me how hard it was to find anywhere that had stayed the same. It must have been easier for someone in England in 1914 to find places that had not changed since 1814, since the age of Jane Austen and the stagecoach. Villages such as William Swift's Churchdown, then physically and economically free of nearby Gloucester and Cheltenham, have merged into towns.

We best seek 1914 not in the cities or in the deserted parts of the country, but in between, places such as the Essex coast as painted by George Rose on holiday; or towns that were small then as now, such as Ledbury, visited by William Swift and his son Leonard for the day on August 6. "It is a fair walk up into the town from the station like it is in Berkeley," Swift wrote. "We lunched on some sandwiches brought by Leonard and some very fair ale." Even then the houses to Swift's eyes were of a 'former age'.

Or, we can enjoy the seaside towns, built to cater for that era: such as Scarborough, Skegness, Southsea and Ilfracombe. Or the grand railway stations where passengers, then as now, changed trains; Carlisle, Bristol, York – to name only places I

236

have lived in. I recall particularly how, when I began work at the evening paper in Carlisle in August, 1995, my walk from home to work could take me through Carlisle railway station, over the platforms, where post trains still stood at night, though the provincial press – whose bundles 'WM' saw at dawn – was, even then, not what it was. Some buildings dating from 1914 – Newark Drill Hall, the Burton-on-Trent museum – still stand, though their use has changed, or ended.

I imagined myself closest to 1914 in Beverley, not in the now pedestrianised shopping streets but the dignified streets off the minster and the market place. I must have been walking where Arthur Ross and the Church Lads Brigade once marched. I was sad to read the short, almost brutally so, list in his journal of his dates home on leave from the war, such a contrast to the comradely feelings that must have prompted him to keep his peacetime journal about his service with the Church Lads. The war killed something inside Arthur Ross, even before his physical death in France.

At the risk of leaving the humbug and deceit intact, sometimes the only dignified response is silence. Hence I did not go into the myth of the 'angel of Mons' and alleged German atrocities, covered ably by John Terraine in the first two chapters of his *The Smoke and the Fire: Myths and Anti-Myths of War 1861-1945* (1981 edition). For evidence of how some Boer War and earlier soldiers liked to place letters home in newspapers, see the article 'Military correspondents in the late nineteenth century press', by Prof Edward M Spiers, in *Archives,* volume 32 (April 2007). Capt J C Dunn, in *The War The Infantry Knew,* wrote for September 20, 1914 (page 65) how soldiers were writing 'lurid' and 'highly coloured' letters home, tongue in cheek, to earn money from newspapers printing their 'adventures'. That said, I would argue that men sending letters home earlier, before they heard of such newspaper offers, and wounded men sent home and interviewed in England, would feel like telling the truth, as best they could, rather than inventing something (and what?).

Later, as the war dragged on, not only the bad things about war, but the fraud – the difference between what was said about it at home and what war was really like – soured men and coarsened life, for long afterwards. August 1914 has a long reach, into this century, even. Princess Marie Louise, a granddaughter of Queen Victoria, who counted King George V and Kaiser Wilhelm II as family, attended the coronation of her great-great-granddaughter, Queen Elizabeth II. She described her August 1914 on pages 140-1 of *My Memories of Six Reigns* (1956; paperback 1961).

Now I can fold away my Bartholomew's 1:1,000,000 scale cloth map of France and the Low Countries (1950). The ten-volume 1895 *Chambers's Encyclopaedia* that my father bought as a not-quite complete set has been a help for its articles and maps. As a good omen, I have not wished for the missing volume four (D to H). As my father has had to learn as an amputee, and as many learned after 1914, a man can go on even when something is missing.

My thanks to Dr Amanda Field of Chaplin Books for bringing my work to print.

Mark Rowe
Burton upon Trent, Staffordshire,
August 2013

Sources by Chapter

Chapter 1: First Shots

Gerald Legge letters from Sudan: Staffordshire record office (Stafford), D 859/1/3/8. Clifford Gothard's diary, Stafford, D4054/2/4. For a description of Kordofan province (about the size of France) in the 1920s, when Staffordshire Regiment soldiers served there, see the *Staffordshire Knot* annual for 1928, pages 11-12.

Alan Brooke's letters from India: Liddell Hart centre for military studies, King's College London (KCL).

Eva Tibbitts' letter from Canada: Gloucestershire record office (Gloucester), D5049/2.

Chapter 2: Ways to Die

William Thomas Pickbourne's journal: Nottinghamshire record office (Nottingham), DD2560/1/5.

Robert Blakeby's diary: City of Westminster archives (Westminster), Accession 1489/7.

Inquest cases from newspapers: Walsall history centre, glue factory worker burned to death, *Walsall Observer*, May 23, 1914; miner's wife died of burns, *Walsall Observer*, April 11, 1914.

William Thomas Swift diary for 1914: Gloucester, D3981/45.

Lord Charles Beresford's unveiling of statue to the captain of the Titanic: Lichfield record office (Lichfield), *Lichfield Mercury*, July 31, 1914.

Chapter 3: What is an Englishman?

Philip Gibbs' story of arrest in Belgrade in 1912: Newcastle central library, *The Graphic*, August 1, 1914. See also his memoir *The Pageant of the Years*, (1946), page 93.

Guy Paget memoir: Leicestershire record office (Leicester), DE 4795/26/1.

Overnight journey by 'WM' to Scotland: Tamworth library, *Tamworth Herald*, August 8, 1914.

Eric Bennett memoir: Stafford, File 4274.

Carpentier-Smith heavyweight boxing fight: Sheffield central library, *Sheffield Daily Telegraph*, July 15 to 18, 1914, among other newspapers of those days.

Arthur Ellerker Ross' scrapbook and account of the Beverley Company of the Church Lads Brigade: East Riding archives (Beverley). For his father Henry's occupation, *Kelly's North and East Riding Directory* (1913), page 466.

Chapter 4: The Quid Pro Quo

Lord St Aldwyn's speech at Sandon: Wolverhampton archives (Wolverhampton), *Express & Star*, July 24, 1914.

Richard Holt MP's journal: Liverpool city archives (Liverpool), 920 DUR 1/10.

Sir Richard Cooper MP's 'frank' speech: *Walsall Observer*, April 11, 1914. Ben Tillett's speech, *Walsall Observer*, May 23, 1914. Philip Ashworth speech, *Lichfield Mercury*, May 1, 1914.

Suffragette assault on Mr McKinnon Wood: *Market Harborough Advertiser*, July 21, 1914, for example. Bow Street magistrate's remarks: Holborn library, London borough of Camden, *St Pancras Gazette*, July 3, 1914. Crowd unfriendly to shouting suffragette outside Buckingham Palace, *Wolverhampton Express & Star*, July 23, 1914, for example.

New Scotland Yard memo and militant suffragettes' photo-parade: Lincolnshire record office (Lincoln), Constab 2/2/3/1.

Chapter 5: On the Brink

Robin Page Arnot, typed memoir, dated 1974: Hull history centre (Hull), U DAR (2)/2/6. With the Fabians for one night only was Leonard Woolf; see his *Beginning Again: An Autobiography of the Years 1911 to 1918*, (1964), page 167.

Gordon Shephard helping with famous delivery of guns to Irish nationalists at Howth: Royal Air Force museum archives, Hendon, north London (RAF Museum), *Memoirs of Brigadier General Gordon Shephard*, privately printed, (1924), edited by Shane Leslie.

Donald Weir's July 1914 letter home from India, '*what with the trouble in Dublin*': Leicester, DE 2913, bundle 2.

Frank Balfour letters from Sudan to '*my dear Irene*': Hull, DDFA /3/6/26.

War reporter E Ashmead Bartlett's journey from London to Sofia: Leeds central library, *Yorkshire Post*, August 15, 1914.

A T Daniel's cycle holiday in France: Uttoxeter library, *Uttoxeter Advertiser and Times*, September 23 and 30 and October 7, 1914.

Chapter 6: The Island Club

Captain Sycamore, towed by the German Kaiser: Essex record office (Chelmsford), *Essex County Standard*, August 15, 1914, a story it admitted it lifted from the *East Anglian Daily Times*.

Maynard Willoughby Colchester-Wemyss' letters to the King of Siam: Gloucester, D37/1.

Grey's line '*the lamps are going out all over Europe*': from *Life, Journalism and Politics* by J A Spender, volume 2, (1927), page 13.

Chapter 7: The Long Bank Holiday

Sir Mark Sykes MP's letter: Hull, U DDSY /x2/1/2f/27.

H C Mitchell in Brussels: *Tamworth Herald*, August 8, 1914.

Colin Davidson sending telegrams to tell the British Empire it was at war: *Memoirs of a Conservative, JCC Davidson's Memoirs and Papers 1910-37*, edited by Robert Rhodes James (1969), page 20.

Prime minister Herbert Asquith on the '*cheering crowds of loafers and holiday-makers*' in Downing Street: August 4 entry in his *Memories and Reflections*, (1928), volume 2.

Emily MacManus in front of Buckingham Palace on the outbreak of war: from her memoir *Matron of Guy's*, (1956), page 87.

Anonymous witness in front of Buckingham Palace: Leeds library, *Pudsey and Stanningley News*, August 14, 1914.

Robert Ramsey diary: London Metropolitan archives, F/Rmy/028. For the suggestion that the crowds in front of Buckingham Palace were not actors in some open-air theatre but were loyally 'hymning to the king', see *The Men From The Greenwood .... Being the War History of the 11th (Service) Battalion Sherwood Foresters*, by Percy Fryer, (1920), page 10. Copy in Nottingham library.

Hearing of the outbreak of war in Wellington, New Zealand: *Sydney Morning Herald*, August 7, 1914. For a remarkable photograph showing Adolf Hitler among the outbreak of war crowd in Munich, see Ian Kershaw's *Hitler: 1889-1936: Hubris* (1998).

'All wars are popular on the day of their declaration': *War Memoirs of David Lloyd George*, volume one, (1933), page 42.

Rhodesia Trading Company's foiled plan to raise prices 15 per cent: Derbyshire record office (Matlock), Microfilm 781, TC 2/520.

George Thorp diary: Hull, L/DIGT. For his home and work addresses, *Kelly's Hull Directory 1914*, pages 68 and 542.

Chapter 8: The News

GC Harper diary: Churchill College archives, Cambridge, HRPR 1/1. James Somerville diary: SMVL 2/1.

Donald Weir, longing *'to have a dig at the Germans'*: Leicester, DE 2913, bundle 2.

Chapter 9: Spies

George Rose diary: Chelmsford, D/DU 418/15.

Burtonians threatened for taking photographs of warships at Grimsby: *Burton Daily Mail*, August 8, 1914.

Bert Faulkner mistaking northerner for a German: *Walsall Observer*, August 22, 1914.

Mr Durose mistaking an Indian prince for a German, and other national defence work by Lincolnshire police: Lincoln, Constab 2/3/1/2/1.

Swearing in of special constables at Newark, and the court case of the missing Southwell shoes: *Newark Advertiser*, September 9, 1914.

Memo by Major Kell to Winston Churchill on the suspect von Bulow: Churchill archives, microfilm, Char 13/44/57.

Chapter 10: Serving Men

Francis Grenfell's farewell letter to Churchill: Churchill archives, microfilm, Char 13/45/22.

A drunk asking Christopher Hollis' father to pray for him: Christopher Hollis, *Along the Road to Frome*, (1958), page 22.

The drunk Frederick Jewitt at Beverley railway station: East Riding archives, *Beverley Guardian*, August 8, 1914.

Herbert Strutt and marching soldiers in near-accident on the road: Derby local history library, *Derby Advertiser*, September 18, 1914.

Chapter 11: Spectators on the Shore

Rev Denys Yonge diary: Chelmsford, D/DCI 358/26.

Dorothy Wright diary: Matlock, D5430/49/5.

Minutes book of the Burton upon Trent branch of the Soldiers and Sailors' Families Association (SSFA): Lichfield, D34/1.

Arthur Bryan letters to his wife: Matlock, D5948/1 microfilm M1029.

Lady Gwendoline Churchill letters to her husband: Churchill archives, PCHL 5/1.

Chapter 12: Politics

The kaiser as a '*poor misguided man*': *Market Harborough Advertiser*, August 11, 1914.

Speeches on Britain having '*clean hands*': *Ashbourne Telegraph*, August 7, and *Lichfield Mercury*, August 21, 1914.

Lord St Aldwyn letters to his son: Gloucester, D 2455/F3/10/1/4.

Lord Milner letter to Philip Lyttelton Gell: Matlock, D3287 MIL 1/657.

Chapter 13: Business as Usual?

Joseph Leslie Dent's diary: from *History of the South Staffordshire Regiment 1705-1923*, by James P Jones, (1923), pages 242-59. Copy in Stafford library.

Harold Cook postcard promising to write from Berlin: Lincoln, LLHS 38/4/2.

Socialists assaulted for speaking in public against the war: Harry Pollitt, *Serving my Time: An apprenticeship to Politics*, (1940), pages 64-66. Herbert Morrison, *An Autobiography*, page 63. For a Scottish socialist against the war (and all for a fight to defend anti-war meetings), see *Pioneering Days* by Thomas Bell, (1941), pages 101-4.

Papers of the supplies in time of war sub-committee of the Committee of Imperial Defence: Liverpool, 920 DUR 14/34.

Francis Meynell's letters to family: Stafford, D861/P/1/12.

J C 'Farmer' White having to work on the farm instead of play cricket for Somerset against Yorkshire at Weston super Mare: Bristol central library, *Western Daily Press*, August 28, 1914.

Chapter 14: Recruiting

Colonel Chichester not seeing any disadvantages to joining the army: Cambridge central library, *Huntingdonshire Post*, September 11, 1914.

Robert Thornewill's talk to his workmen: *Burton Evening Gazette*, September 1, 1914.

Harold Begbie poem, widely reprinted from the *Daily Chronicle*: Cannock library, *Cannock Advertiser*, September 5, 1914.

Miles Thomas shocked, angered and shamed by a white feather: *Out on a Wing. An autobiography*, by Sir Miles Thomas, (1964), page 38-9.

Chapter 15: United?

Labour MP Jimmy Thomas' support for the war: *Derby Mercury*, September 11, 1914. See also *My Story*, by J H Thomas, (1937), pages 37-38.

The letters between Churchill, Lord Charles Beresford and Arthur Lee MP after Beresford shot his mouth off too far at the Carlton

Club: Churchill archives, Char 13/43.

An example of the shout *'shall we be beaten?!'*: *Burton Daily Mail*, August 6, 1914. Also, unrelated, examples of the *'are we downhearted?!'* cry: *Walsall Observer*, August 8, 1914; and British troops shouting it as they landed at Boulogne; *The Times*, August 18, 1914.

Complaints in newspapers of volunteers for the army having to queue: for example, *Sheffield Daily Independent*, September 2, 1914; and *Derby Daily Telegraph*, September 7, 1914 (with official excuse the next day).

Chapter 16: Food

The Charles Dickens quotation comes from The Dent uniform edition of *Dickens' Journalism*, volume 4, The Uncommercial Traveller and other papers 1859-70, edited by Michael Slater and John Drew (2000), page 98.

C W Colchester-Weymss and the woman he almost married, Miss C Quinlon Day, are each named in *Kelly's Gloucestershire Directory* (1914), page 364.

Chapter 17: Rumours

George Lakeman denying he was a German: *Newmarket Journal*, August 22, 1914.

Court case of Ashbourne man warning *'the Germans are coming'*: *Uttoxeter Advertiser*, August 26, 1914.

On rumours of Russian troops passing through England: *Memoirs of Sir Almeric Fitzroy* volume 2, page 569. Robert Bull diary: Chelmsford, T/B 245/3. For his occupation, see *Kelly's Essex Directory* (1914), page 90. Miss Laura Partridge told in France the Russians were coming: *Willesden Chronicle*, September 4, 1914.

Churchill airing the idea of bringing Russian troops to Ostend: *The Churchill Documents* volume 6, (1972), page 31.

Chapter 18: First Returns

William Simpson writing home: *Ashbourne Telegraph*, September 4, 1914.

Colonel Lang with letter from his son in the trenches: *Bristol Times and Mirror*, September 4, 1914.

Dick Wallis posting letter in normal postbox to get round army censorship: Walsall local history centre, 145/4.

Chapter 19: Going

Lieutenant Brian Horrocks cheered off from Chatham: *A Full Life*, by Lieutenant General Sir Brian Horrocks, (1960), page 15.

Ambulance driver Albert Batty's diary and reminisces: Gloucester, D3435.

Walter Bloem's comment on broken down British lorries he passed: *Vormarsch*, by Walter Bloem, (1916), translated from the German by G C Wynne as *The Advance from Mons 1914*, page 102. Copy at RAF Museum, Hendon.

The fatal runaway wagon in Bristol: *Bristol Times and Mirror*, August 11, 1914. For Park Street shops, *Kelly's Bristol Directory* (1914), page 223.

For the farewells and first marches by Territorials: *Ashbourne Advertiser*, August 7, 1914; *Uttoxeter Advertiser*, August 19 and 26, 1914.

Hinckley Territorials' march to Loughborough, with female followers: Aubrey Moore, *A Son of the Rectory*, (1982), page 120.

Description by 'An Old Newarker' of troops leaving Derby: *Newark Advertiser*, August 19, 1914.

Oliver Lyttleton writing to his mother: Churchill archives, CHAN 1/8/2.

Kitchener's outlook as reported in *The Times* of August 15, 1914, and much reported in the press in following days: *The First World War Personal Experiences of Lieutenant Colonel C A Court Repington*, volume one, (1920), pages 21-22. Colonel G S Foljambe 'ashamed' of returned Territorials: *Newark Advertiser*, September 9, 1914.

Inquest of men killed in aeroplane crash at Netheravon: *Bristol Times and Mirror*, August 13, 1914.

Chapter 20: Forward

The uncensored letter by the Woodin brothers on their crossing to Rouen: *Alfreton and Belper Journal*, September 4, 1914.

Private John Harding's story: *Essex County Standard*, September 12, 1914.

Charles Wallbank's diary and notes: Wolverhampton archives, DX-714/1.

Private Dixon's story: *Pudsey and Stanningley News*, September 11, 1914.

Mr and Mrs Taylor of Quievrain's story: *Loughborough Echo*, August 28, 1914.

Private Thomas Cross' story: *Cannock Advertiser*, September 19, 1914.

Private John Jennings' story: *Derby Advertiser*, September 11, 1914.

Bombardier William Simpson's story: *Ashbourne Advertiser*, September 11, 1914.

Private Harry Mason's story: *Walsall Observer*, September 12, 1914.

Private Charles Broadhurst's story: *Walsall Observer*, September 19, 1914.

Privates Charles Dudley Moore and JT Tait's story: *Burton Evening Gazette*, September 10, 1914.

Private Frederick Bruce's story: *Cambridge Daily News*, September 15, 1914.

Private CE McLoughlin's story: *Burton Evening Gazette*, September 16, 1914.

Sgt Crockett's story: *Burton Evening Gazette*, September 9, 1914.

Private Shepherd's story: *Nottingham Guardian*, September 25, 1914 (and lifted by the *Newark Advertiser*, September 30, 1914).

Chapter 21: Back

Lieutenant Macleod's story: *Cambridge Daily News*, September 10, 1914.

Sgt Bird and Private Woolgar's story: *Newark Advertiser*, September 30, 1914.

A bird's eye view of the retreat: *Recollections of an Airman*, by Lieutenant Colonel LA Strange, (first published 1933; 1935 edition), page 41. Copy at RAF Museum, Hendon.

Unidentified sergeant in bayonet fight; and 'searchlights' described: *Sheffield Daily Independent*, September 4, 1914.

Bugler Tom Reeves' story: *Derby Advertiser*, September 11, 1914.

Lance Corporal Ball's story: *Walsall Advertiser*, September 26, 1914.

Sidney Clive's diary: KCL, Clive II/1.

'Lessons of the battle': December 1933, Battle of Le Cateau August 26, 1914 tour of the battlefield, HMSO. Copy at KCL.

Motorcycle messenger J K Stevens' story: *Cambridge Daily News*, September 15, 1914.

Asquith's widely-reported deploring in the House of Commons on August 31 of *The Times'* August 30 report on the 'broken' British army: for example, *Bristol Times and Mirror*, September 1, 1914. That offending Sunday edition of *The Times* is not among the digital editions available at some libraries and archives, but see *We Thundered On: 200 years of The Times 1785-1985*, by Philip Howard, (1985), pages 87-88; and the article by John Terraine, The Impact of Mons, August 1914, in *History Today*, August 1964.

Lady French's appeal for socks: *The Times*, August 29, 1914, and widely reported the following week. Lord Dartmouth's similar appeal in Staffordshire: for example, *Burton Evening Gazette*, September 4, 1914.

Navy wireless operator William Cash's story: *Wolverhampton Express & Star*, August 15, 1914.

Chapter 22: An Outing to Ostend

Copy of George Aston's account of his command of the expedition to Ostend: copy at KCL, Aston 1/8. Admiralty messages to Aston: Churchill archives, Char 13/36.

Chapter 23: To the End of the World

Letters of Gerald Legge to his parents from Gallipoli, and letters of condolence to Lord Dartmouth: Stafford, D 859/1/3/9. For the last days of Legge and hundreds of men in his battalion at Suvla Bay in August 1915, see *The History of the Seventh South Staffordshire Regiment*, edited by Major A H Ashcroft (1919), pages 11-15; copy in Wolverhampton archives.

Some Military Terms and Totals

Brigade = four battalions. Infantry division = 12 battalions, about 20,000 men.

(Source: *The Times*, August 29, 1914)

Battalion = eight companies, each of three officers, captain, lieutenant, and sub-lieutenant, five sergeants, two drummers and buglers, five corporals, 108 privates, and one driver with two horses for the general service wagon.

(Source: *Chambers's Encyclopaedia*, 1895)

Approximate estimates of the peacetime military of the great powers of Europe (in thousands; war footing in brackets)

Austria 350 (1850), France 564 (2350), Germany 457 (3000), Great Britain 210 (717), Italy 280 (2000), Russia 870 (2900).

(Also: peace footing in thousands of Belgium – 52, and Servia, including reserves – 105.)

(Source: *Chambers's Encyclopaedia*, 1895)

The BEF

'The British Expeditionary Force, composed of six divisions and a cavalry division, had a total strength of, roughly, 160,000 men, 60,000 horses, 490 guns, and 7000 vehicles. That part of it sent out in the first instance numbered only about 100,000 men, and consisted of a cavalry division and two army corps each of two divisions.'

From Private to Field-Marshal by Sir William Robertson (1921), page 203.

Index